LIBRARY OF NEW TESTAMENT STUDIES

679

formerly the Journal for the Study of the New Testament Supplement series

Purity in the Gospel of John

Early Jewish Tradition,
Christology, and Ethics

Wil Rogan

t&tclark

LONDON • NEW YORK • OXFORD • NEW DELHI • SYDNEY

T&T CLARK
Bloomsbury Publishing Plc
50 Bedford Square, London, WC1B 3DP, UK
1385 Broadway, New York, NY 10018, USA
29 Earlsfort Terrace, Dublin 2, Ireland

BLOOMSBURY, T&T CLARK and the T&T Clark logo are trademarks
of Bloomsbury Publishing Plc

First published in Great Britain 2023

A catalogue record for this book is available from the British Library.

A catalog record of this book is available from the Library of Congress.
LCCN: 2022057060

ISBN: HB: 978-0-5677-0866-3
ePDF: 978-0-5677-0867-0
eBook: 978-0-5677-0869-4

Series: Library of New Testament Studies, volume 679
ISSN 2513-8790

Typeset by Newgen KnowledgeWorks Pvt. Ltd., Chennai, India

To find out more about our authors and books visit www.bloomsbury.com
and sign up for our newsletters.

To Tiffany

Contents

Preface

Purity in the Gospel of John is a wonder. Only in the Fourth Gospel does Jesus call his disciples pure, wash his disciples' feet, and baptize. At the same time, the Fourth Gospel lacks the kind of attention given to ritual purity in the Synoptic Gospels. There are no people purified of skin disease, no hemorrhaging women relieved of chronic impurity, no disputes between Jesus and his contemporaries over ritual purity, and no impure spirits cast out. I attempt no explanation for the difference between John's Gospel and the Synoptics on this matter, except to say that divergence on purity among the canonical Gospels is not particularly strange, since early Jewish discourse about purity was extraordinarily rich, wide-ranging, and diverse. Instead, my interest settled on how the Fourth Gospel can be located within this dynamic early Jewish discourse on purity. How does the Fourth Gospel adopt biblical and early Jewish traditions related to purity? How does the Fourth Gospel adapt these traditions of purity to make sense of the luminous figure at the center of its narrative and the people to whom he came? The more that I read about varieties of purity in ancient Jewish practice and belief—being especially helped by the work of Mary Douglas, Jacob Milgrom, Jonathan Klawans, Christine Hayes, Mira Balberg, and Moshe Blidstein—the more that I was dissatisfied with the interpretive consensus that in the Fourth Gospel purity is replaced by faith in Jesus. There was something about it that was too dismissive. All this will be discussed in Chapter 1. What I was surprised to discover is that the Fourth Gospel has a certain intelligence about purity that appears in some of its most stunning claims about the identity of Jesus and the significance of his work. In the Fourth Gospel, purity prepares for perception of Jesus's identity with God, makes possible Israel's participation in God's life, and imparts the capacity to keep Jesus's commandment that his disciples love one another in the same way that they were loved by him.

Thanks is owed to Marianne Meye Thompson, who has deeply influenced how I think about the interpretation of the New Testament. Her patient, wise, and incisive reading of my work has made this book better than what I could have produced on my own, not least because the idea for a book on this topic was hers. She graciously entrusted it to me, and I am grateful that she did. I am also grateful for the generous, constructive feedback of Joel Green, Craig Koester, Christopher Blumhofer, James McMichael, and the peer reviewer of earlier drafts of this project. I feel particularly lucky to have so many dear friends whose support and regard in the years I worked on this project made my life full, among whom are Jonathan and Natalie Anderson, Robert Covolo, Cory Willson, Alex Neuss, Ryan Bestelmeyer, Lou Huesmann, Keith and Sherri Douds, Diana Steenbergen, Kurt Simonson, Jeff and Meg Rau, James McMichael, and Susan Davis. During my studies, I worked with the good people at Grace Long Beach as a pastor, and I will always be grateful to God for those years and the people—too many to name here—whom I came to know and love.

This book would never have been written were it not for my mother Maria Rogan and for Ted Petrikis, who was like a father to me. Neither lived to see the completion of this work, and neither is ever far from my thoughts. I hold them in loving and blessed memory!

I dedicate this book to Tiffany, my wife, dearest friend, and closest companion, whose acts of love and care have graced my life these last twelve years. The steadfastness of her support and encouragement throughout my doctoral studies and first years of teaching, my mother's illness and death, and many sorrows and joys besides have reflected to me nothing less than God's loving kindness. Chief among those joys we have shared are the births of our sons Shiloh and Micaiah. What joy to belong with each other. Thank God.

Abbreviations

Ancient Sources

Ag. Ap.	Josephus, *Against Apion*
Alleg. Interp.	Philo, *Allegorical Interpretation*
Ant.	Josephus, *Jewish Antiquities*
Barn.	Barnabas
Cherubim	Philo, *On the Cherubim*
Comm. Jo.	Origen, *Commentarii in evangelium Joannis*
Confusion	Philo, *On the Confusion of Tongues*
Contempl. Life	Philo, *On the Contemplative Life*
Creation	Philo, *On the Creation of the World*
Decalogue	Philo, *On the Decalogue*
Dreams	Philo, *On Dreams*
Drunkenness	Philo, *On Drunkenness*
DSS	Dead Sea Scrolls
1 En.	1 Enoch
Eternity	Philo, *On the Eternity of the World*
Flight	Philo, *On Flight and Finding*
Giants	Philo, *On Giants*
Good Person	Philo, *That Every Good Person Is Free*
Herm. Vis.	Shepherd of Hermas, Vision(s)
Jub.	*Jubilees*
J. W.	Josephus, *Jewish War*
Let. Aris.	Letter of Aristeas
LXX	Septuagint
m. Ber.	Mishnah Berakot
Migration	Philo, *On the Migration of Abraham*
Moses	Philo, *On the Life of Moses*
Names	Philo, *On the Change of Names*
NT	New Testament
Off.	Cicero, *De officiis*
OT	Old Testament
Paed.	Clement of Alexandria, *Paedagogus*
Prelim. Studies	Philo, *On the Preliminary Studies*
Protr.	Clement of Alexandria, *Protrepticus*
Providence	Philo, *On Providence*
Pss. Sol.	Psalms of Solomon
QE	Philo, *Questions and Answers on Exodus*

Sib. Or.	Sibylline Oracles
Smyrn.	Ignatius, *To the Smyrnaeans*
Spec. Laws	Philo, *On the Special Laws*
T. 12 Patr.	Testaments of the Twelve Patriarchs
T. Ash.	Testament of Asher
T. Benj.	Testament of Benjamin
T. Jos.	Testament of Joseph
T. Levi	Testament of Levi
T. Mos.	Testament of Moses
T. Naph.	Testament of Naphtali
T. Reu.	Testament of Reuben
T. Sim.	Testament of Simeon
T. Zeb.	Testament of Zebulun
Tg. Neof.	Targum Neofiti
Tg. Ps.-J.	Targum Pseudo-Jonathan
Unchangeable	Philo, *That God Is Unchangeable*
Worse	Philo, *That the Worse Attacks the Better*

Secondary Sources

AB	Anchor Bible
ABD	*Anchor Bible Dictionary.* Edited by David Noel Freedman. 6 vols. New York: Doubleday, 1992.
ABR	*Australian Biblical Review*
ABRL	Anchor Bible Reference Library
AcBib	*Academia Biblica*
BAR	*Biblical Archaeology Review*
BBR	*Bulletin for Biblical Research*
BDAG	Danker, Frederick W., Walter Bauer, William F. Arndt, and F. Wilbur Gingrich. *Greek–English Lexicon of the New Testament and Other Early Christian Literature.* 3rd ed. Chicago: University of Chicago Press, 2000 (Danker-Bauer-Arndt-Gingrich).
Bib	*Biblica*
BJP	*Brill Josephus Project*
BJS	Brown Judaic Studies
BNTC	Black's New Testament Commentary
BZAW	Beihefte zur Zeitschrift für die alttestamentliche Wissenschaft
CBET	Contributions to Biblical Exegesis and Theology
CBQ	*Catholic Biblical Quarterly*
CBR	*Currents in Biblical Research*
ConBNT	Coniectanea biblica, New Testament
DJG	*Dictionary of Jesus and the Gospels.* Edited by Joel B. Green, Jeannine K. Brown, and Nicholas Perrin. 2nd ed. Downers Grove, IL: InterVarsity Press, 2013.

DSD	*Dead Sea Discoveries*
ECL	Early Christianity and Its Literature
EDEJ	*The Eerdmans Dictionary of Early Judaism*. Edited by John J. Collins and Daniel C. Harlow. Grand Rapids, MI: Eerdmans, 2010.
EJL	Early Judaism and Its Literature
ETL	*Ephemerides theologicae lovanienses*
ExAud	*Ex Auditu*
FAT	Forschungen zum Alten Testament
IDS	*In die Skriflig*
IEJ	*Israel Exploration Journal*
JAJ	*Journal of Ancient Judaism*
JANER	*Journal of Ancient Near Eastern Religions*
JBL	*Journal of Biblical Literature*
JJS	*Journal of Jewish Studies*
JNES	*Journal of Near Eastern Studies*
JQR	*Jewish Quarterly Review*
JSJ	*Journal for the Study of Judaism in the Persian, Hellenistic and Roman Period*
JSJSup	Journal for the Study of Judaism in the Persian, Hellenistic and Roman Period Supplement Series
JSNT	*Journal for the Study of the New Testament*
JSNTSup	Journal for the Study of the New Testament Supplement Series
JSOT	*Journal for the Study of the Old Testament*
JSOTSup	Journal for the Study of the Old Testament Supplement Series
JSP	*Journal for the Study of the Pseudepigrapha*
JTI	*Journal of Theological Interpretation*
JTS	*Journal of Theological Studies*
KD	*Kerygma und Dogma*
LCL	Loeb Classical Library
LHBOTS	The Library of Hebrew Bible/Old Testament Studies
LNTS	Library of New Testament Studies
LS	*Louvain Studies*
MOTP	Bauckham, Richard, James R. Davila, and Alexander Panayotov, eds. *Old Testament Pseudepigrapha: More Noncanonical Scriptures*. 2 vols. Grand Rapids: Eerdmans, 2013–.
MTZ	*Münchener theologische Zeitschrift*
Neot	*Neotestamentica*
NETS	Pietersma, Albert, and Benjamin G. Wright, eds. *A New English Translation of the Septuagint*. New York: Oxford University Press, 2007.
NICNT	New International Commentary on the New Testament
NICOT	New International Commentary on the Old Testament
NovT	*Novum Testamentum*
NovTSup	Supplements to Novum Testamentum

NRSV	Metzger B. M., and R. E. Murphy (eds.), *New Revised Standard Version*. 1989.
NTL	New Testament Library
NTS	*New Testament Studies*
NTTSD	New Testament Tools, Studies, and Documents
OTL	Old Testament Library
OTP	Charlesworth, James H. (ed.), *Old Testament Pseudepigrapha*. 2 vols. New York: Doubleday, 1983–1985.
PBRIP	Purpose-Built Ritual Immersion Pool
PRSt	*Perspectives in Religious Studies*
RB	*Revue biblique*
RBS	Resources for Biblical Study
RNT	Regensburger Neues Testament
SBL	Society of Biblical Literature
SBLDS	Society of Biblical Literature Dissertation Series
SNTSMS	Society for New Testament Studies Monograph Series
SNTSU	Studien zum Neuen Testament und seiner Umwelt
StBibLit	Studies in Biblical Literature (Lang)
STDJ	Studies on the Texts of the Desert of Judah
SVTP	Studia in veteris testamenti pseudepigrapha
TBN	Themes in Biblical Narrative
ThTo	*Theology Today*
TSAJ	Texte und Studien zum antiken Judentum
TynBul	*Tyndale Bulletin*
VT	*Vetus Testamentum*
WBC	Word Biblical Commentary
WUNT	Wissenschaftliche Untersuchungen zum Neuen Testament
ZAW	*Zeitschrift für die alttestamentliche Wissenschaft*
ZNW	*Zeitschrift für die neutestamentliche Wissenschaft*

1

The Fourth Gospel and Early Jewish Purification

The pervasiveness of concern for purity among ancient Jews is evident not only in the many and diverse writings in which the language of purity and impurity is so prominently featured, but also in pools built for ritual washing and stone vessels designed to hold water for ablutions that archeologists have discovered in abundance in the southern Levant.[1] Ancient Jews held Scriptures in common that instructed them about how to purify their bodies from the impurities brought on by skin disease, discharges such as menstrual blood or semen, childbirth, and human corpses. Israel's Scripture also sometimes speaks of how sin produces its own kind of impurity, a stain that washing with water could not remove.[2] Sin's impurity was likened to rust on a pot (Ezek. 24:1–14) or blood on one's hands (Isa. 1:15–16).[3] Extant early Jewish writings reflect a vital, wide-ranging discourse about all these matters of purity. Purity did not always reside at the surface of the river that nourished early Jewish life and belief, but it seems always and everywhere to have been an undercurrent: from the legal sophistication and existential seriousness about purity in the Dead Sea Scrolls, to the hope of divine, eschatological purification in pseudepigraphic texts (see, e.g., Pss. Sol. 17:22, 30–31; 18:5; *Jub.* 1.21–25; 50.5), to the strange conflation of purifying ablutions

---

[1] For a concise argument that archeological remains of stepped pools and stone vessels throughout the southern Levant reflect ancient Jewish concern for purity, even apart from participation in the temple cult, see Yonatan Adler, "Between Priestly Cult and Common Culture: The Material Evidence of Ritual Purity Observance in Early Roman Jerusalem Reassessed," *JAJ* 7.2 (2016): 228–48; see also, Adler, "Watertight and Rock Solid: Stepped Pools and Chalk Vessels as Expressions of Jewish Ritual Purity," *BAR* 47.1 (2021): 44–51.

[2] I use the terms "purity" and "purification" almost interchangeably, with the former term emphasizing purity as a state, and the latter term emphasizing the process of becoming pure. Throughout this book, I will employ Jonathan Klawans's terms "ritual purity" and "moral purity" to denote two distinct, but interrelated kinds of purity in Israel's Scripture and early Jewish belief and practice (on which, § 1.3). Broadly speaking, "ritual purification" describes the removal of bodily impurities through washing with water and the passage of time, and "ritual purity" is the state one must be in to encounter the holiness of God. "Moral purification" describes the removal of moral impurity caused by sins such as bloodshed, sexual misdeeds, and idolatry. What is at stake in moral (im)purity is God's presence with Israel. See Jonathan Klawans, *Impurity and Sin in Ancient Judaism* (Oxford: Oxford University Press, 2000), 22–31. As will be seen, the Fourth Gospel maintains a distinction between ritual purity and moral purity.

[3] For a provocative argument about how the Hebrew Bible represents sin as a stain or impurity in contrast to sin as, say, a burden to be lifted or an account to be repaid, see Joseph Lam, *Patterns of Sin in the Hebrew Bible: Metaphor, Culture, and the Making of a Religious Concept* (New York: Oxford University Press, 2016), 179–206.

and the forgiveness of sins in the Synoptic representation of John the Baptist (to take only one example from the writings now called the New Testament (NT)), to Philo of Alexandria's comprehensive theory of purity's relation to sacrifice and the temple (*Spec. Laws* 1.257–284), to the role that the pollution of Jerusalem by the zealots' bloodshed plays in Josephus's account of the Temple's destruction (*J.W.* 4.314–325), to purity's determinative force in the relation between oneself and the environment in the Mishnah's *Seder Tohorot*—purity was vital to early Jewish practice, theological conviction, and self-understanding.[4]

Purity's pervasiveness ought not to suggest its homogeneity. The river nourishing early Jewish life had many inlets. And, to exhaust the metaphor, the origin of this river was the return from exile. The social fragmentation that came to characterize the early Jewish period arose out of what Shemaryahu Talmon calls the multicentricity and multiformity of postexilic life.[5] Talmon argues that the loss of centralized leadership and political sovereignty over the land meant that postexilic Jewish society was unbounded and decentered.[6] Social divisions emerged between those who had returned from exile in Babylon, those who had never left the land, those who remained in Babylon, those who came to be known as Samaritans, and those who settled in the Elephantine in Egypt, who assimilated to the dominant culture and all but disappeared.[7] While the significance of the prophetic office diminished—its social power having been dependent on the Israelite monarchy—the authority of scribes and interpreters of biblical traditions increased.[8] The phrase "complex common Judaism" may be employed to describe the multiformity and multicentricity of early Jewish practice and belief, which nevertheless held in common the worship of one God, the reading of the Torah, and practices related to Sabbath, circumcision, diet, and purification, among

---

[4]   For a systemic analysis of purity in the DSS, see Hannah K. Harrington, *The Impurity Systems of Qumran and the Rabbis: Biblical Foundations*, SBLDS 143 (Atlanta, GA: Scholars Press, 1993); on purity as an important, overlooked aspect of Pss. Sol., see Bradley Embry, "The Psalms of Solomon and the New Testament: Intertextuality and the Need for a Re-evaluation," *JSP* 13.2 (2002): 99–136; on the Synoptic representation of John the Baptist with respect to purity, see Klawans, *Impurity and Sin*, 138–43; Joan E. Taylor, *The Immerser: John the Baptist within Second Temple Judaism* (Grand Rapids, MI: Eerdmans, 1997), 49–100; on purity in the works of Philo of Alexandria, see Jutta Leonhardt, *Jewish Worship in Philo of Alexandria*, TSAJ 84 (Tübingen: Mohr Siebeck, 2001), 190–272; Jonathan Klawans, *Purity, Sacrifice, and the Temple: Symbolism and Supersessionism in the Study of Ancient Judaism* (New York: Oxford University Press, 2005), 116–23; for the role of purity and pollution in Josephus's account of the temple's destruction, see Jonathan Klawans, *Josephus and the Theologies of Ancient Judaism* (Oxford: Oxford University Press, 2012), 187–91; Steve Mason, "Pollution and Purification in Josephus's Judean War," in *Purity, Holiness, and Identity in Judaism and Christianity: Essays in Memory of Susan Haber*, ed. Carl S. Ehrlich, Anders Runesson, and Eileen M. Schuller, WUNT 305 (Tübingen: Mohr Siebeck, 2013), 181–207; on purity as a discourse in the Mishnah, see the provocative work of Mira Balberg, *Purity, Body, and Self in Early Rabbinic Literature*, S. Mark Taper Foundation Imprint in Jewish Studies (Berkeley: University of California Press, 2014).

[5]   Shemaryahu Talmon, "The Emergence of Jewish Sectarianism in the Early Second Temple Period," in *Ancient Israelite Religion: Essays in Honor of Frank Moore Cross*, ed. Patrick D. Miller, Paul D. Hanson, and S. Dean McBride (Philadelphia, PA: Fortress, 1987), 594–7.

[6]   Talmon, "The Emergence of Jewish Sectarianism," 594–7.

[7]   Talmon, "The Emergence of Jewish Sectarianism," 599–604.

[8]   Talmon, "The Emergence of Jewish Sectarianism," 593.

other things.[9] Indeed, the matters that ancient Jews held in common were precisely those on which they tended to diverge. If the early Jewish period was characterized by sectarianism, it was at least a *Jewish* sectarianism. Thus, Talmon asserts that postexilic life was characterized not by an in-group and out-group dynamic, but rather, an inner-group, in-group, and out-group dynamic.[10] The social question among ancient Jews was not always whether one was in or out of the covenant, but whether one was innermost.

Purity was one matter held in common among ancient Jews that was complex and on which there was divergence. Contemporary scholars may speak of patterns or systems of purity, but may offer no singular definition that captures the idea of purity in that period. There was not *one*. Even where there are no signs of hostility, there may still have been diverse understandings and practices of purity. The surprising insight of Ian Werrett's study of ritual purity in the Dead Sea Scrolls (DSS) is that even among the scrolls one finds divergent requirements regarding ritual purification, some of which reflect the famous stringency of the Temple Scroll and others of which are more lenient than even the biblical texts from which they were derived.[11] Seeing as certain kinds of impurity were thought to work like a contagion that could be transferred by proximity or touch, it is not difficult to imagine that differing views about how to handle such impurities caused social distance among ancient Jews. Another point of divergence, as will be discussed, was how to conceive the relationship between those harmless impurities contracted in daily living and the impurity caused by particularly treacherous sins.[12] Perhaps more significant for early Jewish identity was how purity was thought to disattune early Jewish bodies from those of Gentiles.[13] Christine Hayes has identified two trajectories running through early Jewish writings with respect to the possibility of Gentile inclusion. On the one hand, the boundary that many ancient Jews

---

[9] Martin Hengel and Roland Deines proposed a model of "complex Judaism" which was characterized by stability with respect to outsiders, and conflict among those on the inside; such is their mediating position between E. P. Sanders's "common Judaism" and Jacob Neusner's Judaisms ("E. P. Sanders' 'Common Judaism,' Jesus, and the Pharisees," *JTS* 46.1 [1995]: 54–5). Complementing Hengel and Deines, Stuart S. Miller has proposed a *complex* common Judaism "that maintained enough order or structure to amount to 'common Judaism,' but which was sufficiently 'chaotic' to allow for innovation and individuality" ("Stepped Pools, Stone Vessels, and Other Identity Markers of 'Complex Common Judaism,'" *JSJ* 41 [2010]: 219).

[10] Talmon, "The Emergence of Jewish Sectarianism," 598–9.

[11] Ian C. Werrett observes, for example, that the treatments of skin disease in the Damascus Document are "considerably shorter and more lenient than their biblical counterparts," and are also more lenient than the Temple Scroll (*Ritual Purity and the Dead Sea Scrolls*, STDJ 72 [Leiden: Brill, 2007], 94, see also, 24–35, 169).

[12] On the distinction Jonathan Klawans draws between ritual and moral purity in his book *Impurity and Sin*, see § 1.3.

[13] The thesis of Christine E. Hayes's work on how purity functioned as a boundary between Jews and Gentiles is that "different definitions of Jewish identity, entailing different assessments of the permeability of the boundary between Jews and Gentiles and thus different attitudes to the postexilic phenomenon of conversion, were a major impetus for the formation of sects in the Second Temple period" (*Gentile Impurities and Jewish Identities: Intermarriage and Conversion from the Bible to the Talmud* [Oxford: Oxford University Press, 2002], 9). From ritual theorist Ronald Grimes I have borrowed the archaic word *disattune*, which, along with attunement, he uses as a metaphor for the dynamic way that ritual "implies that bodies (minded, cultured, and gendered) 'vibrate' or 'resonate' with something else: other bodies, environments, whatever is deemed holy" (*The Craft of Ritual Studies*, Oxford Ritual Studies [New York: Oxford University Press, 2013], 309–10).

maintained with Gentiles remained permeable to those Gentiles who abandoned their idols and sexual practices, which were considered a defiling moral influence. On the other hand, some ancient Jews regarded their lineage itself to be holy, which meant that Gentiles could not cross the boundary of intermarriage or conversion, being impure from the standpoint of genealogy.[14] Because purity was essential to daily, bodily life, to the temple and its sacrifices, to the subject matter of Israel's Scripture, and to the identity of the people, the topics associated with purity were vast, the controversies about them wide-ranging, and their implications socially significant. The language and practice of purification were ways that ancient Jews made sense of life in the world before God.

The Fourth Gospel is immersed in this early Jewish stream of purity. It is to be located among other early Jewish writings that reflect the complexity and pervasiveness of purity in early Jewish practice and belief. One cannot fail to notice how often purity in the Fourth Gospel, when it is explicitly mentioned, is directly connected to early Jewish life. The Fourth Gospel includes the detail that the stone jars at Cana were for "the purification of the *Ioudaioi*" (κατὰ τὸν καθαρισμὸν τῶν Ἰουδαίων, Jn 2:6), the observation that many people went to Jerusalem before the Passover of the *Ioudaioi* (πάσχα τῶν Ἰουδαίων) in order to purify themselves (ἵνα ἁγνίσωσιν ἑαυτούς, 11:55), and the remark that the *Ioudaioi* did not enter the praetorium of Pilate so that they would not be defiled during the Passover (ἵνα μὴ μιανθῶσιν, 18:28).[15] The Fourth Gospel's association of purity with the *Ioudaioi* is but one facet of its thoroughgoing concern for matters with which ancient Jews were preoccupied. Adele Reinhartz observes that the Gospel of John's "narrative, its language, and its conceptual framework situate it squarely within the same realm of other first-century Jewish texts written in Greek."[16] And Daniel Boyarin calls the Fourth Gospel a "noncanonical Jewish text."[17] The Fourth

---

[14] Christine E. Hayes, *Gentile Impurities and Jewish Identities*, 68–91.

[15] Because of the fraught nature of the term Ἰουδαῖοι, I use the transliterated Greek terms *Ioudaios* (sg.) and *Ioudaioi* (pl.) to denote the "Jews" as characters in the Fourth Gospel, as other scholars have done. When speaking of contemporary scholarly understanding of the beliefs and practices of Jews living between the conquest of Alexander and the Bar Kokhba Revolt, I use the adjective *early Jewish*, and when speaking in historical terms of Jews in that period, I use the term *ancient Jews*, taking my cue from John J. Collins, "Early Judaism in Modern Scholarship," in *The Eerdmans Dictionary of Early Judaism*, ed. John J. Collins and Daniel C. Harlow (Grand Rapids, MI: Eerdmans, 2010), 1–23. Because of a comment I heard Daniel Boyarin make at the annual meeting of SBL in 2019, I avoid the term Judaism as best I can out of concern that it reifies contemporary scholarly conceptual constructs. For a helpful overview of the critical issues related to the term Ἰουδαῖοι in John's Gospel, see Tom Thatcher, "John and the Jews: Recent Research and Future Questions," in *John and Judaism: A Contested Relationship in Context*, ed. R. Alan Culpepper and Paul N. Anderson, RBS 87 (Atlanta, GA: SBL Press, 2017), 3–38. Unless otherwise noted, quotations of the Greek NT are from Eberhard Nestle et al., eds., *Novum Testamentum Graece*, 28th ed. (Stuttgart: Deutsche Bibelgesellschaft, 2012).

[16] Adele Reinhartz articulates the Jewishness of the Fourth Gospel in order to problematize its anti-Jewishness ("The Jews of the Fourth Gospel," in *The Oxford Handbook of Johannine Studies*, ed. Judith Lieu and Martinus C. de Boer, Oxford Handbooks [Oxford: Oxford University Press, 2018], 121).

[17] Daniel Boyarin, "What Kind of Jew Is an Evangelist?" in *Those Outside: Noncanonical Readings of Canonical Gospels*, ed. George Aichele and Richard G. Walsh (London: T&T Clark, 2006), 131. As a Christian reader I regard the Gospel of John as canonical in the sense that it speaks from a height, and I am taught by John to consider myself as one who does not belong to the fold, but who is brought near by some miracle of hearing (10:16). Thus Boyarin's labeling of John's Gospel as a

Gospel's polemic against the *Ioudaioi* notwithstanding, its narrative and language may be interpreted as belonging within an early Jewish framework.[18] The Fourth Gospel conceptualizes purity within such a framework. Its narrative world simply would not be the same without its interest in purity. But purity in the Fourth Gospel does more than help construct its narrative world. Purity is integral to aspects of its theological claims. John (the Baptist) is said to be sent by God to ablute with water—a purifying act—so that the one to come would be revealed to Israel (ἐν ὕδατι βαπτίζων, 1:31, cf. 1:26, 33). Later, the ablutions of John and Jesus are said to provoke controversy about purification (ζήτησις ... περὶ καθαρισμοῦ), an apparent narrative aside that lays bare an intelligence about purity and its complexity operative throughout the Fourth Gospel (3:25). Arguably, that intelligence about purity underlies the dialogue between Jesus and Nicodemus about birth from water and Spirit (γεννηθῇ ἐξ ὕδατος καὶ πνεύματος, 3:5) as well as the giving of sight to the man born blind through an act of washing (ἐνίψατο καὶ ἦλθεν βλέπων, 9:7). Only in the Fourth Gospel does Jesus say to his disciples, "You are pure" (ὑμεῖς καθαροί ἐστε, 13:10; 15:3), and in the Farewell Discourse the disciples' purity is related to their moral capacity to keep Jesus's commandment to love one another as he has loved them (13:1–38; 15:1–17).

In spite of views that the Fourth Gospel altogether dispenses with purity, what Mira Balberg says about purity in the Mishnah applies equally well to the Fourth Gospel: purity and impurity "live on as powerful conceptual and hermeneutic tools through which ideas about self and other can be manifested."[19] In this book, I argue that the Fourth Gospel employs biblical traditions of purity associated with the revelation of God and restoration of Israel in order to narrate how God's people are prepared for the coming of Jesus and enabled by him to have life before God characterized by love. In the Fourth Gospel, both ritual and moral purity are about what condition humanity must be in to be able to live in the presence of God. In the first scene after the Prologue, as will be argued in Chapter 2 of this book, the Fourth Gospel uses the relation between ritual purity, human perception, and divine revelation forged at Sinai to represent John (the Baptist)'s ablutions with water as a ritual purification that prepares Israel to perceive what God reveals of God in the coming of Jesus. If ritual purification is a preparation for encounter with Jesus in the Fourth Gospel, moral purification is what God provides through Jesus to enable humanity both to receive the life of God and to live in conformity to the pattern of Jesus's love. Chapter 3 of this book locates aspects of the ministry of Jesus in the Fourth Gospel within expectations for the restoration of Israel drawn from the Major Prophets, in which a divine, eschatological work of moral purification was to make human beings capable of participating in God's life. In

---

noncanonical Jewish text rightfully places me outside its immediate frame of reference, even if its cosmic vision ultimately makes room for an outsider such as myself.

[18] Daniel Boyarin, following the work of Talmon cited earlier, argues that the "attack on the *Ioudaioi* in the Fourth Gospel is ... not an attack on Jews or Judaism but on a particular hegemonic sect of Jews" ("What Kind of Jew Is an Evangelist," 130). By contrast, Adele Reinhartz looks beyond historical referents to the rhetoric of the Fourth Gospel, arguing that it was partly designed for disaffiliation between the Fourth Gospel's believers and Jews generally (*Cast Out of the Covenant: Jews and Anti-Judaism in the Gospel of John* [Lanham, MD: Lexington Books – Fortress Academic, 2018], 51–108).

[19] Balberg, *Purity, Body, and Self*, 2.

Chapter 4, I argue that when Jesus tells his disciples, "You are pure" (13:10; 15:2–3), he is making a statement about the moral quality of their lives and their capacity to keep his commandment to love one another as he loved them. The Fourth Gospel's vision of purity is drawn from biblical tradition, conversant with early Jewish discourse about purity, and employed in service of its Christology, soteriology, and ethics.

Johannine scholarship has largely overlooked purity's conceptual power in the Fourth Gospel. The remainder of this chapter explains that this neglect is due to the conceit that purity is replaced by faith in Jesus and that purity's fossilized remains survive only to serve as a contrast to the life that Jesus gives. Against this conceit, a different paradigm for the interpretation of purity in the Fourth Gospel will be offered, in which biblical traditions of purity taken up and carried forward among ancient Jews are drawn on as indispensable theological resources for making sense of the luminous figure at the center of its narrative and those who have come to recognize him in faith.

1.1 Purity's Fossilized Remains? On the Conceit that Purity Is Replaced by Jesus

Since purity is not itself a central theological theme in the Fourth Gospel, only ancillary to central matters, it is unsurprising that it has been neglected by scholars. Neither is it strange that purity has not received the scholarly attention garnered by such important critical issues as the Fourth Gospel's relation to the Synoptic Gospels nor its representation of the *Ioudaioi*. Nevertheless, its neglect is both unfortunate and peculiar—unfortunate, because purity, as we shall see, is so closely related to Christology, soteriology, and the ethics of the Gospel of John; and peculiar, because so much recent scholarship locates the Gospel of John in an early Jewish context, and, where purity does appear in John's Gospel, it is often related explicitly to the *Ioudaioi* (cf., e.g., 1:19–28; 2:6; 3:22–25; 11:55; 18:28).[20] But even as John is interpreted with reference to an early Jewish context, so it is located at a point of fracture between "early Judaism" and "early Christianity," so that possible fault lines between the nascent communities are exploited by scholars.[21] Certain scholars have determined

---

[20] J. Louis Martyn's *History and Theology in the Fourth Gospel* perhaps did the most to locate John within an early Jewish context in the recent history of Johannine scholarship (*History and Theology in the Fourth Gospel*, 3rd ed., NTL [Louisville, KY: Westminster John Knox, 2003]; cf. also Martyn, "The Johannine Community among Jewish and Other Early Christian Communities," in *What We Have Heard from the Beginning: The Past, Present, and Future of Johannine Studies*, ed. Tom Thatcher [Waco, TX: Baylor University Press, 2007], 183–90). Although analysis of the concept of purity in John might be illuminated by comparison to Greco-Roman sources, the present analysis interprets the language of purity in the Fourth Gospel against its early Jewish context, in part because purity is so often related to the *Ioudaioi* in John, and in part because a single book can do only so much.

[21] F. C. Baur argued that John's Gospel reflects the final scission between Judaism and Christianity (F. C. Baur, *The Church History of the First Three Centuries*, trans. Allan Menzies, vol. 1, 3rd ed. [London: Williams and Norgate, 1878], 159). In Martyn's historical reconstruction, the scission was still painfully underway for the Johannine Community, as reflected in the peculiar threat of ἀποσυνάγωγος in John's Gospel (9:22), which mirrors the estrangement between the later Johannine community and the *Ioudaioi*. Martyn's work on the situation of the Johannine Community, influential in Johannine scholarship to the present day, has been critiqued both in its particular historical claims and as a whole hermeneutical project; for a summary of the issues

purity is one such fault line, which leaves no firm ground for constructive readings of the language of purity in the Fourth Gospel. In his work on the representation of the *Ioudaioi* in John's Gospel, Raimo Hakola, for instance, writes that the sign at Cana, in which Jesus makes water for the rites of Jewish purification into wine, "demonstrates that the old religious order of the Jews is replaced by a new one brought by Jesus."[22] The almost total scholarly neglect of purity in the Gospel of John might be explained by the widespread presumption that purity is significant only insofar as it is superseded or replaced, and so, is scarcely significant at all.[23]

and critical assessment, see Edward W. Klink, *The Sheep of the Fold: The Audience and Origin of the Gospel of John*, SNTSMS 141 (Cambridge: Cambridge University Press, 2007).

[22] Raimo Hakola, *Identity Matters: John, the Jews, and Jewishness*, NovTSup 118 (Leiden: Brill, 2005), 88. On the interpretation of the sign at Cana, see § 2.3.

[23] The neglect of purity in John has been *almost* total, but not complete. Five recent essays address purity in John's Gospel directly, concisely, and sympathetically: Ulrich Busse finds that the Fourth Gospel deals with purity positively, and primarily in relation to its temple-Christology ("Reinigung und Heiligung im Johannesevangelium," in *The Scriptures of Israel in Jewish and Christian Tradition: Essays in Honour of Maarten J. J. Menken*, ed. B. J. Koet, S. Moyise, and J. Verheyden, NovTSup 148 [Leiden: Brill, 2013], 141–58); Kent Brower locates purity within John's Christology as well as the mission of the disciples ("Purity in the Gospel of John," in *Purity: Essays in Bible and Theology*, ed. Andrew Brower Latz and Arseny Ermakov [Eugene, OR: Pickwick, 2014], 114–33); Mira Stare speaks of a theme of purity, which entails its transformation from ritual practice to the gift of God ("Die Reinheitsthematik im Johannesevangelium," *SNTSU* 40 [2015]: 79–95); Marianne Meye Thompson's inquiries into the way that ancient non-Jews were likely to have understood language of purification in the Fourth Gospel ("Baptism with Water and with Holy Spirit: Purification in the Gospel of John," in *The Opening of John's Narrative (John 1:19–2:22): Historical, Literary, and Theological Readings from the Colloquium Ioanneum 2015 in Ephesus*, ed. R. Alan Culpepper and Jörg Frey, WUNT 385 [Tübingen: Mohr Siebeck, 2017], 59–78); Wally V. Cirafesi, whose significant work was published after the completion of this manuscript, argues that "Jewish purity practices … form part of [John's] discursive strategy and negotiation of identity," an identity that Cirafesi describes as diasporic and Jesus-oriented; see *John within Judaism: Religion, Ethnicity, and the Shaping of Jesus-Oriented Jewishness in the Fourth Gospel*, Ancient Judaism and Early Christianity 112 (Leiden: Brill, 2021), 145–65, here 146. There are a number of general studies of the role that purity plays in the Gospel of John (Richard Bauckham, "The Holiness of Jesus and His Disciples in the Gospel of John," in *Holiness and Ecclesiology in the New Testament*, ed. Kent E. Brower and Andy Johnson [Grand Rapids, MI: Eerdmans, 2007], 95–113; some historical studies on purity in John (Roland Deines, *Jüdische Steingefässe und pharisäische Frömmigkeit: Ein archäologisch-historischer Beitrag zum Verständnis von Joh 2,6 und der jüdischen Reinheitshalacha zur Zeit Jesu*, WUNT 2/52 [Tübingen: Mohr Siebeck, 1993]; Gary M. Burge, "Siloam, Bethesda, and the Johannine Water Motif," in *John, Jesus, and History*, vol. 3, *Glimpses of Jesus through the Johannine Lens*, ed. Paul N. Anderson, Felix Just, and Tom Thatcher, ECL 18 [Atlanta, GA: SBL Press, 2016], 259–70). Several essays that deal with water imagery and the Holy Spirit also deal with purity (Hannah K. Harrington, "Purification in the Fourth Gospel in Light of Qumran," in *John, Qumran, and the Dead Sea Scrolls: Sixty Years of Discovery and Debate*, ed. Mary L. Coloe and Tom Thatcher, EJL 32 [Atlanta, GA: Society of Biblical Literature, 2011], 117–38; Craig S. Keener, *The Spirit in the Gospels and Acts: Divine Purity and Power* [Peabody, MA: Hendrickson, 1997], 135–89). And there are works that explain the death of Jesus as an act of purification, which draw from 1 John in order to make their argument (Martinus C. de Boer, "Jesus the Baptizer: 1 John 5:5–8 and the Gospel of John," *JBL* 107.1 [1988]: 87–106; *Johannine Perspectives on the Death of Jesus*, CBET 17 [Kampen: Pharos, 1996], 219–310; J. Ramsey Michaels, "By Water and Blood: Sin and Purification in John and First John," in *Dimensions of Baptism: Biblical and Theological Studies*, ed. Stanley E. Porter and Anthony R. Cross, JSNTSup 234 [London: Sheffield Academic, 2002], 149–62). To my knowledge, the only monograph-length study of purity in John is an unpublished dissertation arguing that the Johannine sectarian community redrew social boundaries by reworking and overturning Jewish concern for purity; but it is dated and weighed down by a lengthy discussion of background and method (Edward Roland Bolen, "Purity and Pollution in the Fourth Gospel" [PhD diss., Southern Baptist Theological Seminary, 1993]).

Such a presumption—grounded in unsure foundations long since abandoned by biblical scholars working on other early Jewish writings—obscures the surprising and wonderful ways that the Fourth Gospel reflects and employs biblical and early Jewish traditions of purity as it narrates how humanity is prepared and enabled to live with God through the work of Jesus.

The idea that purity was an older, basically meaningless ritual practice to be replaced by a new, superior, spiritual faith was advanced by William Robertson Smith in his seminal work, *Lectures on the Religion of the Semites*, in which he outlines those features of Semitic religion from which Christian faith and worship originated and developed.[24] Notwithstanding his impressive knowledge of classical and Semitic languages and writings, his clearly articulated arguments, and his careful comparative literary and historical approach to the religious practices of ancient Semitic peoples (all of which, no doubt, account for the enduring influence of his work), Smith's work was the product of the nineteenth-century intellectual milieu. The primary metaphor driving his historical work and warranting his interpretive judgments is that of evolution.[25] The language of evolution—language such as origins, development, survival, primitive, savage, advanced religion, and so on—pervades Smith's analysis of the religious institutions, ritual practices, and beliefs of the ancient peoples who spoke Semitic languages. Smith distinguishes between primitive and advanced religion by categorizing what he considers older, public, bodily, irrational, and ritualistic practices as primitive, and what he considers newer, higher ethical, and spiritual principles as advanced.[26] According to Smith, although traces of primitive and advanced religion are layered together in the OT like fossils in geological substrate, the critical scholar is able to distinguish primitive origins from later development, identify the causes of change, and reconstruct the line of development. Underlying this evolutionary analysis was Smith's intention to present a rational historical argument that the revelation of God was operative in Israel's history, evident in the superiority of the true religion of the OT over its primitive origins.[27]

---

[24] William Robertson Smith, *Lectures on the Religion of the Semites: First Series, The Fundamental Institutions* (New York: D. Appleton, 1889). The second and third series of the lectures he delivered on the religion of the Semites were rediscovered and first published a century after his death (*Lectures on the Religion of the Semites: Second and Third Series*, ed. John Day, JSOTSup 183 [Sheffield: Sheffield Academic, 1995]). Smith's enduring influence is seen in his role as the primary theorist on purity for an influential work on baptism, written some seventy years after his lectures were published, namely, George R. Beasley-Murray, *Baptism in the New Testament* (Grand Rapids, MI: Eerdmans, 1973), 1–16.

[25] Although Smith employs the language of evolution metaphorically, he wrote in an intellectual climate in which history was thought to reflect the actual progress and development of humankind. On the metaphor of evolution in nineteenth-century historiography, see Robert A. Nisbet, *Metaphor and History: The Western Idea of Social Development* (New Brunswick, NJ: Transaction Publishers, 2009), 159–88. Mary Douglas critiques the evolutionary metaphor that Smith uses to interpret purity in Israel's Scripture (*Purity and Danger: An Analysis of the Concepts of Pollution and Taboo* [London: Routledge & Kegan Paul, 1966], 16–17).

[26] Smith, *Lectures on the Religion of the Semites: First Series*, 1–28.

[27] On Smith's apologetic intent, which is evident in one of his later letters referring to his Burnett Lectures, see J. W. Rogerson, *The Bible and Criticism in Victorian Britain: Profiles of F. D. Maurice and William Robertson Smith*, JSOTSup 201 (Sheffield: Sheffield Academic, 1995), 146–9.

With evolutionary analysis and apologetic intent, Smith conceptualizes purity as fossilized remains that show the vitality of Israel's later religious ideals. In his lecture, "Holy Places and Their Relation to Man," and its accompanying note, "Holiness, Uncleanness and Taboo," Smith reconstructs the development of holiness from a cultic concept to an ethical ideal by arguing that the distinction between holiness and impurity marks an advance over Semitic religion. According to Smith, holiness in Semitic religion governed the relation between humanity and the gods in particular holy places, sanctuaries where priestly representatives of the gods would regulate participation in the cult according to arbitrary rules designed to enculturate reverence for the sacred and to avoid offense to the divine.[28] Like holiness in its merely cultic form, purity involves arbitrary and irrational rules that "belong to magical superstition—the barrenest of all aberrations of the savage imagination," and which are "founded only on fear."[29] Whereas holiness, in Smith's view, eventually developed out of its primitive cultic origins into ethical ideals of god-likeness, the laws regulating purity and impurity never found a place in advanced religion. He writes that "rules like this have nothing in common with the spirit of Hebrew religion," and "the irrationality of laws of uncleanness, from the standpoint of spiritual religion or even of the higher heathenism, is so manifest that they must necessarily be looked on as having survived from an earlier form of faith and of society."[30] For Smith and those located in his interpretive trajectory, the supersession of concern for purity marks a distinctive advancement and sign of superiority over older, ancient Semitic forms of ritual practice. Smith's work on purity is the distant warrant for the moral judgment (and it is a *moral* judgment) that it is good for concern with the old religious institution of purity to be replaced by the new spiritual form of faith.

Of all the seemingly superfluous details narrated in the Gospel of John, perhaps none is as fascinating as the identification of the six stone vessels holding the water that Jesus made wine as those set apart for the purification of the *Ioudaioi* (2:6). Biblical interpreters, never inclined to consider any detail superfluous, have offered varying explanations for its significance. The most strange and colorful explanations come from ancient Christian interpreters: lest someone think the water acquired flavor from the residue of wine in the vessels, the evangelist proves the authenticity of the sign by noting that the vessels must have been pure; whereas the creation of wine *ex nihilo* would have symbolized the repudiation of Scripture, the transformation of water for purification into wine reflects the fullness of meaning that Christ brings to Israel's Scripture; and the turning of pure water into wine verifies the claim that eucharistic wine becomes blood.[31] After the

---

[28] Smith, *Lectures on the Religion of the Semites: First Series*, 132–49, 427–35.

[29] Smith, *Lectures on the Religion of the Semites: First Series*, 144.

[30] Smith, *Lectures on the Religion of the Semites: First Series*, 428, 430.

[31] Whereas Chrysostom was absorbed with the authenticity of Jesus's sign, Augustine is interested in its hermeneutical significance, and Cyril of Jerusalem in its eucharistic mystagogy (see Joel C. Elowsky, ed., *John 1–10*, Ancient Christian Commentary on Scripture, New Testament 4a [Downers Grove, IL: IVP Academic, 2006], 95–8). In his own reading of the pericope, Thomas Aquinas reflects all these explanations (*Commentary on the Gospel of John: Chapters 1–5*, trans. Fabian R. Larcher and James A. Weisheipl, Thomas Aquinas in Translation Series [Washington, DC: Catholic University of America Press, 2010], 139–40).

nineteenth-century debates about whether the Gospels were to be read mythically, supernaturally, or rationalistically receded into the background, something of a consensus emerged that the replacement of water for ritual purification with wine signals the replacement of early Jewish rituals of purification with (faith in) Jesus.[32] In the more recent commentary tradition, the explanatory language of *replacement* and *supersession*, along with the idea that the *old* is replaced by the *new*, reflects the evolutionary paradigm of Robertson Smith and presumes that it would have been (and *is*) a sign of superiority that concern with purity be abandoned for faith in Jesus.[33] The dominant interpretation of this one detail typifies the scholarly approach to purity in the Fourth Gospel as a whole: early Jewish concepts of purity and practices of purification are replaced by faith in Jesus, a replacement that distinguished the Johannine Christians and elevated them above those whom John called the *Ioudaioi*.[34] In this view, purity plays an entirely negative role in the Gospel of John; purity is like the night sky against which stars shine so brightly, or the negative space against which the form of Jesus is so clearly seen.

---

[32] On the interpretation of Cana in the nineteenth century, see, for example, Augustus Tholuck, *Commentary on the Gospel of John*, trans. Charles P. Krauth, 7th ed. (Philadelphia, PA: Smith, English, 1859), 101–5. The original groundwork for the interpretation that purity is *replaced* by Jesus may have been Baur's assertion that in John's reading of Scripture, "the type ceases to be what it is as soon as the substance to which it refers has come" (*The Church History*, 159). On the idea that (faith in) Jesus replaces purity, see, for example, R. H. Lightfoot, *St. John's Gospel: A Commentary*, ed. C. F. Evans, Oxford Paperbacks 5 (London: Oxford University Press, 1960), 100; C. H. Dodd, *The Interpretation of the Fourth Gospel* (Cambridge: Cambridge University Press, 1953), 299; Raymond E. Brown, *The Gospel according to John*, AB 29 (Garden City, NY: Doubleday, 1966), 1:104–5; C. K. Barrett, *The Gospel according to St. John: An Introduction with Commentary and Notes on the Greek Text*, 2nd ed. (Philadelphia, PA: Westminster, 1978), 192; George R. Beasley-Murray, *John*, 2nd ed., WBC (Nashville, TN: Thomas Nelson, 1999), 36; Craig S. Keener, *The Gospel of John: A Commentary* (Peabody, MA: Hendrickson, 2003), 509–13; Craig R. Koester, *Symbolism in the Fourth Gospel: Meaning, Mystery, Community*, 2nd ed. (Minneapolis, MN: Fortress, 2003), 182; Andrew T. Lincoln, *The Gospel according to Saint John*, BNTC (Grand Rapids, MI: Baker Academic, 2013), 129, 131; Michael Theobald, *Das Evangelium nach Johannes*, RNT (Regensburg: Friedrich Pustet, 2009), 214. Three recent commentators demonstrate a more sympathetic view of purity in the Gospel of John: J. Ramsey Michaels, *The Gospel of John*, NICNT (Grand Rapids, MI: Eerdmans, 2010), 148–9; Jo-Ann A. Brant, *John*, Paideia Commentaries on the New Testament (Grand Rapids, MI: Baker Academic, 2011), 61–2; and Marianne Meye Thompson, *John: A Commentary*, NTL (Louisville, KY: Westminster John Knox, 2015), 62–4.

[33] The replacement of Jewish rites of purification by Jesus is related by Brown and others to a theme of replacement in the book of signs, which includes the replacement of the temple and feasts (Brown, *The Gospel according to John*, 1:lxx–lxxv; 1:cxliii). More recently, on the theme of the replacement of the temple by Jesus in the Fourth Gospel, see Alan R. Kerr, *The Temple of Jesus' Body: The Temple Theme in the Gospel of John*, JSNTSup 220 (London: Sheffield Academic, 2002), 102–35; 167–204.

[34] Hakola claims that the Johannine Community was to understand the replacement of purity as a mark of their superiority over the practice of the *Ioudaioi* (*Identity Matters*, 87–112). Making a more global claim, Daniel H. Weiss and Holger Zellentin argue that early Christians rejected the discourse of purity altogether, believing that concern for purity was itself a sign of impurity ("Purity and the West: Christianity, Secularism, and the Impurity of Ritual," in *Purity and Danger Now: New Perspectives*, ed. Robbie Duschinsky, Simone Schnall, and Daniel H. Weiss [Abingdon: Routledge, 2017], 181–200). By contrast, for a careful demonstration of the continuing significance of purity from Paul to Origen, see Moshe Blidstein, *Purity, Community, and Ritual in Early Christian Literature*, Oxford Studies in the Abrahamic Religions (New York: Oxford University Press, 2017), esp. 107–236.

1.2 Purity Remains: The Place of Purity in the Fourth Gospel

To be sure, the Fourth Gospel neglects the particular elements of purity that one finds in the portrayal of Jesus's ministry in the Synoptic Gospels. This neglect must be part of the rationale for Barrett's judgment that "John cares (and perhaps knows) little about the details of Jewish ablutions."[35] For all of Jesus's controversies with the *Ioudaioi* in the Fourth Gospel, not a single one focuses on ritual purification. No attention is given to the innovative practice of washing one's hands before a meal or to Jesus's judgments about what truly defiles (cf. Mk 7:1–23; Mt. 15:1–20).[36] Neither does Jesus in the Fourth Gospel rebuke the Pharisees for purifying only the outside of the cup (Lk. 11:39; Mt. 23:25–26) nor for straining out a gnat, only to swallow a camel, the latter, of course, being a forbidden food also (Mt. 23:23–24; Lev. 11:4).[37] Unlike the Synoptic Gospels, the ministry of Jesus in the Fourth Gospel does not involve the purification of the chronically impure, such as those afflicted with skin disease (cf., e.g., Mk 1:40–44; Mt. 8:1–4; Lk. 5:12–16; 17:11–19) or the woman with the flow of blood (Mk 5:25–34).[38] Neither does Jesus cast out a single impure spirit in the Fourth Gospel, which in the Synoptic Gospels expresses the eschatological victory of God over a demonic kind of impurity (cf., e.g., Mk 1:21–28; 5:1–20; Mt. 12:28; Lk. 11:20).[39] Matthew Thiessen has recently argued that these elements of the Synoptic Gospels' portrayal of Jesus—his healing of those afflicted with skin disease and the woman with the flow of blood, his raising of the recently deceased, and his expulsion of impure spirits—work to represent Jesus as one who overcomes the forces of death that cause ritual impurity.[40] By contrast,

---

[35] Barrett's comment was inspired by the Fourth Gospel's mention of a controversy over purification (3:25) without any apparent specification of its subject matter (*The Gospel according to St. John*, 221).

[36] Yair Furstenberg helpfully interprets the conflict between Jesus and the Pharisees over handwashing as a halakhic debate over the innovative idea that food could be defiled by defiled hands, and that the consumption of defiled food would defile the body, against which Jesus maintains a levitical position that the body itself is the source both of ritual and moral impurity ("Defilement Penetrating the Body: A New Understanding of Contamination in Mark 7.15," *NTS* 54.2 [2008]: 192–8).

[37] In an insightful essay on the role of purity in the Gospel of Matthew, Anders Runesson argues that ritual purity is represented as indispensable, but not as weighty as the matters of moral impurity that Jesus accuses the Pharisees of neglecting; see "Purity, Holiness, and the Kingdom of Heaven in Matthew's Narrative World," in *Purity, Holiness, and Identity in Judaism and Christianity: Essays in Memory of Susan Haber*, ed. Carl S. Ehrlich, Anders Runesson, and Eileen M. Schuller, WUNT 305 (Tübingen: Mohr Siebeck, 2013), 144–80.

[38] Thomas Kazen argues that a woman with an unceasing flow of blood would have had the most severe form of ritual impurity possible at the time, since the practice of *tevul yom*, which some ancient Jews thought reduced impurity caused by corpses or skin disease, did not pertain to a discharge of blood (*Issues of Impurity in Early Judaism*, ConBNT 45 [Winona Lake, IN: Eisenbrauns, 2010], 91–112).

[39] On the relation between demons and impurity in the Hebrew Bible, early Jewish writings, and the Synoptic Gospels, see Thomas Kazen, *Jesus and Purity Halakhah: Was Jesus Indifferent to Impurity?*, rev. ed., ConBNT 38 (Winona Lake, IN: Eisenbrauns, 2010), 300–9.

[40] Matthew Thiessen, *Jesus and the Forces of Death: The Gospels' Portrayal of Ritual Impurity within First-Century Judaism* (Grand Rapids, MI: Baker Academic, 2020). For the connection between death and ritual impurity, Thiessen depends on the work of Jacob Milgrom. Thiessen takes a literary and theological approach to purity in the Synoptic Gospels. On purity and the historical Jesus, see John P. Meier, *A Marginal Jew: Rethinking the Historical Jesus*, Vol. IV: *Law and Love*, ABRL (New York: Yale University Press, 2009), 342–477; Kazen, *Jesus and Purity Halakhah*.

the Fourth Gospel is silent about ritual impurity at certain moments that the matter could have been directly addressed in a theologically significant way. The levitical dietary laws are at most implicit in the scandal of Jesus's challenge to eat his flesh and drink his blood (Jn 6:52–59; cf. Lev. 11; 17:10–14). And the concern that was articulated about removing the stone from Lazarus's grave was not about the possibility of corpse impurity being transmitted to those present, but rather, about the stench (11:38–44).[41]

Nevertheless, reflected in the Fourth Gospel is a surprisingly detailed knowledge of purity in early Jewish life in the southern Levant. For example, the six jars (ὑδρίαι) at the wedding at Cana are said to be made of stone (λίθιναι), and for "the purification of the *Ioudaioi*" (τὸν καθαρισμὸν τῶν Ἰουδαίων, 2:6). Archeologists have found that stone vessels such as these were distributed widely throughout "Jerusalem, Judea, the Jordan valley, Jewish-inhabited parts of Perea, Galilee, and Western Golan," with fewer discoveries in Samaria and none throughout the diaspora.[42] That is, the use of stone vessels was distinctive to early Jewish daily life in those places. The dominant scholarly explanation for the apparently wide circulation of stone vessels among ancient Jews depends on the Mishnah's presumption that stone vessels were impervious to impurity.[43] In other words, among the reasons for the use of certain kinds of stone vessels was the desire of ancient Jews to be ritually pure in daily life, even apart from worship in the temple.[44] So the Fourth Gospel's inclusion of the details that these jars

---

[41] Thiessen appeals to the raising of Lazarus as the only evidence of concern for ritual impurity in the Fourth Gospel, tentatively noting that John's Gospel may have "abandoned all concern for ritual impurities" (*Jesus and the Forces of Death*, 120). But if the raising of Lazarus was to make a theological point about how Jesus's life-giving work abolishes corpse impurity, then it does so in only the most indirect, underdeveloped way.

[42] Jürgen K. Zangenberg, "Pure Stone: Archeological Evidence for Jewish Purity Practices in Late Second Temple Judaism [Miqwa'ot and Stone Vessels]," in *Purity and the Forming of Religious Traditions in the Ancient Mediterranean World and Ancient Judaism*, ed. Christian Frevel and Christophe Nihan, Dynamics in the History of Religions 3 (Leiden: Brill, 2013), 546; see also, Adler, "Between Priestly Cult and Common Culture," 240–5. For a comprehensive catalogue of stone vessels found by archeologists up to the early 1990s that includes their geographic distribution throughout southern Levant, see Deines, *Jüdische Steingefäße*, 39–165. Yonatan Adler has authored and co-authored a number of articles cataloguing and interpreting more recent archeological findings related to purity, including Yuval Gadot and Yonatan Adler, "A Quantitative Analysis of Jewish Chalk Vessel Frequencies in Early Roman Jerusalem: A View from the City's Garbage Dump," *IEJ* 66.2 (2016): 202–19; Yonatan Adler, "Ritual Purity in Daily Life after 70 CE: The Chalk Vessel Assemblage from Shu'afat as a Test Case," *JSJ* 52.1 (2020): 39–62. The latter article convincingly demonstrates that, contrary to previous thought, stone vessels continued to be manufactured and used after the destruction of the temple.

[43] See Zangenberg's summary of the literary and archeological evidence on the purity of stone vessels, with the important qualification that purity alone does not account for the widespread use of all stone vessels, adding ethnic and economic factors for consideration ("Pure Stone," 551–4).

[44] So argues Eyal Regev, "Pure Individualism: The Idea of Non-Priestly Purity in Ancient Judaism," *JSJ* 31.2 (2000): 176–202; also John C. Poirier, "Purity beyond the Temple in the Second Temple Era," *JBL* 122.2 (2003): 247–65. Both of these scholars build on E. P. Sanders' claim that ancient Jews sought "purity for its own sake," as opposed to imitating priestly purity (*Jewish Law from Jesus to the Mishnah: Five Studies* [London: SCM, 1990], 184). Regev and Poirier too hastily connect ritual purification to holiness as an explanation for why it was so widely practiced. I suggest, following Gedalyahu Alon, that some ancient Jews found exegetical basis in Leviticus for the practice of ritual purity apart from the temple (Wil Rogan, "Purity in Early Judaism: Current Issues and Questions," *CBR* 16.3 [2018]: 323–8); similarly, Miller, "Stepped Pools, Stone Vessels"; Adler, "Between Priestly Cult and Common Culture," 245–8.

were made of stone and for Jewish purification reflects an intimate knowledge of early Jewish practice and tradition.[45]

The Fourth Gospel also makes reference to the way that ancient Jews would go to Jerusalem sometime before the Passover in order to purify themselves (ἁγνίζω, 11:55), a practice attested in Philo of Alexandria:[46]

> As for the body, it purifies it with ablutions and sprinklings (λουτροῖς καὶ περιρραντηρίοις καθαίρει) and does not allow the person to be sprinkled and washed once for all (οὐκ ἐᾷ περιρρανάμενον εἰς ἅπαξ ἢ ἀπολουσάμενον) and then pass straightway within the sacred precincts, but bids him stay outside for seven days and be twice sprinkled (περιρραίνεσθαι) on the third and seventh day, and after that, when he has bathed himself (λουσαμένῳ), it gives him full security to come within and offer his sacrifice. (*Spec. Laws* 1.261)[47]

Philo apparently felt the need to explain to his diasporic Jewish audience that one must spend a week in the process of purification prior to offering sacrifice in the temple, instead of being washed once for all (ἅπαξ). The inclusion of this detail in the Fourth Gospel some decades after the destruction of the Jerusalem temple is evidence of familiarity with practices of purity during pilgrimage feasts.

Furthermore, although somewhat less explicitly, the Fourth Gospel features stepped pools built for ritual purification in the healings performed by Jesus on the man who was paralyzed (Jn 5:1-9) and the man who was born blind (9:1-7). Danielle Fatkin coined the charming acronym PBRIP to describe pools such as these: purpose-built ritual immersion pools.[48] Fatkin observes that the construction of these pools was a technological feat, and one not necessitated by biblical instructions about washing for purification, which do not prescribe the place in which one must wash.[49] The purpose for which the pools were built was ritual purification—not hygiene or leisure—as is evident in the Hasmonean Buried Palace at Jericho, in which a PBRIP was discovered adjacent to a bathtub.[50] These pools quickly became part of the built environment of areas of the southern Levant occupied by Jews, and further evidence the lengths to which ancient Jews would go in their pursuit of ritual purity.[51] Although the Fourth

---

[45] So Deines, *Jüdische Steingefäße*, 248-9; John Christopher Thomas, "The Fourth Gospel and Rabbinic Judaism," *ZNW* 82.3-4 (1991): 162-5.

[46] As helpfully noted by Busse, "Reinigung und Heiligung," 151-2.

[47] Throughout this book, all quotations of Philo's *Spec. Laws* and *Decalogue* are taken from Philo, *On the Decalogue. On the Special Laws, Books 1-3*, trans. F. H. Colson, LCL 320 (Cambridge, MA: Harvard University Press, 1937).

[48] At stake in this terminology is which historical and cultural contexts are determined to be most relevant to interpreting these archeological remains. Danielle Steen Fatkin prefers the descriptive acronym PBRIP to the term *miqweh*, because the latter term puts one at risk of anachronistically deducing the meaning and function of stepped pools built in the first-century B.C.E. with recourse to literary evidence from the second-century C.E. ("Invention of a Bathing Tradition in Hasmonean Palestine," *JSJ* 50 [2019]: 157-60).

[49] Fatkin, "Invention of a Bathing Tradition," 159-61.

[50] Fatkin, "Invention of a Bathing Tradition," 161-3.

[51] For recent work on the geographic distribution of such pools, see Adler, "Between Priestly Cult and Common Culture," 232-40. For a somewhat dated but nevertheless helpful catalogue of archeological discoveries of such pools, see Jonathan David Lawrence, *Washing in Water: Trajectories*

Gospel does not explicitly connect the pools of Bethesda and Siloam with purification, there are indications that this is what those pools were for.[52] That Bethesda was a stepped pool is indicated by the use of the verb καταβαίνω to describe how one would enter the pool (κολυμβήθρα, 5:7). And Jesus's command to the man born blind to go to the pool of Siloam in order to wash construes that pool as a place for washing (νίπτω, 9:7), just as one might go to a grave as a place for weeping (cf. 11:31). These features of the Fourth Gospel reflect a knowledge of early Jewish practices and beliefs about ritual purification.

Even if the Fourth Gospel reflects a certain historical knowledge of early Jewish ritual purification, the question remains as to how purification serves its literary and theological aims, if it does at all. This question brings us back to the proposal, mentioned earlier, that purity is located within what may be regarded as a theme of replacement in the Fourth Gospel. Scholars have argued that the replacement of purity is intended to demonstrate the superiority of faith in Jesus over the rituals that preceded him, as well as to reflect the ambivalence of the Johannine community toward the rites of purification they had previously practiced.[53] However, the idea that purity is replaced by faith in Jesus is as perplexing as it is problematic. To the extent that faith in Jesus represents something called Christianity and purity represents something called Judaism, claims about replacement ought to be challenged on the grounds that they do no justice to the complex negotiation of Jewish and Christian identity that lasted for centuries after the writings that became the NT were produced.[54] When one considers the claim about purity's replacement historically, one must recognize its magnitude, namely, that Johannine Christians ceased from practices of purification altogether (with the possible exception of the singular event of Christian baptism), which would have separated them not only from all ancient Jews, but also from all peoples in the ancient Mediterranean world.[55] When replacement appears to stand for something

of Ritual Bathing in the Hebrew Bible and Second Temple Literature, AcBib 23 (Atlanta, GA: Society of Biblical Literature, 2006), 251–68.

[52] Gary M. Burge helpfully summarizes the controverted archeological evidence about whether the pools of Siloam and Bethesda were intended for ritual purification, which seems particularly likely in light of the prevalence of PBRIPs throughout the southern Levant ("Siloam, Bethesda, and the Johannine Water Motif," 259–65). See also, Urban C. von Wahlde, "The Pool(s) of Bethesda and the Healing in John 5: A Reappraisal of Research and of the Johannine Text," *RB* 116.1 (2009): 111–36.

[53] See, for example, Brown, *The Gospel according to John*, 1:lxx and 1:103–4; Hakola, *Identity Matters*, 87–8.

[54] See Annette Yoshiko Reed's recent, wide-ranging collection of essays that problematize the use of the categories "Judaism" and "Christianity" to describe social history of ancient Jews, Christians, and Jewish Christians (*Jewish-Christianity and the History of Judaism: Collected Essays*, TSAJ 171 [Tübingen: Mohr Siebeck, 2018]). See also Megan Hale Williams's insightful essay reviewing the works of Boyarin, Lieu, and Becker and Reed on early Jewish-Christian relations ("No More Clever Titles: Observations on Some Recent Studies of Jewish-Christian Relations in the Roman World," *JQR* 99.1 [2009]: 37–55).

[55] On purity in the ancient Mediterranean world, see Christian Frevel and Christophe Nihan, eds., *Purity and the Forming of Religious Traditions in the Ancient Mediterranean World and Ancient Judaism*, Dynamics in the History of Religions 3 (Leiden: Brill, 2013). On Hellenistic perspectives on and concern for purity, see Robert Parker, *Miasma: Pollution and Purification in Early Greek Religion* (Oxford: Clarendon, 1983). See also Thompson, "Baptism with Water and with Holy Spirit," 59–78. Although there is second-century evidence of Christian polemic against Jewish purification of various kinds, early Christian rejection of early Jewish ritual purification was neither universal nor absolute. For example, Christian practice of various kinds of Jewish purificatory washings is

theological, then it must be asked whether purification with water really reflected the theology that interpreters suppose it did. There is no evidence, for example, that purification with water was understood as "everything by which man thinks he can live and which yet fails him when put to the test," or even as that which was accomplished by human effort rather than God's action.[56] Neither is purity ever evaluated in the Fourth Gospel as old, defective, burdensome, or legalistic.

The Fourth Gospel does not recapitulate the discussions of purity in the Synoptic Gospels, but this does not indicate its lack of concern for purity. What, then, is the place of purity in the Fourth Gospel? The Fourth Gospel seems not only to receive a wide-ranging early Jewish discourse about purity, which is reflected in its references to stone vessels (2:6), pools for immersion (5:2; 9:7), washings with water (1:19–34; 3:22–4:3; 11:55; 13:1–11), and evaluations of the disciples' purity (13:10–11; 15:2–3), but it also seems to produce such discourse. In other words, what is reflected in the Fourth Gospel is not simply historical reminiscence about purity, but an early Jewish discourse of purity employed to serve its literary and theological aims. Among ancient Jews, purity was a bodily practice as well as a discursive one. Bodies were washed with water and altars were sprinkled with blood as ancient Jews prepared to encounter the Holy One of Israel in worship, and the language of purity was then used to interpret these actions socially and theologically. Early Jewish discourses of purity and impurity both exceeded and outlasted the practices of purity involved in worship in the Jerusalem temple, as they became (to quote Balberg again) "powerful conceptual and hermeneutic tools through which ideas about self and other can be manifested."[57] The Fourth Gospel assumes and employs aspects of early Jewish discourses on purity as hermeneutical tools for interpreting what happened for God's people in the coming of Jesus. Critical analysis of how purity was immured in early Jewish cosmology and theology ought to warrant interpretive judgments regarding purity in John's Gospel, instead of well-worn treatments of purity as a symbol of burdensome, legalistic, and essentially meaningless religious rituals replaced by Jesus. The approach of this book is to analyze how the Fourth Gospel drew from conceptually robust, wide-ranging, and diverse biblical and early Jewish traditions of purity in order to develop its claims about the identity and work of Jesus.

In the next section, I attempt to map these biblical and early Jewish traditions of purity, which the Gospel of John inherited and with which it engaged. The work of Mary Douglas and Jonathan Klawans helps to outline the conceptual frameworks for how different varieties of purity were practiced, understood, and spoken about. As will be seen, the two primary patterns for conceiving of purity may be referred to as *ritual purity* and *moral purity*. These patterns are derived from Israel's Scripture,

---

reflected in the Pseudo-Clementines, *Didascalia apostolorum*, and Protoevangelium of James, on which see Blidstein, *Purity, Community, and Ritual*, 185–202.

[56] The quote is from Rudolf Bultmann, *The Gospel of John: A Commentary*, trans. George R. Beasley-Murray (Philadelphia, PA: Westminster, 1971), 120. Ernst Haenchen suggests the sign of wine made from water grants freedom from the purificatory rites by which "man attempted to make himself clean before God" (*John: A Commentary on the Gospel of John*, trans. Robert W. Funk [Philadelphia, PA: Fortress, 1984], 1:179).

[57] Balberg, *Purity, Body, and Self*, 2.

carried forward in multiple conflicting directions by ancient Jews, and both inherited and reproduced in the Fourth Gospel.

1.3 "Where There Is Dirt There Is System": Mapping Early Jewish Purities

Over the past five decades, in no small measure because of the explanatory power of Mary Douglas's anthropological approach to purity in her 1966 monograph *Purity and Danger*, biblical scholars have discovered how vital purity is for understanding the social and theological dimensions of early Jewish life.[58] How the laws of purity might be understood together as embodied theology, how the categories of ritual and moral impurity were appropriated and related to each other, how purity conceptualizes spaces or practices as sacred, and how conceptions and practices of purity worked to inscribe distinctive social identities—careful work on questions like these has yielded a plethora of illuminating studies on a wide range of ancient and early Jewish literature, with the notable exception of the Gospel of John. In short, the study of purity has become a crucial undertaking in interpreting and evaluating early Jewish life, practice, and belief, as well as the writings that ancient Jews produced and, in some sense, were produced by.

What made *Purity and Danger* a landmark work in the study of purity was its exposure of the conceptual limits imposed by the metaphor of evolution, thereby marking a significant shift in the study of purity and making way for a more comprehensive, undistorted, and sympathetic understanding of ancient Jewish purity than that set forth by William Robertson Smith. The evolutionary metaphor, which predominated in religious studies in the late nineteenth and early twentieth centuries, plotted modern western society at the apex of social development, a conceit that severely curtailed understanding of ancient rituals of purification.[59] As seen in the work of Smith, the concept and practices of purity were understood as irrational, arbitrary, and meaningless. Douglas's critique of the work of Smith showed that contemporary western concerns about hygiene are no more rational than the so-called primitive concerns about purity, and, moreover, that the tendency to distinguish sharply between different areas of existence—such as hygiene and religion—is distinctly modern.[60] Finding that

---

[58] Douglas's work was appropriated and introduced to biblical studies through Jacob Neusner, *The Idea of Purity in Ancient Judaism* (Leiden: Brill, 1973). Similarly influential has been Jacob Milgrom's three-volume commentary on Leviticus, which interprets the laws of ritual purity in the Priestly source in terms of a symbolic system (*Leviticus: A New Translation with Introduction and Commentary*, 3 vols., AB 3 [New York: Doubleday, 1991]). For helpful introductions to matters of purity in early Judaism, see Susan Haber, *"They Shall Purify Themselves": Essays on Purity in Early Judaism*, ed. Adele Reinhartz, EJL 24 (Atlanta, GA: Society of Biblical Literature, 2008), 9–71; or, more recently, Rogan, "Purity," 309–39.

[59] In the words of Grimes, metaphors "are not mere illustrations but either generative forces, creating new insights, or inhibitive blockers, obstructing insight" (*The Craft of Ritual Studies*, 183). On metaphor as understanding, see George Lakoff and Mark Johnson, *Metaphors We Live By* (Chicago, IL: University of Chicago Press, 1980).

[60] Douglas, *Purity and Danger*, 8–35.

any approach to purity that evaluates each law of purity on its own is futile, Douglas sets out to understand the total system in which ancient or contemporary practices of purity become intelligible. For Douglas, dirt is "matter out of place."[61] This definition implies an ordering and classification of human experiences and of the cosmos, so that, "where there is dirt there is system."[62] The metaphor of system is defined by the dual movement between the parts and the whole, the interrelationships between individual elements making up processes of purification, and the total symbolic system in which those elements are intelligible. One ought not to underestimate how influential the metaphor of system has been in the study of purity in early Jewish thought and practice.[63] Where the metaphor of evolution had once obstructed vision, the metaphor of system has opened up vistas.

It is difficult, if not impossible, to (re)construct a single, universally applicable concept of purity in early Jewish life because of the diversity of thought and practice about purity evident in the extant literature. The ambiguity and complexity of the language of purity in Leviticus (not to mention the rest of Israel's Scripture) came to be interpreted in diverse ways and became a source of conflict among ancient Jews, who were divided on a variety of questions, ranging from the most punctilious attention to how the laws of purity were to be observed to theological concerns about the life of Israel before God: What are the sources of defilement and how are different kinds of defilement removed? For what liturgical or quotidian practices must one become pure? In what sense are Gentiles impure? What is the relation of impurity to sin? Are the sacrifices of a defiled temple acceptable to God? What is to become of purity in Jewish worship after the destruction of the temple? For this reason, it is better to forsake the search for a single idea of purity and search for the conceptual frameworks or symbolic systems that ancient Jews may have held in common.

Jonathan Klawans has advanced the most useful proposal regarding the common conceptual system within which purity was both understood and debated among ancient Jews. The point of departure of his monograph, *Impurity and Sin in Ancient Judaism*, is Douglas's insight that purity is to be understood as a symbolic system.[64] Whereas Douglas sought to find a single system of impurity that could illuminate all the priestly laws regarding impurity, Klawans argues that there are two distinct and interrelated systems of impurity in the priestly tradition—what he calls *ritual impurity* (cf. Lev. 11–15; Num. 19) and *moral impurity* (cf. Lev. 18–20)—which, on account of

---

[61] Douglas, *Purity and Danger*, 44.

[62] Douglas, *Purity and Danger*, 44.

[63] On the ongoing significance of *Purity and Danger* and its critical appropriation by anthropologists, psychologists, and scholars in the humanities, see Robbie Duschinsky, Simone Schnall, and Daniel H. Weiss, eds., *Purity and Danger Now: New Perspectives* (Abingdon: Routledge, 2017). On critical appropriations of the metaphor of system in the study of purity by biblical scholars, see Rogan, "Purity," 310–19; Jonathan Klawans, "Methodology and Ideology in the Study of Priestly Ritual," in *Perspectives on Purity and Purification in the Bible*, ed. Baruch J. Schwartz, David P. Wright, Jeffrey Stackart, and Naphtali S. Meshel, LHBOTS 474 (New York: T&T Clark, 2008), 84–95.

[64] Klawans writes that "what must be studied, and then compared, are systems of defilement: the totalities of things that pollute, and the ways in which pollution can be conveyed" (*Impurity and Sin*, 8).

the ambiguity of biblical language, were interpreted in various ways by ancient Jews.[65] Since mostly the same language for impurity was used in Leviticus to refer to two different conceptual systems, Klawans distinguishes one system of impurity from the other by considering how individual ritual elements (i.e., the sources of impurity, the objects rendered impure, the agents of purification, the rites of purification, and whether the impurity is contagious through touch) interrelate and work together as a total system of purification and defilement.[66]

According to Klawans, Leviticus represents ritual impurity, on the one hand, as contracted temporarily through natural processes such as discharges of semen or menstrual blood, childbirth, affliction with skin diseases, and contact with corpses. While it is not sinful, ritual impurity renders a person unfit to enter the temple to offer worship.[67] Ritual impurity is removed by washing with water and the passage of time. The opposite of ritual impurity is the ritual purity requisite for participation in holy places and activities. Moral impurity, on the other hand, is contracted through certain sins with a defiling force, particularly idolatry, sexual immorality, and bloodshed.[68] Moral impurity pollutes not the individual who commits sin, but the sanctuary and land.[69] Moral impurity is more like pollution than contagion. Not unlike plastic pollution today, moral impurity is cumulative and permanent, but not transferable through touch. It affects the land as well as the people of the land, and the two are never completely separable.[70] Interestingly, moral impurity does not restrict individual worshippers from approaching the temple. Odd as it may seem, worship in the temple carried on even when Israel was defiling the temple through idolatry, bloodshed, and sexual immorality. The prophets of Israel recognized such situations as genuine cultic crises, and critiqued the sacrificial cult accordingly, for as the Proverbs say, "The sacrifice of the wicked is an abomination to the LORD" (Prov. 15:8).[71] Although the impurity of the temple as a result of sin is somewhat alleviated by sacrifice, ultimately the temple's defilement by the people's sin renders its sacrifices ineffective and results in the people's exile from the land (cf. Lev. 18:24–30). In one of Ezekiel's oracles of judgment, for example, the Lord says, "When I purified you in your filthy lewdness, you did not become pure from your filth; you shall not again be purified until I have satisfied my fury upon you" (24:13 NRSV, trans. mod.).[72] The opposite of moral

---

[65] In distinguishing between ritual impurity and moral impurity, Klawans acknowledges his indebtedness to the work of David Hoffman, Jacob Milgrom, Tikva Fymer-Kensky, and David P. Wright (*Impurity and Sin*, 13–17). Klawans carries forward their work by querying the differing reception these purity systems received in ancient Jewish communities as well as by standardizing terminology for each of these systems.

[66] See Klawans's presentation of ritual and moral impurity in Leviticus (*Impurity and Sin*, 22–31).

[67] Klawans, *Impurity and Sin*, 23–6.

[68] Klawans, *Impurity and Sin*, 26–31.

[69] Klawans, *Impurity and Sin*, 26–31.

[70] Bohdan Hrobon argues that the concept that the land is defiled by sin in the Law and Prophets depends on a sense that the Lord owns the land, which the people of Israel occupy only as "aliens and tenants" (Lev. 25:23); see *Ethical Dimension of Cult in the Book of Isaiah*, BZAW (Berlin: de Gruyter, 2010), 53–71.

[71] Klawans, *Purity, Sacrifice, and the Temple*, 75–100. Unless otherwise noted, all English translations of the Bible throughout this book are from the NRSV.

[72] Following the observation of Yitzhaq Feder that purity and cleanness are not interchangeable terms in English, and that the former term aligns more closely with the semantic possibilities of ancient

impurity is the holiness of people and temple needed for the divine presence to abide there. Klawans's distinction between the interrelated systems of ritual impurity and moral impurity disentangles the contagious defilement contracted by Israelites from sources that are not sinful from the lasting defilement of the temple, the land, and the people caused by certain defiling sins. As will be seen, the Fourth Gospel has concepts of both ritual and moral purity that are intelligible in terms of these systems of purity reflected in Israel's Scripture and early Jewish writings.

It may be helpful to attempt to visualize the workings of these systems of ritual and moral purification, as well as the way that different elements of the systems were often lexicalized in the LXX and early Jewish writings.[73] Of course, any generalization about how ritual and moral purification were conceived among ancient Jews will fail to represent their complexity and variety, but these patterns may nevertheless illuminate how the language of purity often functioned. The first distinction to make is between ritual purity and holiness. One may notice the two sets of antonymic relations in Lev. 10:10, between the holy and profane and the pure and impure: "You are to distinguish between the holy [שֹׁדֶק; ἅγιος] and the common [חֹל; βέβηλος], and between the impure [אֵמֵט; ἀκάθαρτος] and the pure [רֹהָט; καθαρός]" (NRSV, trans. mod.). The relationship between ritual purity and holiness may thus be visually as given in Figure 1:[74]

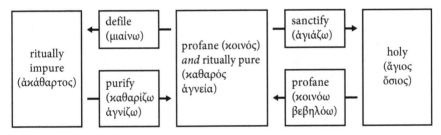

Figure 1 Ritual Purity and Holiness.

terminology for purity, throughout this book I modify English translations of the Bible and early Jewish sources that use the words *clean, cleanse,* and *unclean* to *pure, purify,* and *impure,* always noting that I have done so ("The Semantics of Purity in the Ancient Near East: Lexical Meaning as a Projection of Embodied Experience," *JANER* 14 [2014]: 88).

73   In the paragraphs on ritual and moral purity that follow, I owe an intellectual debt to Jonathan Klawans, *Impurity and Sin,* 3–60; Klawans, *Purity, Sacrifice, and the Temple,* 49–73, since he has more than any other scholar shaped the way I understand and synthesize the vast and unwieldy biblical and early Jewish traditions of purity, including the relationship of impurity to sin and the interrelation between purity, sacrifice, and the temple.

74   This chart is adapted from Bauckham, "The Holiness of Jesus and His Disciples in the Gospel of John," 96, who, in turn, had adapted his chart from Gordon J. Wenham, *The Book of Leviticus,* NICOT (Grand Rapids: Eerdmans, 1979), 19. Philo of Alexandria, commenting on Lev. 10:10, also upholds the distinction: "Again, it is the special task of law and instruction to 'distinguish' [διαστέλλειν] the profane from the sacred [βέβηλα ἁγίων] and the impure from the pure [ἀκάθαρτα καθαρῶν], just as conversely it is the way of lawlessness and indiscipline to mix and confuse everything and thus force under the same head things which are in conflict with each other" (*Drunkenness,* 143 [Colson and Whitaker]).

The term for purity in the Hebrew Bible, טהר, in the LXX translates to καθαρίζω ("purify") and the term for impurity, טמא, translates to μιαίνω ("make impure; defile") and ἀκαθάρτος ("impure").[75] The two terms used most often for washing in the Hebrew Bible are רחץ and כבס. In the LXX, רחץ usually translates to λούω ("bathe") but also to πλύνω ("wash [something other than one's body]"), and νίπτω ("wash [part of the body]"), and כבס translates solely to πλύνω.[76] The term signifying consecration or holiness, קדשׁ, is almost always translated either as ἅγιος or ἁγιάζω ("holy" or "sanctify or dedicate" depending on whether it is rendered as a noun or verb), and in some contexts is translated with the term ἁγνίζω ("purify"; see, e.g., Exod. 19:10; Isa. 66:17; 1 Chron. 15:12–14; 2 Chron. 29:6, 15–19).[77]

We may make three observations about ritual purity in relation to holiness. First, while ritual purity is needed for a person, vessel, or place to be fit for holiness, ritual purity is not equivalent to holiness.[78] One may be ritually pure but not consecrated as holy. Sanctification is what moves one from ritual purity to holiness. And holiness is not reducible to subjective experiences of transcendence, sociological codes of inviolability, or principles of ethical life, even if all these play significant roles in grasping at holiness's meaning.[79] God's presence is determinative for holiness, and what is God's derives its holiness from that living presence.[80] The people of God are to be ritually pure for an encounter with holiness because the holy presence of God dwells among them.

Second, ritual impurity is not equivalent to sin.[81] To be sure, contact between ritual impurity and holiness was thought to result in cultic and moral disaster. Since ritual impurity was unavoidable, the disaster was not whether a person designated as holy might become ritually impure. There were, after all, special ablutions designated for priests alone, such as the washing of hands and feet (Exod. 30:18–21). The moral, cultic disaster happened when a ritually impure person partook in holy food or sacred worship in the temple. An Israelite who ate sacred sacrifices while ritually impure was to be "cut off from their kin" (Lev. 7:20), and the people of Israel were to be attentive to their impurities so as not to defile the temple and die (15:31). That is, what was sin was not ritual impurity itself, but the failure to separate ritual impurity from holiness.

Third, ritual purity and holiness were vitally, dialectically related. Participation in holy places and sacred practices was necessarily preceded by ritual purification, and ritual purification had the effect of designating certain places or practices as holy. Thus, when Josephus speaks of the "seven purities" (τάς ἑπτὰ ἁγνείας, *J.W.* 1.26) he recounts

---

[75] See BDAG, s.v. "καθαρίζω"; "μιαίνω"; "ακαθάρτος."
[76] See BDAG, s.v. "λούω"; "πλύνω"; "νίπτω." On terminology for purity and washing in the Hebrew Bible, see Lawrence, *Washing in Water*, 25–42.
[77] See BDAG, s.v. "ἅγιος"; "ἁγιάζω"; "ἁγνίζω."
[78] As Bauckham observes, the distinction between ritual purity and holiness has become more widely recognized of late, but one does still occasionally find the uncritical conflation of the two in NT scholarship ("The Holiness of Jesus," 95–8).
[79] Markus Bockmuehl " 'Keeping It Holy': Old Testament Commandment and New Testament Faith," in *I Am the Lord Your God: Christian Reflections on the Ten Commandments*, ed. Christopher R. Seitz and Carl E. Braaten (Grand Rapids, MI: Eerdmans, 2005), 95–124.
[80] So Bockmuehl, "Keeping It Holy," 103.
[81] See Klawans, *Impurity and Sin*, 24–5.

instructions about where one may not go depending on what rendered him or her ritually impure (*J.W.* 5.193–199, 227–229, 236). Increasing levels of ritual purity were needed to cross through eight circles of increasing holiness as a man or woman drew nearer to the holy of holies in the temple in Jerusalem.[82] And, as mentioned before, ritual purification was observed even apart from participation in worship in the temple.[83] Scholars have puzzled over the rationale for the observance of ritual purification apart from the temple, often debating whether it was an imitation of priestly purity or was simply regarded as good to be ritually pure.[84] While the matter will not be settled here, what ought not to be overlooked is how some early Jewish texts feature ritual purification that precedes meals, prayer, and the reading of Torah, all daily practices that may have been thought to bring one into contact with the holiness of God.[85] That is, even if the state of ritual purity was not always related to the temple, it seems always to have been related to the possibility of encounter with the holy presence of God.

What this dynamic between ritual purity and holiness does not take into account is sin.[86] The sins that cause moral impurity are not simply the worst ethical violations imaginable, though idolatry, bloodshed, and sexual misdeeds are indeed agonizingly violating to those who suffer from them. They are those sins that also most violate the faith that God shares with Israel, and Israel shares with God. Where sin's impurity is present, the divine presence is likely to depart from the temple and people, and the people are likely to be deported from the land. This is most transparent in Ezekiel's account of the departure of glory from the temple (Ezek. 8–11). In a vision, Ezekiel sees

---

[82] Matan Orian helpfully analyzes Josephus's seven purities, discerning in them a hierarchy of impure persons (with those afflicted by skin disease and men with discharges being most impure) and a hierarchy of pure persons (with pure women most restricted in their access to the temple and the high priest the least restricted); he also notices how Josephus designates eight geographic thresholds that each require more ritual purity to cross ("Josephus's Seven Purities and the Mishnah's Ten Holinesses," *JSJ* 47.2 [2016]: 183–93).

[83] In an influential essay, first published in Hebrew in 1937, Gedalyahu Alon identifies two conflicting traditions of interpretation running through early Judaism as regards the spatial boundaries in which ritual purity was practiced: the "restrictive" tradition, represented by the Sadducees and some rabbinic halakha, tends to limit concern for ritual purity to participation in the temple cult and the laws of purity pertaining to priests. The "expansionist" tradition, represented by Josephus, Philo, and the Essenes, found exegetical basis for the practice of ritual purity outside of the temple (cf., e.g., Lev. 11:8, 14:34–53) and did so ("The Bounds of the Laws of Levitical Cleanness," in *Jews, Judaism, and the Classical World: Studies in Jewish History in the Times of the Second Temple and Talmud*, trans. Israel Abrahams [Jerusalem: Magnes, 1977], 190–234).

[84] Jacob Neusner argues that the Pharisees sought to imitate priestly purity and distinguish themselves as a purity sect (*Judaism in the Beginning of Christianity* [Philadelphia, PA: Fortress, 1984], 56–8). E. P. Sanders argues that the Pharisees were concerned primarily with the study of the Torah, but that they also pursued "purity for its own sake" (*Jewish Law from Jesus to the Mishnah*, 235–6). The debate between them, I have argued, concerns the question of the social and geographical bounds in which ritual purity was a concern (Rogan, "Purity in Early Judaism," 323–8).

[85] See Poirier, "Purity beyond the Temple," 253–9. Of those ancient Jews who practiced ritual purification indiscriminately, Alon says that they applied "sanctity to all Jews (even those who were not priests) and to all places (apart from the Temple) and at all times" ("The Bounds of the Laws of Levitical Cleanness," 233).

[86] Klawans helped me see how idolatry, bloodshed, and sexual misdeeds are represented in Scripture as sins that defile, and helped me make connections between the defilement of sin and Israel's worship in the temple (*Impurity and Sin*, 26–30; *Purity, Sacrifice, and the Temple*, esp. 3–174). He has deeply influenced my thought in the sense that his work informs how I read biblical texts, so in the paragraphs that follow I owe him an intellectual debt.

the seventy elders of the house of Israel in the outer court of the temple worshipping images of creatures impure to eat (8:10–12), then women in the temple weeping for Tammuz (8:14–15), and then twenty-five men in the temple's holy place prostrating themselves before the sun (8:16). For Ezekiel, all these acts of idolatry are closely associated with how the house of Judah fills the land with violence and bloodshed (8:17; 9:9; 11:6).[87] Thus, entangled in the cultic violation of idolatry is the ethical violation of bloodshed. The people's presumption that "the LORD has forsaken the land" instantiates itself in the disfigurement of holiness through idolatry in worship and bloodshed in society (8:12; 9:9). These defiling sins were incommensurable with the presence of Israel's Lord. Therefore, these sins provoked the withdrawal of God's glory from the holy place, which is narrated as glory's regression from the inner court (8:3–4), to the temple's threshold (9:3), through the east gate (10:18–19), and finally east of the city (11:23). The prophecy that completes this visionary sequence in the text's final form is alternatively the severe judgment of exile from the land (11:5–12, 21) and the improbable mercy of regathering a renewed people to the land (11:13–20). Although the language of purity is only implicit in this vision of sin, judgment, and mercy in Ezek. 8–11, it becomes explicit later in one of Ezekiel's oracles of restoration that idolatry and bloodshed defiled the land and provoked Israel's deportation, but that God will remove sin's impurity in Israel's restoration:

> Mortal, when the house of Israel lived on their own soil, they defiled it [μιαίνω] with their ways and their deeds; their conduct in my sight was like the impurity [ἀκαθαρσία] of a woman in her menstrual period. So I poured out my wrath upon them for the blood that they had shed upon the land, and for the idols with which they had defiled it. I scattered them among the nations, and they were dispersed through the countries; in accordance with their conduct and their deeds I judged them. (36:17–20 NRSV, trans. mod.)

The promise that follows the judgment is that sin's impurity will finally be removed from Israel when God purifies them and restores them to the land: "I will sprinkle pure water [ὕδωρ καθαρόν] upon you, and you shall be pure from all your impurities [καθαρισθήσεσθε ἀπὸ πασῶν τῶν ἀκαθαρσιῶν ὑμῶν], and from all your idols I will purify you [καθαριῶ ὑμᾶς]" (Ezek. 36:25, see also vv. 22–36). God's removal of sin's impurity appears here not as an iterative act of forgiveness for regular offenses, but as a final restoration to holiness, the renewal of the people so that they can sanctify the name of God (36:23) and keep God's commandments (36:27).

That idolatry, bloodshed, and sexual misdeeds pollute the land and the people, and provoke God's judgment and mercy is evident also in Jeremiah and Isaiah. Jeremiah indicts Israel for defiling itself by going after Baal (μιαίνω, 2:23), for the robes stained with the blood of the poor (2:34), and for its sexual misdeeds that polluted the land (ἐμίανας τὴν γῆν ἐν ταῖς πορνείαις σου, 3:1–3, 9). The indictment is perhaps most

---

[87]   On this reading, see Walther Zimmerli, *Ezekiel 1: A Commentary on the Book of the Prophet Ezekiel, Chapters 1–24,* ed. Leonard J. Greenspoon, trans. Ronald E. Clements, Hermeneia (Philadelphia, PA: Fortress, 1979), 240–5.

pointed when the Lord says, "I brought you into a plentiful land ... But when you entered you defiled my land [ἐμιάνατε τὴν γῆν μου] and made my heritage an abomination [βδέλυγμα]" (2:7 LXX).[88] Both the land and the people are represented as defiled by these sins. But the ablutions of the people with soap and water will not remove the stains of their injustices (2:23). Ritual purification will not remove the sins of idolatry, or sexual misdeeds, or bloodshed. Sin's stain remains after washing. It must finally be removed by God's act of purification in Israel's restoration, when God will purify (καθαρίζω) them from their sin (33:8).

While Isaiah also envisions the sin of the people as defiling and finally to be removed by God (cf., e.g., Isa. 4:4), one also finds in Isaiah that the sacrifices of people defiled by bloodshed are loathsome to God (cf., also, Hag. 2:13–14). For this reason, Bohdan Hrobon speaks of the "ethical dimension of cult" in Isaiah.[89] Rather than interpreting Isaiah's critiques of cultic practice a critique of ritual *per se* (see, e.g., 1:10–17; 43:22–28; 58:1–14), Hrobon argues that cultic practices were rendered ineffective by the moral impurity of the people. For instance, the prophet speaks of the Lord's rejection of Israel's sacrifices on account of their iniquity and bloodstained hands (1:13, 15). The people had hoped to appear before God's presence with their offerings and convocations (1:12), but God hides from them because of their defiling sin (1:15).[90] Their sacrifices are not represented as removing their sins.[91] Instead, their sins repel God's presence from them in worship, the divine presence which their sacrifices were meant to maintain. Their cultic practice becomes acceptable, it seems, only if they are purified of their sins, not by a cultic act of washing, but by the washing away of evil deeds: "Wash yourselves; make yourselves pure [καθαροὶ γένεσθε], remove the evil of your doings from before my eyes" (1:16 LXX).[92] Thus, for Isaiah, moral impurity undermines Israel's worship of God and moral purification is needed for Israel's worship to be acceptable to God again.

---

[88] Unless otherwise noted, English translations of the LXX follow Albert Pietersma and Benjamin G. Wright, eds., *A New English Translation of the Septuagint* (New York: Oxford University Press, 2007). However, as noted above with respect to the NRSV, I do replace the terms *clean, cleanse,* and *unclean* with their near-synonyms *pure, purify,* and *impure* for the sake of accuracy and consistency, always noting I have done so by the formula, NETS, trans. mod. When NETS is the translation cited, the LXX is the version being cited.

[89] Hrobon, *Ethical Dimension*, 37–52.

[90] Hrobon argues that idolatry is the referent of the word אָוֶן (1:13), which, if true, would further signify that the defilement of the people is the problem with their worship. He also reads לֵרָאוֹת פָּנַי as "see God's face," rather than "appear before me" (1:12), which would render God's pledge to hide from them even more devastating (1:15). More importantly, through close analysis of Isa. 1:10–17, he argues that the people's moral impurity cannot be removed by cultic practice and must be ameliorated by the removal of their evil deeds (*Ethical Dimension*, 75–115). He overlooks septuagintal Isaiah's astonishing translation of 1:14, which supports his argument: "no longer will I forgive your sins" (οὐκέτι ἀνήσω τὰς ἁμαρτίας ὑμῶν)!

[91] The relation of sacrifice to purity and the temple is a vast, controverted discourse. I follow Klawans, Hrobon, and others who view the sacrifices of the temple as "joyful and productive" offerings that maintain the presence of God in the temple, which defiling sins threaten (see, e.g., Klawans, *Purity, Sacrifice, and the Temple*, 71–2; Hrobon, *Ethical Dimension*, 13–17).

[92] For an analysis of the metaphor of washing away sin in the Hebrew Bible, see Lesley DiFransico, "Identifying Inner-Biblical Allusion through Metaphor: Washing Away Sin in Psalm 51," *VT* 65 (2015): 542–57. DiFransico finds this metaphor only in Isa. 1:16; 4:4; Jer. 2:23; 4:14; and Ps. 51:4, 9, although she acknowledges something like it is present also in Ezek. 36:22–25 and Zech. 13:1.

The purification of sin's impurity is irreducible to other language that interpreters might be inclined to use, such as forgiveness or atonement. As Joseph Lam has shown, moral impurity has its own metaphorical integrity in the Hebrew Bible.[93] Metaphors, he says, have a systematicity, a pattern to them constituted by their linguistic associations.[94] For instance, when sin is spoken of as a burdensome weight, its removal consists in a bearing away, which comes to be lexicalized as forgiveness. Or when sin is figured as a deviation from a path or goal, its correction involves a turning, or a different way.[95] Too much conceptual freight is lost when interpreters uncritically conceptualize moral purification as forgiveness, since moral purification is a dynamic element in Israel's embodied theology and worship. Even if the opposite of moral impurity is holiness, moral purity is not simply personal holiness or morality; it is something more like the corporate, covenantal faithfulness that maintains the holy presence of the God of Israel in the temple and sustains the efficacy of the cultic rites of the temple.[96] In other words, there is not *one* system of purity (ritual purity), the language of which is removed from the context of cultic worship and applied to another context called morality, but *two* systems of purity—ritual and moral purity.[97] Sin's defilement of the land and people, the resulting divine judgment or divine purification from sin, and the restoration of Israel that comes as a result—all these hang together on the same broad conceptual framework in the Law and Prophets.[98]

While the language of purity is often the same both with respect to moral purification and ritual purification, unique to contexts where moral impurity is in view are the terms חנף ("pollute," translated in the LXX as μιαίνω and μολύνω) and תועבה ("abomination," most often translated in the LXX as βδέλυγμα, but with some regularity in Ezekiel as ἀνομία).[99] The distinction Klawans has codified is one not explicitly made in the text of Scripture, but is a heuristic device to distinguish between what are evidently two interrelated systems of purity operative in Israel's Scripture.

Now, to be sure, the work of Klawans on ritual and moral purity has its limitations. His symbolic, systemic approach to ritual and moral purity is just not as comprehensive as he first supposed, as shown by the work of Christine Hayes on genealogical impurity (which is, in Ezra-Nehemiah, another kind of impurity altogether) and Jordan Rosenblum on the dietary laws (which simply defy the categories of ritual and moral impurity).[100] Moreover, scholars such as Thomas Kazen, Yitzhak Feder, and T. M.

---

[93]   Lam, *Patterns of Sin*, 179–206.
[94]   Lam, *Patterns of Sin*, 10–14.
[95]   Lam, *Patterns of Sin*, 16–86, 156–78.
[96]   On this reading of moral purity, see Klawans, *Purity, Sacrifice, and the Temple*, 68–72.
[97]   On there being two symbolic systems related to purity, see Klawans, *Impurity and Sin*, 36–8. In my view, the cultic (in)consequence of moral purity is really what is at stake in the debate between Neusner, Klawans, and Kazen on the metaphorical and real in relation to ritual and moral purity (cf. Neusner, *The Idea of Purity in Ancient Judaism*, 11–16; Klawans, *Impurity and Sin*, 32–3; Kazen, *Jesus and Purity Halakhah*, 205). For a careful analysis of the metaphorical character of sin as impurity, see Lam, *Patterns of Sin*, 188–91, 201–5.
[98]   Hrobon argues that the cultic, priestly conception of the land's belonging to God and its possible defilement by sin is operative also within the Prophets, particularly Hosea, Jeremiah, Ezekiel, and Isaiah (*Ethical Dimension*, 53–71).
[99]   Klawans, *Impurity and Sin*, 26–8.
[100] Hayes, *Gentile Impurities and Jewish Identity*; Jordan D. Rosenblum, *The Jewish Dietary Laws in the Ancient World* (New York: Cambridge University Press, 2016). Klawans acknowledges

Lemos have set forward important critiques delineating the limitations and drawbacks of approaching purity as a symbolic system, most significantly, that the approach sometimes obscures particular aspects of biblical texts that resist scholars' theorizing about purity.[101] Kazen and Lemos advocate for the abandonment of a symbolic, systemic approach to purity. Kazen argues that a "bio-psychological approach" that attends to the role of disgust in human emotion and the cognitive character of metaphorical language better explains (im)purity in biblical texts than the systemic approach of Douglas and Klawans.[102] On the one hand, Kazen and Lemos rightly warn against theoretical constructs that predetermine the interpretation of texts. That is, one cannot assume that what Klawans says about the meaning of ritual purity constitutes the Fourth Gospel's theory of purity, for example.[103] On the other hand, Kazen's bio-psychological approach has its own limitations. It offers no help for the explanation of purity in the Fourth Gospel because the Fourth Gospel nowhere connects purity with anything that might be considered "disgust triggers," such as skin disease, corpses, genital discharges, or swarming creatures.[104] More substantively, Kazen's approach to explaining purity in biblical texts with a bio-psychological approach assumes a western, scientific metaphysics in such a way that may obscure the alterity of these biblical texts.[105] What Kazen does not appreciate about the symbolic, systematic approach is

---

the difficulty of categorizing dietary laws in terms of ritual or moral purity (*Impurity and Sin*, 31–2).

[101] Thomas Kazen, "Levels of Explanation for Ideas of Impurity: Why Structuralist and Symbolic Models Often Fail While Evolutionary and Cognitive Models Succeed," *JAJ* 9.1 (2018): 75–88; T. M. Lemos, "Where There Is Dirt, Is There System?: Revisiting Biblical Purity Constructions," *JSOT* 37.3 (2013): 283–9. Yitzhak Feder, "Contagion and Cognition: Bodily Experience and the Conceptualization of Pollution (*Ṭumʾah*) in the Hebrew Bible," *JNES* 72.2 (2013): 151–67; Feder, "The Semantics of Purity." For more analysis of Kazen and Lemos, see Rogan, "Purity," 315–18.

[102] Kazen, "Why Structuralist," 92–100; Thomas Kazen, "Dirt and Disgust: Body and Morality in Biblical Purity Laws," in *Perspectives on Purity and Purification in the Bible*, ed. Baruch J. Schwartz, David P. Wright, Jeffrey Stackart, and Naphtali S. Meshel, LHBOTS 474 [New York: T&T Clark, 2008], 43–64; Kazen, *Issues of Impurity in Early Judaism*, 13–40. In a similar vein, but with a different angle, Feder draws on embodiment theory to argue that the roots of biblical laws about impurity are in the repeated bodily experiences of contagious infection and of objects that are susceptible to stains, which developed through metaphorical integration into metaphysical concepts such as the stain of bloodshed ("Contagion and Cognition," 151–67).

[103] Klawans, like others, has explained the logic of the laws of ritual impurity in their connection to sex and death, which may both be taken as conditions of finite, mortal, human life, since the former makes for a life's beginning, and the latter its end (Klawans, *Purity, Sacrifice, and the Temple*, 53–68). In making that claim, Klawans is following David P. Wright, "Clean and Unclean (OT)," *ABD* 6:729–41. The theory is that ritual purification is a practice in *imitatio Dei*, symbolically and temporarily removing the conditions of mortality to come into the presence of the living God (Klawans, *Purity, Sacrifice, and the Temple*, 56–8). Although I find this theory of ritual purity helpful and provocative, the meaning of purity in the Fourth Gospel must be surmised exegetically, as much as possible.

[104] Kazen, "Levels of Explanation," 92–5.

[105] Kazen argues that in contrast to the symbolic, structuralist approach of scholars such as Mary Douglas and Jonathan Klawans, the "evolutionary, contextual, and cognitive models … do not try to provide ideological superstructures" ("Levels of Explanation," 100). It seems plain to me, however, that to employ such models for explaining purity, one must assume quite a lot about theology, cosmology, and anthropology. Of course, as Kazen rightly observes, symbolic, structuralist approaches are not innocent of contemporary cultural assumptions either. But they do seem better designed to understand, insofar as possible, ancient writings about purity on their own terms. For the insight that the need for explanation is often a sign of different ontologies, I am indebted to Grimes, *The Craft of Ritual Studies*, 70.

what draws me to it, namely, its capacity to open up the imagination of the interpreter to the otherness of the text. There is also the question of subject matter. The psychology of disgust aims to explain the ancient persons who practiced rituals of purification, but this can be done only insofar as those persons are able to be reconstructed from texts. By contrast, cognitive linguistics can certainly help illuminate the language of purity in biblical texts, and, interestingly, such analysis often moves toward a distinction between ritual and moral purity.[106]

My own concern is not to explain purity in terms of contemporary western forms of thought, so much as it is to interpret purity in the Fourth Gospel in such a way that its particularity is preserved. The approach of this book is synchronic and textual. It is a synchronic, literary study in the sense that the subject matter is the Fourth Gospel's representation of persons, concepts, and events, and not the things themselves. It is also a historical study in recognition that the Fourth Gospel is a narrative produced in a particular historical context.[107] To conceive of the Fourth Gospel as an early Jewish writing involves attention to its constraint and mobility within that cultural context, its assumed traditions and its studied innovations.[108] The work of Klawans is helpful for interpretation not because the system he speaks about is *there* in the text, but because it opens up interpretive questions and possibilities that to this point have been obscured by evolutionary paradigms of thought or the failure to distinguish ritual and moral impurities.

Given that John's Gospel is a narrative that does not offer an explicit account of purity, how does one tell what conceptions and practices of purity are reflected in the language of purity used in it? Among biblical scholars there is a growing interest in the interdisciplinary field of ritual studies to interpret and evaluate ritual concepts and practices such as purification.[109] In this study, I do not employ a particular theory of ritual in order to explain purity in John's Gospel, since all too often, in Catherine Bell's judgment on the ritual theory as it was practiced in the early nineties, "the theoretical construction of ritual becomes a reflection of the theorist's method and the motor of a discourse in which the concerns of theorist take center stage."[110] Biblical scholars have access only to how rituals are represented in texts, as well as access to whatever

---

[106] Feder's cognitive linguistic work on impurity results in an understanding of impurity that is remarkably similar to Klawans's distinction between ritual and moral impurity (Feder, "Contagion and Cognition," 164–6). Lam helpfully uses a cognitive linguistic approach to metaphor in his work on sin as a stain in the Hebrew Bible and also comes to make a similar distinction (*Patterns of Sin*, 1–15, 179–206).

[107] This is what Joel B. Green refers to as the particular kind of historical-criticism consisting in the "study of the historical situation within which the biblical materials were generated, including the sociocultural conventions they take for granted" ("Rethinking 'History' for Theological Interpretation," *JTI* 5.2 [2011]: 161).

[108] On a text's relation to culture as a matter of constraint and mobility, see Stephen Greenblatt, "Culture," in *Critical Terms for Literary Study*, ed. Frank Lentricchia and Thomas McLaughlin (Chicago, IL: University of Chicago Press, 1990), 225–6.

[109] Frank H. Gorman, "Ritual Studies and Biblical Studies: Assessment of the Past, Prospects for the Future," *Semeia* 67 (1994): 13–36.

[110] Catherine Bell prefers to analyze the strategies of ritualization with as much attention to cultural particularity as possible, a sensibility I hope to have gained from her work (*Ritual Theory, Ritual Practice* [New York: Oxford University Press, 1992], 54).

material culture has been recovered through archeological work.[111] In other words, biblical scholars are unable to study rituals themselves, because only representations of the rituals are available to them. Thus, the questions supplied by what ritual theorist Ronald Grimes calls representation criticism and exegetical criticism prove helpful: What about ritual practice is selected for representation, what is left out, and for what reasons? In what ways is the ritual interpreted? What beliefs, values, and stories are presupposed in the representation of the ritual?[112] Attention to the way ritual is represented textually demands careful exegesis. Rites of purification and the language of purity are conceptualized in the Fourth Gospel in connection to biblical and early Jewish beliefs, stories, values, and controversies. As was demonstrated at the beginning of this chapter, the Fourth Gospel may be located within a stream of early Jewish writings in which questions, concerns, and stories related to purity were discussed in relationship to some of the most important social and theological questions of their time. For this reason, intertextual analysis will be done throughout this book, which attends not only to precursor texts related to purity alluded to in the Fourth Gospel, but also the way these texts were interpreted and received in early Jewish writings.[113] All this to say, this study of purity in the Fourth Gospel will proceed exegetically, with particular sensitivity to how the Fourth Gospel employs biblical traditions of purity to narrate how human beings are prepared for the coming of Jesus and enabled by him to have life with God.

The conceptual system of purity constructed by Klawans is particularly useful for the interpretation of purity in narratives, since narratives draw on cultural knowledge

---

[111] What is sometimes overlooked is that biblical scholars do not have direct access to rituals in the way that ritual theorists studying contemporary cultures do, as in T. M. Lemos, "Where There Is Dirt," 293. On the issue of *what* the object of study is in the study of purity—whether rituals or their textual representations—see Frank H. Gorman, "Pagans and Priests: Critical Reflections on Method," in *Perspectives on Purity and Purification in the Bible*, ed. Baruch J. Schwartz, David P. Wright, Jeffrey Stackart, and Naphtali S. Meshel, LHBOTS 474 (New York: T&T Clark, 2008), 102–10. Because biblical scholars have access only to the representation of ritual, what Grimes calls representation criticism, exegetical criticism, and tradition criticism are the most helpful tools offered to biblical scholars by ritual studies (*The Craft of Ritual Studies*, 74–5).

[112] These questions come from Grimes, *The Craft of Ritual Studies*, 74–5. Insofar as narratology aids close reading and supplies language for the critical analysis of narrative, it is used for attending to the way the Fourth Gospel represents purity as a ritual and a concept. Narratologically, I am most influenced by Mieke Bal, *Narratology: Introduction to the Theory of Narrative*, 3rd ed. (Toronto: University of Toronto Press, 2009); Bal, "The Point of Narratology," *Poetics Today* 11.4 (1990): 727–53. R. Alan Culpepper influentially brought structural narratology to bear on the interpretation of the Fourth Gospel (*Anatomy of the Fourth Gospel: A Study in Literary Design* [Philadelphia, PA: Fortress, 1983], 60).

[113] Robert L. Brawley helpfully critiques and expands on the criteria given by Hays for determining intertextual echoes. He argues that recurrence, thematic coherence, historical plausibility, history of interpretation, and satisfaction are simply variations on availability and volume. Brawley expands volume to include not only lexical correspondence, but also "the form, genre, setting, and plot" of both text and supposed intertext (*Text to Text Pours Forth Speech: Voices of Scripture in Luke-Acts* [Bloomington: Indiana University Press, 1995], 13). For Richard B. Hays's exposition of his seven criteria, see *Echoes of Scripture in the Letters of Paul* (New Haven: Yale University Press, 1989), 29–32. In her appreciative critique of Hays' work on intertextuality in the Gospels, Marianne Meye Thompson says "one must take stock of the Jewish interpretive traditions … that shape how the arguments about Scripture and about Jesus are formed" ("Hearing Voices: Reading the Gospels in the Echo Chamber of Scripture," *JTI* 11.1 [2017]: 47).

of purity without making explicit the whole concept to which they refer.[114] His account of purity is helpful because it enables interpreters, insofar as possible, to read early Jewish writings on their own terms with regard to purity. Klawans's construct of purity—an interrelated dual system of impurity and purification, grounded in Israel's Scripture and then diversely appropriated by ancient Jews—is both stable and indeterminate enough for individual texts to reflect and stand in tension with it. The flexibility of this construct is apparent in his elucidating comparative analysis of how these systems of ritual impurity and moral impurity were appropriated in early Jewish writings, particularly the writings of Qumran, the tannaitic rabbis, and the NT. He demonstrates that, although the conceptual framework referred to by ritual and moral impurity was carried forward by ancient Jews, these systems of impurity were defined and related to each other in numerous different and conflicting ways. For instance, ritual purification is the bodily analogue of the purification of the soul from vice (Philo of Alexandria); moral impurity is conflated with ritual impurity, such that ritual impurity is produced by sin and corrected through both ritual purification and repentance (the later sectarian literature of Qumran); and ritual impurity and moral impurity are separated and compartmentalized (the *halakhic* material of the tannaitic literature).[115] In other words, without offering a recklessly general theory of purity that obscures its historical and literary particularities, Klawans's work outlines the boundaries of early Jewish discourse on purity, within which the Gospel of John might be interpreted.

When considered in light of the preceding map of ritual and moral purity in Israel's Scripture and early Jewish writings, the Fourth Gospel may be regarded both as traditional in its approach to ritual and moral purity, and also innovative in the way it employs language about purity to advance its claims about Jesus's divine identity and God's work of salvation effected through Jesus's work. For the sake of clarity, it may be helpful to offer tentative, working definitions of ritual and moral purity and purification as reflected in the Gospel of John. I use the term *purity* when speaking about a state or condition, and I use the term *purification* when referring to the process by which something moves from impurity to purity. I will here provide working definitions of ritual and moral purity, explore the interrelation of ritual and moral purity in the Fourth Gospel, and acknowledge the Fourth Gospel's relative neglect of the gendered aspects of purity.

---

[114] The study of purity in early Jewish narratives is still underdeveloped; even where purity may play a significant role, cultural knowledge is assumed and unexplained. As a result, only a paucity of studies on purity in early Jewish narratives have been written. Steve Mason observes that no monograph on purity in the writings of Josephus has yet been written, even though impurity is an indispensable aspect of *Jewish War* ("Pollution and Purification in Josephus's *Judean War*," 181–207). Likewise, Beate Ego notices how scholarship on purity in early Judaism has accorded scant attention to purity in the deuterocanonical writings and so-called Old Testament Pseudepigrapha, because, in these writings, "recourse to the topic of purity takes place *en passant* in the narrative context" ("Purity Concepts in Jewish Traditions of the Hellenistic Period," in *Purity and the Forming of Religious Traditions in the Ancient Mediterranean World and Ancient Judaism*, ed. Christian Frevel and Christophe Nihan, Dynamics in the History of Religions 3 [Leiden: Brill, 2013], 477).

[115] Klawans, *Impurity and Sin*, 43–134.

First, in the Fourth Gospel, ritual purity is brought into effect through washing with water and is the preparation needed for humanity to be able to perceive God's revelation. Unlike in the Synoptic Gospels, the Fourth Gospel's focus on ritual purity is not on the removal of ritual impurities such as skin disease, chronic genital discharges, or corpse impurity, or on the expulsion of impure spirits. Instead, the Fourth Gospel conceptualizes ritual purity positively as a state that prepares one to perceive what God reveals of God in Jesus. As will be argued in Chapter 2, the Fourth Gospel's concept of ritual purity—particularly as it relates to John's ablutions with water for the revealing of Jesus to Israel—is reminiscent of Israel's preparation for the revealing of God in the Law at Sinai (Exod. 19:10). Having been prepared by washing with water, the Israelites would be able to see the voice of God in the giving of the Law without experiencing the fearsome consequences of being ritually impure in the presence of God's holiness. Jesus comes to Israel, and Israel must be ritually pure to be able to perceive just who Jesus is. So ritual purity does not have to do with the absence of sin. One can be ritually pure and caught in sin, as those who delivered Jesus to Pilate presumably were (18:28; cf. 13:10–11).

In the Fourth Gospel, moral purity is the condition that enables those who trust Jesus to see, enter, and act out the life of God. This moral purity is the result of God's work in Jesus, who, by his word, removes sin and ablutes with the Holy Spirit, and so makes his disciples morally pure. The disciples' moral purity is not only indicative of their having seen and entered God's life, but also of the moral quality of their lives, which is actualized as they keep the commandment given to them by Jesus, so that their lives are patterned after his own. Having been made morally pure and morally capable of keeping Jesus's commandment, they will bear the fruit of love. Moral purity is effected by the work of God in Jesus and evident in the moral quality of the disciples' lives.

The distinction between ritual purity and moral purity is maintained in the Fourth Gospel, such that washing with water is nowhere represented as the means by which sin is removed or ameliorated.[116] At the same time, ritual purity and moral purity correspond to one another. The ablutions of John with water—a kind of ritual purification—correspond to the ablutions of Jesus with the Holy Spirit—a kind of moral purification. As I will argue, this correspondence between ritual and moral purity is also found in the giving of sight to the man born blind by an act of washing with water (9:39–41) and the washing of the disciples' feet with water (13:1–11). To summarize, throughout this book, I will use *ritual purity* and *moral purity* as technical terms. Ritual purity always has to do with the condition arrived at through the washing of the body with water, and moral purity has to do with the absence of defiling sin and the presence of holiness. Both ritual and moral purity, each in its own way, concern human life in the presence of God.

The Fourth Gospel's focus on purity lacks attention to purity's gendered qualities.[117] This inattentiveness to the purity of gendered bodies is best summed

---

[116]   Against the claim that Jesus's washing of the disciples' feet has to do with the removal of post-baptismal sins, see Richard Bauckham, *The Testimony of the Beloved Disciple: Narrative, History, and Theology in the Gospel of John* (Grand Rapids, MI: Baker Academic, 2007), 191–206.

[117]   For an analysis of how the language of purity "helps to construct and maintain human and bodily gendering" in Lev. 12 and 15 and its reception in the LXX, see Dorothea Erbele-Küster, *Body,*

up by Jesus's proverbial statement about ritual purification at the footwashing: "One who has bathed does not need to wash, … but is entirely pure" (Jn 13:10a).[118] That is, although Leviticus delineates different practices for the removal of ritual defilements caused by semen, menstrual blood, or childbirth (see Lev. 12, 15), in John's Gospel all that matters is that bathing with water results in ritual purity.[119] The Fourth Gospel leaves out the way that practices of purity mark bodies as gendered.[120] Readers learn *that* John and Jesus had ministries of ablution (1:19–34; 3:22–4:2), but they are not told whether those who were abluted included both men and women or whether men and women underwent different rites to become ritually pure. When the Fourth Gospel does focus on purity, however, male characters are exclusively in view, namely, John, Jesus, and Jesus's male disciples who were present with him at the footwashing. Arguably, the connection between maleness and purity is coincidental rather than integral to the Fourth Gospel's portrayal of purity, since Jesus, John, and the male disciples are all characters whose activities (abluting) or situations (being in Jerusalem at Passover) are open to being interpreted with the language of purity.

But the Fourth Gospel's exclusive connection between purity and male characters did not need to be the case, since a number of the Gospel's female characters are also proximate to matters of purity. Jesus's mother prompted the sign at Cana (2:3), the Samaritan woman meets Jesus as one whose living water satisfies thirst rather than purifies (4:4–42), Mary and Martha meet Jesus as resurrection and life when they were likely defiled by their brother's corpse (11:17–44), and the women present with Jesus at the crucifixion were apparently unconcerned about becoming ritually impure for the Passover (19:25; cf. 18:28). While the same silence about purity affects minor male characters like Lazarus (who had been a corpse) or a paralyzed man healed by a pool, the puzzle of the Fourth Gospel's silence about the (im)purity of all of its female characters remains.[121] As I attend to the way Fourth Gospel represents purity and

---

Gender and Purity in Leviticus 12 and 15, LHBOTS 539 (London: T&T Clark, 2017), 87–150, here 87. Erbele-Küster emphasizes how Leviticus construes male and female flesh (בָּשָׂר) as the same, except that male flesh is marked by circumcision (89–102). Purity's power in constructing gender continued into late antiquity. As Charlotte Elisheva Fonrobert's work has shown, discourse on menstrual purity in ancient Jewish and Christian writings was a site of gender politics; see *Menstrual Purity: Rabbinic and Christian Reconstructions of Biblical Gender*, Contraversions: Jews and Other Differences (Stanford: Stanford University Press, 2002).

[118] On the interpretation of this sentence as a proverb, § 4.2.1.

[119] For an argument that the difference in semen and menstrual blood explains the differences between purificatory rites to remove them in Leviticus, see Thomas Kazen, *Issues of Impurity*, 41–62.

[120] The grammatical gender of "the one who has bathed" (ὁ λελουμένος) is masculine (Jn 13:10a), but the Fourth Gospel often employs such participial phrases in a gender inclusive way, as when Jesus tells Martha that "the one who believes in me … will live" (ὁ πιστεύων εἰς ἐμὲ κἂν ἀποθάνῃ ζήσεται, Jn 11:25), then asks her if she believes it.

[121] Colleen M. Conway argues that a generative approach to gender in the Fourth Gospel can be conducted through comparison of male and female characters; see "Gender and the Fourth Gospel," in *The Oxford Handbook of Johannine Studies*, ed. Judith Lieu and Martinus C. de Boer, Oxford Handbooks (Oxford: Oxford University Press, 2018), 220–36. Though it is beyond the scope of this project, I wonder what would surface in a comparison between the way the male disciples' purity is evaluated by Jesus and Jesus's silence about the purity of his female disciples.

purification, I replicate its limited focus on purity in connection to John, Jesus, and the (male) disciples and its general neglect of gendered aspects of purity.

1.4 Conclusion

There is more to be said about purity in the Fourth Gospel than has yet been said. An intelligence about purity is at work in the Fourth Gospel, evident not only in the early Jewish cultural knowledge about purity inscribed in the text, but also in the way purity appears to be integral to its theological claims. The particular ways that the Fourth Gospel draws on early Jewish concepts of purity to show how one is prepared to perceive God's revelation, made able to participate in God's life, and enabled to keep the commandment of Jesus will be explored in the chapters to follow. It was first necessary to problematize the dominant interpretation of purity in the Fourth Gospel, namely, that it was replaced by faith in Jesus. If the replacement of purity is the theological substance of the sign at Cana, there is nothing more to be said about purity in the Fourth Gospel. I have argued that this interpretation is influenced by William Robertson Smith's theory of purity, which is conceived in terms of evolutionary development. For Smith, purity represents the old, irrational, ritualistic elements of Israel's religion that were bound to be superseded by a new, spiritual form of faith. Purity is to him nothing more than fossilized remains. Scholars of John's Gospel located in Smith's trajectory were sometimes inclined to find in the replacement of purity evidence for the parting of the ways between early Jews and early Christians. There is little reason to think, however, that Smith's theory of purity is still a helpful interpretive schema to bring to the Fourth Gospel. A theoretical construction of purity derived from Israel's Scripture and its diverse interpretation among ancient Jews is more promising for the interpretation of the Fourth Gospel, since its language of purity is both bound by its early Jewish context and generative within it. The grammar of early Jewish discourse about purity is what Klawans contributes to scholarship, particularly in his critical appropriation of Douglas's work on purity as a symbolic system. Although Klawans's construction of two interrelated systems of ritual and moral purity cannot account for all the phenomena related to purity and ought not to predetermine the interpretation of particular texts, the distinctions drawn between kinds of (im)purity and the connections made between ritual elements and cultic systems are of good help for interpreting texts in their own terms, to the extent that it is possible. As will be seen, purity remains a vital theological resource that the Fourth Gospel employs to make sense of the work of God in Jesus.

2

That He Might Be Revealed: John, Ritual Purity, and Revelation

In the Fourth Gospel, ritual purification is a matter of preparing Israel for perception of divine revelation, as it was in the giving of the Law at Sinai (Exod. 19–34) and in certain early Jewish traditions related to God's self-disclosure (see, e.g., Philo, *Migration*, 36–52; Sir. 51:19–20; Wis. 7:24–25; 1 QS 8.11–18; Aramaic Levi). The association between ritual purity and revelation is carried through the Fourth Gospel. Jesus's glorification, *the* moment of revelation in the Fourth Gospel, is during the only Passover it associates with ritual purification (Jn 11:55; 13:10–11; 18:28). By instructing him to wash in the pool of Siloam, Jesus gives eyesight to a man born blind (9:7), an act by which "the works of God are revealed in him" (φανερωθη τὰ εργα του θεου ἐν αυτω, 9:3–4) and the means by which the man was ultimately able to perceive the identity of Jesus.[1] The stone vessels that held water for ritual purification at Cana were filled to the brim, and that water becoming wine is the sign by which Jesus first "revealed his glory" to his disciples (ἐφανέρωσεν τὴν δόξαν αὐτοῦ, Jn 2:11). The disciples who first perceived the glory of Jesus at Cana were formerly disciples of John, whose ablution with water— an act of ritual purification—was the way that Jesus was to be "revealed to Israel" (φανερωθῇ τῷ Ἰσραὴλ, 1:31).[2] The Fourth Gospel does not replace the practice of ritual purity with faith in Jesus. Instead, it appeals to biblical and early Jewish traditions of ritual purity related to human perception and divine revelation to serve its Christology. In John's Gospel, ritual purification becomes a hermeneutic for interpreting who Jesus is: none less than the revelation of Israel's God.

In the last chapter, I outlined two missteps one might take in the study of purity in the Fourth Gospel. On the one hand, one might focus on how the Fourth Gospel neglects the kinds of concerns about ritual impurity taken up in the Synoptic Gospels

---

[1]   The giving of sight to the man born blind will be discussed in Chapter 3, since the ritual purification with water undertaken at Siloam appears to be a sign for the moral purification with the Spirit through which the man is born from above. See § 3.4.

[2]   Throughout this book, I render the term βαπτίζω and its cognates as ablute, ablution, and ablutionary. The transliteration of βαπτίζω as *baptize* is misleading, since the word *baptize* carries so much Christian theological freight. The obscure English term *ablute* is a good match for βαπτίζω, since the latter was itself an obscure term for washing (its synonym λούω is used roughly ten times more often in the LXX). Furthermore, as will be seen, both βαπτίζω and *ablute* tend to describe reflexive activities, but, oddly, in the Fourth Gospel βαπτίζω is an active verb that takes a direct object.

or the DSS, then conclude that purity was either irrelevant or displaced in the Fourth Gospel. But the intelligence about purity reflected in the Fourth Gospel suggests otherwise, namely, that the Fourth Gospel brings its distinctive theological interests into a discourse on purity that was wide-ranging and controversial among ancient Jews. In matters of purity also, one must "let John be John."[3] On the other hand, one might impose theories of purity on the Fourth Gospel that either obstruct vision or obviate complexity. The conceptual power of the thought that purity is replaced by faith in Jesus comes from a theory of purity in which purity is a survival of old, primitive religion that is to be replaced by higher, spiritual ideals like faith.[4] The way to avoid these missteps is, as ritual theorist Ronald Grimes recommends, to interrogate what stories, metaphors, or images the ritual is associated with when it is represented in written form.[5] This approach to analyzing ritual purity in the Fourth Gospel's narrative and theology proves generative, particularly for the way ritual purity is employed in service of Christology.

The interrelation of ritual purity, human perception, and divine revelation in the Fourth Gospel is attested in biblical and early Jewish traditions about God's self-disclosure, particularly those related to the giving of the Law at Sinai. In other words, the stories, metaphors, and images with which the Fourth Gospel associates ritual purity are adapted from biblical traditions of washing in preparation for the revelation of God. Ritual purification prepared human bodies for encounter with a holy God. In one sense, ritual purification was a preparation undertaken to avoid the consequences of ritual impurity colliding with holiness, just as one would prepare for dangerous activity by taking safety precautions.[6] In another sense, ritual purification prepared one with what was needed to encounter God, just as preparing an oven provides the heat necessary to bake bread.[7] In traditions of purity concerned with human perception and divine revelation, purification focuses not so much on the removal of impurities as on the attainment of the state of purity that prepares people to perceive what God reveals.

The interrelation of purity, perception, and revelation found in biblical and early Jewish traditions of God's self-disclosure is most evident in the Fourth Gospel's account of the ablutions of John (1:19–34), which are intended to reveal Jesus to Israel (1:31) and are later interpreted in terms of ritual purity (3:25). As I will argue, this account, which immediately follows the Prologue, intertwines John's ablutions with allusions to the giving of the Law at Sinai (1:14–18), and so represents Jesus as the revelation of God's Word for which Israel is to be ritually purified. Before turning to the Fourth

---

[3] Jörg Frey has recently reiterated James D. G. Dunn's motto that scholars ought to "let John be John," underlining the need to recognize that John "tells [the story of Jesus] from a theological conviction about who Jesus really is" (*Theology and History in the Fourth Gospel: Tradition and Narration* [Waco, TX: Baylor University Press, 2018], 141).

[4] I understand replacement as the substitution of one thing for another thing like it, to the effect that what is replaced is no longer needed. On the evolutionary theory of purity mentioned here, see § 1.1.

[5] So, Grimes, *The Craft of Ritual Studies*, 74–5.

[6] On ritual purification as a merciful and protective practice for God's people, see the helpful treatment by Thiessen, *Jesus and the Forces of Death*, 9–12, 18–19. See also § 1.3.

[7] Philo, for example, thought that those who are pure are most capable of perceiving God's revelation (see, e.g., *Spec. Laws* 1.45–46).

Gospel, this constellation of three elements—purity, perception, and revelation—will be explored, from the giving of the Law at Sinai (Exod. 19–34) to its appearance in other contexts in early Jewish writings.[8] Following that, the Fourth Gospel's distinct account of John's ablutions will be analyzed in light of these biblical and early Jewish traditions of purity, and this analysis will be carried through to ritual purification in the Fourth Gospel more broadly.

2.1 Synesthesia at Sinai: Purity, Perception, and Revelation in Early Jewish Writings

In his monograph *Washing in Water*, Jonathan Lawrence outlines three roles that washings for ritual purification played in Israel's Scripture: (1) general washings, which were for the removal of ritual impurities caused by corpses, skin diseases, and genital discharges, and which concerned participation in the temple cult by Israelites (cf. Lev. 11–15); (2) priestly washings, which only priests were required to undergo, and only for the sake of their temple service (cf. Exod. 29:4; 30:18–21); and (3) washings in preparation for theophanies, which the whole people of Israel undergo in preparation for the revealing of the God of Israel, as in the giving of the Law at Sinai (Exod. 19:10–11) and Israel's crossing of the Jordan (Josh. 3:5).[9] In this third case, ritual purification is required to prepare the people of Israel to perceive God's revelation. To be sure, the association of purity, perception, and revelation is on the margins of early Jewish practice. Lawrence says there is nearly no evidence that washings before theophanies were *practiced* in the early Jewish period.[10] Nevertheless, in early Jewish readings of the theophany at Sinai, one does find a close discursive association maintained between purification, human perception, and divine revelation. Purification's function as preparation for divine revelation gives the rationale for why the Fourth Gospel narrates the ablutions of John as the preparation of Israel for the revelation of Jesus.

2.1.1 Washing to See God's Voice at Sinai

Early Jewish interpretations of the Sinai account foreground the way the Lord is revealed in the giving of the Law to a people whom Moses has purified, even as they maintain that no mortal is able to see God (cf. Exod. 33:20). The revelation at Sinai begins when the Lord sends Moses to purify the people in order to prepare them for the divine descent on Mount Sinai:

---

[8] Methodologically, I am following the path of Hindy Najman, who suggests tracing "constellations of features or elements" through generically diverse early Jewish writings, on which see "The Idea of Biblical Genre: From Discourse to Constellation," in *Prayer and Poetry in the Dead Sea Scrolls and Related Literature: Essays in Honor of Eileen Schuller on the Occasion of Her 65th Birthday*, STDJ 98 (Leiden: Brill, 2011), 316.

[9] Lawrence, *Washing in Water*, 26–32.

[10] Lawrence mentions the washings before the heavenly visions in the Aramaic Testament of Levi as a possible exception (*Washing in Water*, 77).

> And the Lord said to Moyses, "When you go down, testify solemnly to the people, and purify them [ἅγνισον αὐτούς; וְקִדַּשְׁתָּם] today and tomorrow, and let them wash their clothes [πλυνάτωσαν τὰ ἱμάτια], and be prepared for the third day. For on the third day the Lord will come down upon the mountain Sina before all the people. (Exod. 19:10–11 LXX)

Although the LXX tends to translate the term קדשׁ with the language of holiness or consecration (e. g., ἅγιος, ἁγιαζω), the term קדשׁ is here translated with ἁγνίζω, which is typically used to denote the activity of purification (cf., also, Num. 8:21; 19:11–13; 2 Chron. 30:17–18). The term קדשׁ in Exod. 19:10 was apparently also understood as a reference to bathing in water in the Temple Scroll (11Q19 49.21).[11] The narrative context and close connection to washing clothing suggested to early interpreters that Moses was being asked to purify Israel with water. However, unlike other ritual purifications in which one bathes oneself, *Moses* is to purify Israel (see, e.g., Lev. 14:8–9; 15:5–11; 17:15–16). The purification of the people is interpreted as preparation for the revelation of the Lord on Sinai. On the third day, after the people had been prepared and purified, the mountain was charged with fire and smoke and thunderous sounds that blasted like trumpets, and the Lord spoke words to all Israel. After the Decalogue was given, there is a report of how the people *saw* (ὁράω) "the sound [φωνή; קוֹל] and the flashes and the sound of the trumpet and the mountain smoking" (Exod. 20:18 LXX). Because the people were said to *see* the *voice*, the giving of the Law came to be interpreted by Philo and the *targumim* as the revealing of the Lord to the people.

Early Jewish interpretations of the giving of the Law at Sinai tend to conflate the giving of the Law with the vision of God's voice, so that to see God revealed is to see the voice of God in the Law.[12] In other words, there was synesthesia at Sinai. In his account of the giving of the Law, Philo expands on how the people prepared themselves through ritual purification for the revealing of God:

> Nearby stood the people. ... They had cleansed themselves with ablutions and lustrations [λουτροῖς τε καὶ περιρραντηρίοις καθηράμενος] for three days past, and moreover had washed their clothes [τὰς ἐσθῆτας ἀποπλυνάμενος] ... Then from the midst of the fire that streamed from heaven there sounded forth to their utter amazement a voice, for the flame became articulate speech in the language familiar to the audience, and so clearly and distinctly were the words formed by it that *they seemed to see rather than hear them*. What I say is vouched for by the law

---

[11] This claim depends on the argument that the Temple Scroll expands the instructions about removing corpse impurity in Num. 19:11–22 with recourse to Exod. 19:10 (Werrett, *Ritual Purity and the Dead Sea Scrolls*, 138 fn. 76). Harrington also notes that קדשׁ is used with reference to Bathsheba's bathing after menstruation, which suggests it may also be used in Exod. 19:10 as a reference to bathing ("Purification in the Fourth Gospel," 131 fn. 46; cf. 2 Sam. 11:4).

[12] So Steven D. Fraade, who comes to this conclusion by comparing the reception of this scene in the LXX, early rabbinic sages, and Philo ("Hearing and Seeing at Sinai: Interpretive Trajectories," in *The Significance of Sinai: Traditions about Sinai and Divine Revelation in Judaism and Christianity*, ed. George J. Brooke, Hindy Najman, and Loren T. Stuckenbruck, TBN 12 [Leiden: Brill, 2008], 247–68.)

in which it is written, "All the people saw the voice." (*Decalogue* 45–47, emphasis mine; cf. Exod. 20:18 LXX)

Philo interprets the term ἁγνίζω in Exod. 19:10 LXX with terms yet more explicitly associated with ritual purification by noting that the people purified themselves with ablutions and sprinklings. Philo, however, supposes that the people purified themselves, perhaps harmonizing Exod. 19:10–11 with the contemporary practice of bathing oneself, rather than having a ritual agent somehow involved in bathing others. Only after having been ritually purified do the people see a voice. The fire that descended on Sinai takes form as the words of the written Law, so that in hearing the Law, the people see the voice of God.

The *targumim* also take note of how the Israelites were instructed by Moses to be prepared for the revealing of God by washing their clothing.[13] Like Philo, they appear to conflate the giving of the Law and the appearance of God at Sinai. Most striking among the *targumim*, perhaps, is Tg. Neof. Exod. 19:10–11 and 20:2:

> And the Lord said to Moses: "Go to the people and sanctify them this day and tomorrow and let them wash their garments, and they shall be in readiness for the third day, because on the third day the Glory of the Shekinah of the Lord will be revealed to the eyes of all the people upon Mount Sinai. ... The first word that went out from the mouth of the Holy One, may his name be blessed, (was) like shooting stars and lightnings and like torches of (fire), a torch of fire to the right and a torch of fire to the left. It flew and winged swiftly in the air of the heavens and came back! and all Israel saw it and feared; and returning, it became engraved on the two tables of the covenant and said: "My people, children of (...)." And it came back and hovered over the camps of Israel and returning it became engraved on the tables of the covenant and all Israel beheld it. (*Tg. Neof.* Exod. 19:10–11; 20:2).[14]

Moses sanctifies the people, and they wash their clothing in order prepare to for the revealing of the glory of God at Sinai. There is no vision of God *per se*, but rather, a spectacular vision of the "Glory of the Shekhinah of the Lord," which takes the form of the first two commandments of the Decalogue, visibly appearing as shooting stars and flames of fire. The first two commandments of the Decalogue are precisely those that reveal the identity of God in relation to Israel. The first is this:

---

[13] Charles Thomas Robert Hayward compares how the LXX and *targumim* have qualified and interpreted the claim to see God in Exod. 24:10, observing also that the *targumim* "regard Exod. chapters 19 and 24 as one continuous narrative" ("The Giving of the Torah: Targumic Perspectives," in *The Significance of Sinai: Traditions about Sinai and Divine Revelation in Judaism and Christianity*, ed. George J. Brooke, Hindy Najman, and Loren T. Stuckenbruck, TBN 12 [Leiden: Brill, 2008], 269, cf., also, 280). On the writings of the NT and the *targumim* being located together within a variegated and developing stream of first-century Jewish thought, so that questions of precise dating and influence may fall into the background, see Géza Vermès, "Jewish Literature and New Testament Exegesis: Reflections on Methodology," *JJS* 33 (1982): 361–76.

[14] Unless otherwise noted, translations of Tg. Neof. follow Martin McNamara, Kevin Cathcart, and Michael Maher, eds., *Targum Neofiti 1, Exodus*, trans. Martin McNamara (Collegeville, MN: Liturgical Press, 1994).

My people, children of Israel, I am the Lord, your God, who redeemed you and led you out redeemed from the land of Egypt, from the house of slavery. (Tg. Neof. Exod. 20:2)

And the second is this:

My people, children of Israel, you shall have no other God beside me … I am the Lord, your God, a jealous and revenging God who takes revenge with zeal on the wicked … but I observe grace and goodness to thousands of generations for the just who love him and for those who observe my commandments. (Tg. Neof. Exod. 20:3b, 5–6)

In short, as Fraade eloquently puts it, "God is revealed through the revelation of his Torah," and not directly through sense perception (cf. Exod. 33:20).[15] Thus, when Moses and Aaron, Nadab and Abihu, as well as seventy elders are said to "see the God of Israel" (אלהי ישראל ויראו את, 24:10) in the MT, the LXX reads that they "saw the place, there where the God of Israel stood" (τὸν τόπον, οὗ εἱστήκει ἐκεῖ ὁ θεὸς τοῦ Ἰσραηλ), and Tg. Neof. Exod. 24:10 reads that they saw "the glory of the Shekinah of the God of Israel." No one had seen God, but in the giving of the Law God was made known. And God was made known only after the people became ritually pure. Ritual purification makes for a people who are prepared to perceive God's self-disclosure in the Law (ἕτοιμος, Exod. 19:11 LXX).

2.1.2 Blessed Are the Pure in Heart, for They Shall See God

The constellation of elements forged at Sinai—purity, human perception, and divine revelation—appear in a variety of early Jewish writings, but in different literary and theological contexts. Attention will be given to how these three elements are bound together in Philo, deuterocanonical wisdom literature, and the DSS. As will be apparent, whereas the washing of the people at Sinai seems only to have been an act of ritual purification, the ritual purity associated with revelation in these early Jewish writings seems also to have included a consideration of the moral purity of a person's life—purity, that is, from sins of various kinds. In these texts, then, it seems that purity entails more than ritual purification with water, but not less. Like these writings, the Fourth Gospel brings together purity with human perception of divine revelation. Unlike them, in its portrayal of John's ablutions as that which prepares Israel for the revealing of Jesus, the Fourth Gospel limits this connection to ritual purity, since only Jesus can make people morally pure.

It is most clear in Philo's *On the Migration of Abraham* that the association between purity, perception, and revelation is derived from the account of the giving of the Law at Sinai and subsequently applied elsewhere. Philo brings up purity in connection to human capacity to perceive and receive divine revelation (*Migration* 36–52). He

---

[15] Fraade, "Hearing and Seeing," 247.

inquires into why God tells Abraham and Moses that they will be shown (δείκνυμι) what they will not possess (43–44; cf. Gen. 12:1; Deut. 34:4). He writes:

> For how is it possible to become possessed of things whose allotted place is nearer to the divine? Yet to see them is within the bounds of possibility [οὐκ ἀδύνατον]: though not for all. It is exclusively for the purest and most keen-eyed class [τῷ καθαρωτάτῳ καὶ ὀξυωπρεστάτῳ γένει], on whom the Father of all things, by shewing [ἐπιδεικνύμενος] to them His own works, bestows an all-surpassing gift. … Whereas the voice of mortal beings is judged by hearing, the sacred oracles intimate that the words of God are seen as light is seen; for we are told that "all the people saw the voice." (*Migration* 46–47 [Colson and Whitaker]; cf. Exod. 20:18 LXX)

For Philo, God's revelation is a gift that cannot be possessed. It can be received only through a particular kind of sight. However, not all are capable of seeing what God shows, but only those who are most pure. Although Philo is commenting on Gen. 12:1, he develops his ideas about how purity makes possible the perception of God's revelation with reference to Israel at Sinai. This exegetical move suggests that Philo developed his ideas about human perception of divine disclosure with reference to Sinai, and so with reference also to the purity of the perceivers.

Purity, perception, and revelation appear together elsewhere throughout Philo's writings. At times, the (im)purity of a person is what inclines God to reveal or withhold heavenly knowledge (*Dreams* 1.148; *Eternity* 2; *Cherubim* 48–9). More often, Philo speaks anthropologically about how the purity of one's soul or mind prepares one to attain true knowledge of God. For Philo, Moses is the paradigm for how purity helps one to perceive and receive the knowledge of God. Allegorically speaking, Moses represents the purest mind (νοῦς ὁ καθαρώτατος, *Names* 208; cf. *Prelim. Studies* 132), which is capable of apprehending what God reveals of God without recourse to any created, sensate thing (*Spec. Laws* 1.45–46; *Alleg. Interp.* 3.100–101; *Confusion* 92; *Flight* 109–10). More broadly, those who are pure are initiated into Moses's teaching of holy mysteries (*Giants* 54) and are able to receive a knowledge of God that cannot be derived from sensate phenomena (*Dreams* 1.84; cf. *Alleg. Interp.* 3.200). But those who are not pure cannot behold the things of God (*Flight* 81). Philo's writing on purity and perception is no doubt influenced by the Platonic concept that being pure from passion makes possible the perception of eternal forms.[16] At the same time, however, Philo most often develops the relation between purity, perception, and revelation theologically and exegetically with reference to Sinai and Moses.

In Sirach and the Wisdom of Solomon, it is those who are pure that receive wisdom from God. Sirach closes with a first-person account of how Sirach sought and finally found wisdom. After recounting how he looked for wisdom through prayer and obedience to the Law (51:13–18), he speaks of the moment he finally found wisdom:

---

[16] On which, see Scott D. Mackie, "Seeing God in Philo of Alexandria: Means, Methods, and Mysticism," *JSJ* 43.2 (2012): 161.

> I spread out my hands to the heavens, and lamented my ignorance of her. I directed
> my soul to her, and in purity I found her [ἐν καθαρισμῷ εὗρον αὐτήν]. With her
> I gained understanding from the first; therefore I will never be forsaken. (Sir.
> 51:19b–20 NRSV)

Randal Argall suggests that in this sentence we are given an answer to the rhetorical
question posed at the beginning of Sirach: "The root of wisdom—to whom has it been
revealed?" (1:6).[17] Such wisdom is revealed to those like Sirach who, for everything else
that can be said about their pursuit of wisdom, are pure. The wisdom that Sirach found
through purity is the wisdom that exists always with God (1:1), that God employed in
the world's creation (24:1–34), and that was given uniquely to Israel in the form of the
Torah (16:24–17:23).[18] Thus, in Sirach human beings who are pure are those to whom
the wisdom of God is revealed. Similarly, in the Wisdom of Solomon, only those who
are pure are able to access the wisdom of God:

> For wisdom moves more freely than any movement; she pervades and penetrates
> all things because of her pureness [διὰ τὴν καθαρότητα]. For she is a breath of
> the power of God and an emanation of the pure glory of the Almighty; therefore
> nothing defiled [οὐδὲν μεμιαμμένον] gains entrance into her. (Wis. 7:24–25 NRSV)

Wisdom's own purity and its nearness to divine glory makes it impossible for defiled
persons to access it. Because wisdom is pure and is from God, those who attain it must
also be pure. Wisdom is what is revealed by God in these texts, and purification gives a
person what is needed to seek wisdom in such a way that it can be found.

In the DSS, the direct association between purity and divine revelation is not made
as often as one might expect.[19] However, the Rule of the Community (1QS) brings
together the location of the community in the wilderness, the study of the revelation of
God through Moses, and the necessity of purity to access the community's knowledge:

> And every matter hidden from Israel but which has been found out by the
> Interpreter, he should not keep hidden from them for fear of a spirit of desertion.
> And when these exist / as a community / in Israel / in compliance with these
> arrangements / they are to be segregated from within the dwelling of the men of
> sin to walk to the desert in order to open there His path. As it is written: "In the
> desert, prepare the way of ****, straighten in the steppe a roadway for our God."
> This is the study of the law which he commanded through the hand of Moses, in

---

[17]   Randal A. Argall, *1 Enoch and Sirach: A Comparative Literary and Conceptual Analysis of the Themes
of Revelation, Creation, and Judgment*, EJL 8 (Atlanta, GA: Scholars Press, 1995), 71. I interpret Sir
51:19 differently than Argall.

[18]   On wisdom in relation to creation and law in Sirach, see the helpful treatment in Ari Mermelstein,
*Creation, Covenant, and the Beginnings of Judaism: Reconceiving Historical Time in the Second
Temple Period*, JSJSup 168 (Leiden: Brill, 2014), 16–37.

[19]   Harrington notes that one must make logical deductions to define the relationship between
ritual purity and the study of divine revelation at Qumran, but that there is good reason to do so
("Purification in the Fourth Gospel in Light of Qumran," 130).

order to act in compliance with all that has been revealed from age to age, and according to what the prophets have revealed through his holy spirit. And anyone of the men of the Community, the covenant of the Community, who insolently shuns anything at all commanded, *cannot approach the pure food* [יגע בטהרת] *of the men of holiness, and cannot know anything of their counsels until his deeds have been cleansed from every depravity* [יזכו מעשיו עול], *walking on the perfect path* [(1QS 8.11–18, emphasis mine)[20]

In this passage is an appeal to Isaiah as rationale for the community's desert location (Isa. 40:3). This is significant because, as Najman has noted, the wilderness was a geography of suffering, purification, and revelation.[21] The Rule of the Community teaches that life in the desert involves both purification and the study of God's revelation in the Law and Prophets. Because what is revealed is revealed through God's Holy Spirit, only those who are pure are allowed to access the knowledge of what has been revealed. This text is similar to Josephus's description of the Essenes. He writes that "there are some among them who profess to foretell the future, being versed from their early years in holy books, various forms of purification [διαφόροις ἁγνείαις] and apophthegms of prophets; and seldom, if ever, do they err in their predictions" (*J.W.* 2.159 [Thackeray]). Josephus understands the Essenes' accurate knowledge of the future to be a function of their ritual purity and their study of Scripture. At Qumran, the knowledge of God's revelation was protected by the purity of those who were to perceive it.

There are several instances in which the purity of an individual prepares them to receive what God will reveal. First, preserved only in fragmentary form is an account of Levi's heavenly vision, for which he prepared himself by washing in water:

Then I washed my clothes and purified them in pure water, and I washed completely in running water and I made all my paths straight. Then I raised my eyes and my face to heaven and spoke and I spread out the fingers of my hands and my hands to the truth before the sanctuary. And I prayed and I said: O Lord, You know all hearts, and You alone understand all thoughts of insights. And now my children are with me. [...] Let there be revealed to me, Master, the holy spirit, and give me counsel and wisdom and knowledge and power to do the things pleasing to You and to find grace before you and to praise Your words with me, O Lord. [...]Then I was shown a vision ... in a vision of visions, and I saw the hea[vens] ... under me, high until it clung to the heave[ns] ... to me the gates of heaven and a single angel.[22]

[20] Unless otherwise noted, all translations of the DSS throughout this book follow Florentino García Martínez, *The Dead Sea Scrolls Translated: The Qumran Texts in English*, trans. Wilfred G. E. Watson, 2nd ed. (Leiden: Brill, 1996). For the Hebrew text of the DSS, I rely upon Devorah Dimant and Donald W. Parry, eds., *Dead Sea Scrolls Handbook* (Leiden: Brill, 2014).
[21] Hindy Najman, "Towards a Study of the Uses of the Concept of Wilderness in Ancient Judaism," *DSD* 13.1 (2006): 99–113.
[22] Aramaic Levi; trans. James R. Davila, *MOTP* 1:134–5. The ellipses in square brackets indicate where I have skipped text; the other ellipses represent gaps in the original manuscripts. I did not preserve the stylistic formatting used by Davila to indicate which parts of the text are preserved in

The bathing of the body as well as the washing of clothes reminds one of Israel at the base of Sinai (Exod. 19:10). Levi's vision of heaven is a divine response to his purification with water ("I washed"), his moral purity ("I made all my paths straight," cf. Isa. 40:3), and his prayer. Second, and somewhat less clearly, the divine appearance in which Jacob was renamed Israel is preceded by his purification. Jubilees rewrites the story in Genesis in which Jacob commanded those who were with him to purify themselves, change their clothes, and to put away their idols (*Jub.* 31.1; cf. Gen. 35:2), an act undertaken in the expectation that God would appear to him again at Bethel (*Jub.* 32.16–26; cf. Gen. 35:9–15).

Third, and most obscurely, Daniel's desire that "he not be defiled" (μὴ συμμολυνθῇ, Dan. 1:8 LXX) resulted in a vegetarian diet and physical health for him and his companions. The conclusion to this strange foray into dietary matters is that "the Lord gave the young men knowledge and clever insight in every literary art. And to Daniel he gave insight into every vision and dreams and in all wisdom" (Dan. 1:17 NETS). Perhaps Daniel's desire not to be defiled by food shows how pure his whole life was, with the result that God imbued Daniel and his companions with wisdom. Josephus both naturalizes and theologizes the account. He describes Daniel and his companions as those "whose souls were in this way kept pure [καθαρῶν] and fresh for learning and their bodies more vigorous for arduous labour" because of their diet, giving a natural explanation for their learning. Then, unexpectedly, Josephus adds a theophany: "the Deity manifested Himself to him" (τὸ θεῖον αὐτῷ φανερὸν ἐγίνετο, *Ant.* 10:194 [Marcus]). Finally, one cannot forget the saying of Jesus in Matthew about those who are blessed: "Blessed are the pure in heart, for they will see God" (μακάριοι οἱ καθαροὶ τῇ καρδίᾳ, ὅτι αὐτοὶ τὸν θεὸν ὄψονται, 5:8). In Matthew, to be pure in heart is to to be free from the defiling sins that proceed from the heart, and so is a matter of moral purity (cf. 15:18–20). Even so, in each of these instances, it was pure individuals who are to perceive what God reveals of God.

Five points of significance may be derived from the constellation of purity, perception, and revelation in early Jewish writings dealing with divine self-disclosure. First, these elements are most tightly bound together in the biblical account of the giving of the Law at Sinai and its interpretation in early Jewish writings. The interrelation of purity, perception, and revelation at such a significant moment in Israel's story explains why one finds purity related to perception and revelation in a variety of early Jewish writings, even outside of comments on the giving of the Law. Second, while ritual purification is clearly in view in the giving of the Law and its interpretation, there is a sense in Philo, Wis, Sir, and the DSS that the kind of purity needed to perceive divine revelation also entails an upright life. By contrast, the Gospel of John more narrowly relates *ritual* purification to perception and revelation, particularly in its representation of John's ablutions with water. Third, purification prepares a person with what is needed to perceive what God reveals. That is, purity is a human state that is particularly suited to perception of God's revelation. Fourth, in every context where purification is related to the perception of revelation, there is little or no focus on what

which manuscripts, but it is worth noting that the majority of this text comes from the Mt. Athos manuscript, which overlaps with 4QLevi[b] (see *MOTP* 1:123).

ritual impurities or sins are removed. Not all discourse on ritual (im)purity among ancient Jews was focused on sources of impurity and mechanisms of its removal. The relation of (ritual) purification to revelation is an attested tradition within biblical and early Jewish traditions of purity. Fifth, most significantly for ritual purity and the Fourth Gospel's Christology, there is no instance in which purification prepares for the revelation of a human being or the impartation of human knowledge. Ritual purification concerns only what is revealed to human beings from God. Whether knowledge of God, wisdom from God, or understanding of the Law and Prophets, purification prepares one to receive from God what comes from God.

2.2 Made Pure to See the Glory of the Word Made Flesh

The constellation formed by purity, perception, and revelation in certain early Jewish writings about God's revelation is visible also in the Fourth Gospel's account of John's ablutions. John's act of washing with water is represented as a particular kind of ritual purification, performed to prepare Israel to perceive what God was to reveal in Jesus. As will be seen, the purpose of John's ablutions with water is that Israel would be ritually pure for the revealing of Jesus to Israel (1:31). The Fourth Gospel develops its account of John's ablutions in close connection to the giving of the Law at Sinai, which further strengthens the contention that John's ablutions are represented as a ritual purification preparing Israel for the revelation of God in the Word.

2.2.1 God Sent John Abluting that Jesus Might Be Revealed to Israel

Because John's ablutions with water are related explicitly to the revelation of Jesus to Israel rather than more conventional matters of ritual purification, some interpreters have supposed that the Fourth Gospel's representation of John's baptism "diminishes, if not excludes, any purification or initiation of the baptisands" (cf. Jn 1:31).[23] Others distinguish John's ablutions and witness, suggesting that the former are eclipsed by the latter.[24] In each case, the assumption is that early Jewish ritual purification and the revelation of Jesus are mutually exclusive. However, as just seen, a vibrant association between purification, human perception, and divine revelation is attested in early Jewish discourse. The Fourth Gospel holds together purification and revelation in its portrayal of John's ablutions with water.[25] To be more precise, in the Fourth Gospel,

---

[23] Larry P. Jones, *The Symbol of Water in the Gospel of John*, JSNTSup 145 (Sheffield: Sheffield Academic, 1997), 50. Edwyn C. Hoskyns positions John (the Baptist) between "the messianic baptism of water and Spirit" and "Jewish purification," writing that "John's baptism dissolves the latter, for it is the final call of God to repentance, and anticipates the former, for the Messiah has come and is even now standing in their midst"; (*The Fourth Gospel*, ed. Francis Noel Davey [London: Faber and Faber, 1947], 175).

[24] Culpepper, *Anatomy of the Fourth Gospel*, 60.

[25] Similarly, Cornelis Bennema, who argues that the baptism of John accomplishes both revelation and purification ("Spirit-Baptism in the Fourth Gospel: A Messianic Reading of John 1:33," *Bib* 84.1 [2003]: 37–8).

John enacts his witness to Jesus through his ablutions with water, which prepare Israel to perceive what God reveals in Jesus.

The claim that John's ablutions are ritually purifying is helped by the word chosen to describe John's activity of abluting people with water, namely, βαπτίζω (1:25, 26, 31, 33; 3:23; 10:40). This term, rarely used in early Jewish writings in Greek, tends to describe one of two activities. In Josephus, Philo, and the Sibylline Oracles, βαπτίζω denotes total submersion underwater, to the point that ships sink (Josephus, *Ant.* 9.212; *J. W.* 3.368; *Life* 1.15; cf. Philo, *Good Person*, 1.97), people drown (Isa. 21:4 LXX; Philo, *Free*, 1.97; Josephus, *Ant.* 15:55; *J. W.* 1.437, 525–527), or the sun itself is extinguished in the ocean (Sib. Or. 5.477–478).[26] But in the LXX and the portrayals of Jewish practice in the Synoptic Gospels, the term βαπτίζω describes ritual ablution for the sake of purification (2 Kgs 5:14; Sir. 34:25; Jdt. 12:7–9; see also Mk 7:3–4; Lk. 11:38–39).[27] In these instances, a causal relationship is constructed between ablution in water (lexicalized by βαπτίζω) and the resulting state of purity (lexicalized by καθαρίζω or καθαρός, or else suggested by context). For example, Naaman ablutes in the Jordan and finds himself purified of his skin disease (2 Kgs 5:14), Judith ablutes in a spring of water and enters her tent pure (Jdt. 12:7–9), and Jesus responds to the Pharisee's amazement that he did not ablute himself prior to eating with instruction about outer and inner purity (Lk. 11:37–41; cf. Mk 7:2–4). Within the Fourth Gospel, the ablutions of John and Jesus occasion a "controversy about purification" between John's disciples and a *Ioudaios* (ζήτησις … περὶ καθαρισμοῦ, 3:25). This suggests that even if John's ablutions were controversial, the controversy was understood as a matter of early Jewish purification (3:22–25).[28]

Of course, terminology is not everything. The Fourth Gospel, the Synoptic Gospels, and Josephus all use the term βαπτίζω and its cognates to describe John's ablutions, but offer different perspectives on the purpose of his ablutions. In the Synoptic Gospels, John's ablution is called "an ablution of repentance for the forgiveness of sins" (βάπτισμα μετανοίας εἰς ἄφεσιν ἁμαρτιῶν, Mk 1:4; Lk. 3:3) or an ablution "with water

---

[26] The term βαπτίζω in the sense of total submersion is occasionally extended metaphorically to describe becoming "overwhelmed" by something. Alcohol, for example, might overwhelm the mind (Philo, *Contempl. Life* 1.46; *Providence* 2.67; Josephus, *Ant.* 10.169) and passions might overwhelm the soul (Philo, *Alleg. Interp.* 3.18; *Worse*, 1.176; *Migration*, 1.204).

[27] Ferguson also observes that βαπτίζω was often used in connection to purification, and includes the use of βαπτίζω in Josephus and Philo for the sense of "drown" or "overwhelm," see *Baptism in the Early Church: History, Theology, and Liturgy in the First Five Centuries* (Grand Rapids, MI: Eerdmans, 2009), 56–9.

[28] Everett Ferguson both acknowledges that the term βαπτίζω was related to ritual purification among ancient Jews and that John's ablutions may be understood as a kind of early Jewish ritual purification, but on the grounds of Jn 3:25 suggests that in the Fourth Gospel "John's baptism had a different kind of purification in view from that in Jewish baptisms"; see *Baptism in the Early Church*, 93. Ferguson's phrase "Jewish baptisms" construes early Jewish ablutions as monolithic and uncontroverted, an impression that the considerable debate over purity in extant early Jewish literature does not allow. One alternative is offered by Joel Marcus, who speculates that the debate over purification may have concerned the kinds of legal debates found about purity in early Jewish sources, and notes that early Christians continued to question how ritual purity was to be practiced, on which see *John the Baptist in History and Theology*, Studies on Personalities of the New Testament (Columbia: The University of South Carolina Press, 2018), 155–6. See my own treatment of the controversy in § 3.3.3.

for repentance" (βαπτιζω ἐν υδατι εις μετανοιαν, Mt. 3:11). Ablution with water for the forgiveness of sins was a strange, anomalous practice for ancient Jews. As Klawans argues, in the sectarian texts from Qumran sin results in ritual impurity and repentance involves ritual purification, but the Synoptic Gospels give no indication that sins caused a kind of ritual impurity that was removed through John's ablutions. Instead, the Synoptics represent John's ablutions as an eschatological, moral purification that takes place in the guise of ritual purification.[29] Josephus relates John's ablutions to moral life differently than do the Synoptics, indicating that those who came to John for ablutions had already come to a state of inward purity through repentance (*Ant.* 18.116–119). For Josephus, the ablutions of John did nothing but symbolize a moral reformation that had already taken place.[30] By contrast, the Fourth Gospel is the only early source to gesture toward the connection between John's ablutions and early Jewish practices of purity (Jn 3:23–25), and the only one not to interpret his ablutions in relation to repentance from sin. In a way, the Fourth Gospel's portrayal of John's ablutions has more precedent in early Jewish writings on purity than either of the others.[31]

If the reference to John's ablutions in close connection to a controversy over purification suggests that they were a kind of ritual purification, the emphasis on water also supports this contention. The three times that John refers to his own ablutions, he repeats that he ablutes *with water* (ἐν ὕδατι, Jn 1:25, 31, 33). John's emphasis on water warrants his denial that his own ablutions carry the particular kind of eschatological significance that those who come to him inquire about (1:19–25). To put it differently, John's ablution with water represents for him an absolute distinction between him and the one to come after him. The one to come after him would "take away the sin of the world" (1:29) and would "ablute with the Holy Spirit" (1:33). But John's ablutions with water do not take away sin or make one pure with the Holy Spirit. This distinction between the ablutions of John and Jesus suggests that the Fourth Gospel does not conflate ritual and moral purification. Whereas John ablutes with water for ritual purification, Jesus ablutes with the Holy Spirit for moral purification, that is, for the removal of sin and restoration to holiness. In other words, the Fourth Gospel distinguishes John's ablution from that of Jesus by pointing to the medium with which John ablutes—water—and so conceptualizes John's ablution as ritual purification.[32]

---

[29] This conclusion comes from Klawans's analysis of the ablutions of the historical John the Baptist in relation to early Jewish ritual purifications, especially those at Qumran (*Impurity and Sin*, 75–88, 138–43).

[30] Klawans draws attention to Josephus's attempt to downplay the innovative quality of John's ablutions by rendering them "symbolic, legally inconsequential, perhaps even quaint, and certainly harmless" (*Josephus and the Theologies of Ancient Judaism*, 173).

[31] The implications of my argument for the reconstruction of the historical John the Baptist are not my concern, but it seems that the Fourth Gospel's distinctive construal of John's ablutions is a creative theological interpretation of his activity that draws heavily from early Jewish tradition, which shows that the author(s) of the Fourth Gospel worked carefully with early Jewish conceptual resources in the development of the Fourth Gospel's Christology. For explorations of the Fourth Gospel's engagement with early Jewish writings and concepts in its presentation of Jesus as the Messiah, see Benjamin E. Reynolds and Gabriele Boccaccini, eds., *Reading the Gospel of John's Christology as Jewish Messianism: Royal, Prophetic, and Divine Messiahs*, Ancient Judaism and Christianity 106 (Leiden: Brill, 2018).

[32] It is often assumed that John's baptism was a one-time, initiatory event, and, for that reason different from early Jewish practices of ritual purification, which were repeated. There is, however,

John's ablutions, then, are located squarely within the realm of ritual purification—a washing with water by which one becomes ritually pure, and so prepared to encounter God's holy presence in one's mortal body.

In the Fourth Gospel, John's ablutions have nothing to do with repentance, the forgiveness of sins, or moral reformation. But John's ablutions were not for nothing. John relates his ablutions to Israel's perception of the one whom God would reveal. "I myself did not know him; but I came baptizing with water for this reason, that he might be revealed to Israel" (ἵνα φανερωθῇ τῷ Ἰσραὴλ διὰ τοῦτο ἦλθον ἐγὼ ἐν ὕδατι βαπτίζων, 1:31). Soon after, John's confession, "I myself did not know him," gives way to his visual perception of Jesus. The prominence of the language of vision on the second day of John's witness is striking (1:29–34): John sees Jesus coming toward him (βλέπω, 1:29); he calls people to behold the lamb of God (ἴδε, 1:29); he sees the Spirit descend on Jesus (θεάομαι, 1:32; ὁράω, 1:33); and he declares that he has seen that Jesus is the Son of God (ὁράω, 1:34). John, whose ablutions were performed so that Jesus would be revealed to Israel, is the one from Israel who first perceives the one whom God revealed.[33] In this passage we find that same constellation of purity, perception, and revelation visible across a spectrum of early Jewish writings, with the caveat that John's Gospel more narrowly relates *ritual* purity to revelation. The ablutions of John purify. Israel is purified in preparation for the revealing of Jesus.[34] And Jesus's revelation to Israel is first perceived by John and, within a week of Jesus's arrival, perceived by John's former disciples at Cana (2:11). This suggests that the Fourth Gospel narrates John's ablutions and their purpose by drawing from an early Jewish discourse in which (ritual) purity prepares Israel to perceive what God reveals.

John's ablutions are controversial in the Fourth Gospel, and it is necessary to explore why (1:19–28; 3:25). If John's ablutions were simply a ritual purification, one may wonder why they provoked a delegation sent from Jerusalem to inquire about whether John was the Messiah, Elijah, or the Prophet (1:19–28). After all, washing with water for ritual purification was regularly practiced by ancient Jews. There is evidence that ancient Jews purified themselves with water not only to prepare for worship in the Jerusalem temple (see, e.g., Jdt. 16:18; Philo, *Spec. Laws* 1.257–266), but also before

---

no positive evidence in the Fourth Gospel that John's baptism was undergone only once by those who came to him. In fact, the use of the imperfect periphrastic construction in narrative summaries of John's practice of baptism (ἦν ... βαπτίζων, 1:28; 3:23) may suggest otherwise—that John's baptism was repeated and that the same people "kept coming to him and being baptized" (παρεγίνοντο καὶ ἐβαπτίζοντο, 3:23). But the evidence is inconclusive one way or another, because the imperfect tense cannot carry such heavy interpretive weight, and it is unclear if the *same* people were undergoing John's baptism time and again.

[33] We might assume that as one abluting others, John himself was also in a state of ritual purity. This might have been achieved by John doing what ancient Jews tended to do, namely, by abluting himself with water—but it is not narrated.

[34] Strictly speaking, what is narrated in the first scene after the Prologue is not John's activity of abluting, but the purpose and outcome of that activity. John's abluting is related to readers only in direct discourse (1:25, 26, 31, 33) and a narrator's summary (1:28). Although readers later find out that people were being abluted by John (3:23), in the first account of John's witness readers only know *that* John abluted and that the ablutions were for the purpose of someone being revealed to Israel (1:31). It is unlikely that John abluted every person in Israel. But John's ablutions were apparently sufficient for the sake of revealing Jesus to Israel, as is implied by Jesus's coming and John's recognition of him.

eating (see, e.g., Mk 7:3–4; Lk. 11:38; Jos. *J.W.* 2.129–132; Tg. Ps.-J. Exod. 22:30), before prayer (see, e.g., Jdt. 12:7–9; Let. Aris. 305–306), and immediately after contact with a corpse (see, e.g., Tob. 2:7–9).[35]

What, then, made John's ablutions of such interest, if they were only a ritual purification? As it so happens, bathing for ritual purification was always an activity that one performed on oneself. Thus, when the term βαπτίζω is used to signify ritual ablution for purification, it always appears in the middle or passive voice (2 Kgs 5:14; Jdt. 12:7; Sir. 34:25; Mk 7:4; Lk. 11:38).[36] But in the Fourth Gospel, John is the subject of the verb βαπτίζω in an active voice, which suggests that he was somehow involved in abluting others with water (1:25, 26, 31, 33; 3:23; cf., e.g., Mt. 3:11; Mk 1:8; Lk. 3:16). Furthermore, people came to John to be abluted (βαπτίζω), which suggests again that John's involvement in these ablutions was indispensable. Involvement of two people in ablutions—one abluting and one abluted—was strange, and for that reason may have been controversial. Noting the utter peculiarity of John's agency in abluting others, Joan E. Taylor observes that the only extant example outside of the NT of a person abluting someone else is the case of the servants of Herod, who ablute the high priest Aristobulus III in water … until he drowns (*J.W.* 1.437).[37] Although John's ablutions were hardly the act of drowning anyone, Taylor suggests the image evoked in performing such ablutions is pushing someone down underwater, or perhaps going underwater with them (cf. Acts 8:38).[38] To the extent that early Christian visualizations of baptism have continuity with the ablutions of John the Baptist, Taylor's contention is supported. Early Christian depictions of baptism from the third to fifth centuries always feature an administrator of the baptism, often a man whose hand is on the head of the baptisand, as if to push the one being baptized down into the waters.[39] But it may have been that John's agency in abluting others was simply a matter of his authorizing the ablutions of those who came to him.[40] What exactly John's involvement in abluting others may have looked like, however, is beside the point.

---

[35] I am indebted to Poirier for this concise summary of ways purification extended beyond the temple ("Purity beyond the Temple," 256–9). It should be noted that some of these practices were innovative and contested, as, for instance, in the controversy between Jesus and the Pharisees about hand-washing before meals reflected in Mark 7. There, Jesus and his disciples are portrayed as taking a conservative, levitical approach to purity in contrast to the innovative halakhic approach of the Pharisees (Furstenberg, "Defilement Penetrating the Body," 176–200). The practice of washing with water immediately after contact with a corpse to mollify corpse impurity was also innovative and disputed (Kazen, *Issues of Impurity*, 63–90).

[36] The same can be said for the term λούω, which is used about ten times more often than βαπτίζω in the LXX to denote bathing for ritual purification—it is almost always used to refer to a reflexive activity. The one exception is when Moses washes the sons of Aaron as part of their rite of consecration to priesthood (Exod. 29:4; 40:12; Lev. 8:6).

[37] The text in Josephus reads that Aristobulus III "was, consequently, sent by night to Jericho, and there, in accordance with instructions, plunged [βαπτίζω] into a swimming-bath by the Gauls and drowned" (*J.W.* 1.437 [Thackeray]).

[38] Taylor, *The Immerser*, 50, 56.

[39] Robin M. Jensen, *Living Water: Images, Symbols, and Settings of Early Christian Baptism*, Supplements to Vigiliae Christianae 105 (Leiden: Brill, 2011), 149–51. Jensen notes that as early as Ignatius of Antioch there was concern about who was allowed to administer Christian baptism (Ign. *Smyrn.* 8.2).

[40] That John's agency in ablution was a matter of authorization or presiding may be suggested by the fact that Jesus is said to have abluted (3:22, 26; 4:1), with the qualification that "it was not Jesus

It is John's own involvement in abluting others with water that explains why his purifying ablutions were controversial, as well as why the controversy was about his identity.[41] After John denies being any eschatological figure associated with Israel's restoration, the Pharisees ask him "Why, then, are you abluting, if you are not the Messiah, nor Elijah, nor the Prophet?" (τί οὖν βαπτίζεις εἰ σὺ οὐκ εἶ ὁ χριστὸς οὐδὲ Ἠλίας οὐδὲ ὁ προφήτης, 1:25). The emphatic pronoun σύ in their question is matched with an emphatic ἐγώ in every statement John makes about his ablutions. So John answers them, "*I baptize with water*" (ἐγὼ βαπτίζω ἐν ὕδατι, 1:26). The next day he repeats, "*I came baptizing with water*" (ἦλθον ἐγὼ ἐν ὕδατι βαπτίζων, 1:31). These emphatic pronouns function both to separate his own ablutions from those of the one to follow him, as well as to underscore his own agency in abluting with water. John's identity is under scrutiny because *he* is baptizing others, and the Pharisees are perplexed that he would do such a thing if he did not claim to be the Messiah, or Elijah, or the Prophet.[42] By his own account, John ablutes in the wilderness to straighten the way of the Lord (1:23; cf. Isa. 40:3) and to reveal to Israel the one to come after him (1:31).

What provoked controversy about the ablutions of John in the Fourth Gospel is not the fact that ablutions were taking place—such ablutions with water for ritual purification were common—so much as the involvement of another person in these ablutions with water, namely, John.[43] Such active involvement in abluting others with water is without precedent, except for Moses's administration of Israel's purification at Sinai and his washing of Israel's priests as they were initiated into their work in the tabernacle (Exod. 19:10, 16; 29:4; 40:12; Lev. 8:6). Risto Uro draws from ritual and cognitive theory to describe the ablutions of John as "a special agent ritual."[44] That is to say, the involvement of *John* in the ablution of others mattered more than the particular way the ablutions were administered or performed. His role as a ritual agent in ritual purification was an innovation that drew crowds of people, caught the attention of the Pharisees, and made them wonder whether John thought he was one of the figures associated with Israel's restoration. John's status as a special agent also

---

himself but his disciples who abluted" (4:2 NRSV, trans. mod.). In other words, Jesus's agency in ablution may have been to authorize the ablutions that his disciples administered, and the same may be true of John the Baptist.

[41] The "controversy about purification" in Jn 3:25 also appears to be about the question of *who* is authorized to ablute, with the disciples of John doubting whether it is good for Jesus to supplant John as the agent involved in the ablutions of Israel, on which, see § 3.3.3.

[42] The Messiah, Elijah, and the Prophet, in other words, may not have been associated with ablutions, but were connected with the restoration of Israel, which included expectation of Israel's moral purification. See § 3.1 for how early Jewish hope for an eschatological, moral purification by God is focused onto Jesus in the witness of John (cf., e.g., Isa. 1:15-17; 4:1-4; Ezek. 36:25-27; Pss. Sol. 17-18; 1QS 4:20-22). It is conceivable that the Pharisees wondered whether John's ablutions involved claim to be a visual enactment of God's moral purification of Israel.

[43] In the words of Risto Uro, the difference between John's ablutions with water and ritual purification as it was usually practiced was that ritual purification was usually "self-administered, while in John's immersion there is an agent of the ritual (John or his disciple) *and* a ritual patient (someone who came to him to be baptized)"; see *Ritual and Christian Beginnings: A Socio-Cognitive Analysis* (Oxford: Oxford University Press, 2016), 85.

[44] Uro, *Ritual and Christian Beginnings*, 86.

positions him to interpret the purpose of his own ablutions for the Fourth Gospel's readers.

John ablutes with water because he understands himself to have been sent from God to do so. In the Fourth Gospel, John is not the Messiah, but he is unique. He is the only living human mentioned in the Prologue besides the Word made flesh (1:6–8, 15). And John is called a man "sent from God" (ἀπεσταλμένος παρὰ θεοῦ, 1:6; cf. 3:28), which is said of no other human being in the Fourth Gospel except for Jesus. Having been sent, John "came as a witness [ἦλθεν εἰς μαρτυρίαν] to testify to the light, so that all might believe through him" (1:7). These aspects of John's characterization are voiced by the narrator, who cannot be wrong about John's singular significance in his witness to Jesus.[45] The account of John's witness that follows the Prologue gives John's own understanding of why he was sent and what he came to do. John refers to God as "the one who *sent me* to baptize with water" (ὁ πέμψας με βαπτίζειν ἐν ὕδατι, 1:33). And, again, John says, "I *came* baptizing [ἦλθον ἐγὼ … βαπτίζων] with water for this reason, that he might be revealed to Israel" (1:31). John's self-identification echoes and develops what was said of his being sent and coming in the Prologue—his witness to the light was to be enacted through ablutions with water. Even as John denies that he is the Messiah and diminishes himself in relation to the one to come, he regards his action of abluting with water as divinely commissioned. John's witness to Jesus is inseparable from his ablutions with water because they are a preparation for Jesus to be revealed to Israel (1:19–34).

To put it all together, the Fourth Gospel's use of the term βαπτίζω to lexicalize John's ablutions, its reference to John's ablutions in relation to purity, its emphasis on water as the medium of John's ablutions, and its interpretation of John's ablutions as a preparation for the one whom God would reveal all work together to locate the Fourth Gospel's portrayal of John among early Jewish writings in which purification precedes divine disclosure. In those early Jewish writings, however, Israel is prepared by ritual purification for the revelation of God in the Law of God, the wisdom of God, or the knowledge of God. But in the Fourth Gospel, ritual purification prepares Israel for God's revelation in a mortal man called Jesus, whom the Fourth Gospel claims is the Word of God and the Son of God (1:1–18). This is why John's ablutions themselves can be understood as integral to his witness (1:19, 34). It is immediately after the Prologue that the Fourth Gospel poses its christological question, and it does so through the ablution of John: who is this mortal that requires ritual purification before his appearance? As with early Jewish writings that associate purity, perception, and God's self-disclosure, the Fourth Gospel draws on the story and images of God's revelation at Sinai to develop its claims about how people are prepared for God's revelation. In the Fourth Gospel's case, however, God's self-revelation is the word made flesh—Jesus.

---

[45] James L. Resseguie argues that the narrator of the Fourth Gospel is "a third-person omniscient and intrusive narrator," who, among other things, establishes the ideological perspective by which characters are represented or evaluated ("Point of View," in *How John Works: Storytelling in the Fourth Gospel*, ed. Douglas Estes and Ruth Sheridan, RBS 86 [Atlanta, GA: SBL Press, 2016], 79–96, here 83).

2.2.2 Echoes of Sinai Seen beyond the Jordan

The constellation of purity, perception, and revelation in the Fourth Gospel's account of John's ablutions will be more clearly seen by attending to the glimpses of Sinai in it (Jn 1:19–34). The Fourth Gospel subtly and effectively binds together the ablutions of John that reveal Jesus with the revelation of God in the giving of the Law at Sinai. Richard Hays writes that, in his use of Scripture, the Fourth Evangelist is "the master of the carefully framed, luminous image that shines brilliantly against a dark canvas and lingers in the imagination. … His intertextual sensibility is more visual than auditory."[46] The reference to the giving of the Law in the final sentences of the Prologue prepares readers to see John's ablutions as the kind of purification that Moses performed for Israel at Sinai, which would prepare them to perceive what God revealed in the Law. In the Fourth Gospel, however, what is revealed after this purification is not the written Law, but the Word made flesh.

In remarkably few words in the final sentences of its Prologue, the Fourth Gospel recalls not only the revelation at Sinai (Jn 1:17; Exod. 19–24), but also the limited human ability to perceive what God reveals of God (Jn 1:18; Exod. 33:20).[47] The recollection of Sinai appears in alternating parallel statements, which move between the revelatory event at Sinai and the revelatory event of the word become flesh:[48]

> The law indeed was given through Moses; [x]
> grace and truth came through Jesus Christ. [y]
> No one has ever seen God. [x]
> It is God the only Son, who is close to the Father's heart, who has made him
> known. [y] (1:17–18)

The first "x-y" set juxtaposes what is given from God through Moses and through Jesus, and the second juxtaposes what is or is not perceived in each instance. As with early Jewish interpretations of Sinai, what Israel sees at Sinai is not God, but the Law through which God is revealed (Exod. 20:18). The "x" statements in the alternating parallelism suggest that the Fourth Gospel is like other early Jewish literature in supposing that Israel received the Law at Sinai but did not see God directly.[49]

---

[46] Richard B. Hays, *Echoes of Scripture in the Gospels* (Waco, TX: Baylor University Press, 2016), 284.

[47] Craig A. Evans documents five parallels between Jn 1:14–18 and Exod. 33–34: (1) the reference to the giving of the Law (Jn 1:17); (2) Moses's request to see God's glory (Exod. 33:18; Jn 1:14); (3) the claim that no one can see God (Exod. 33:20; Jn 1:18); (4) the reversal between Moses's sight of God's back and the sight of what is in front of God, that is, the one toward the Father's chest; and (5) the phrase "full of grace and truth" (Exod. 34:6; Jn 1:14); see *Word and Glory: On the Exegetical and Theological Background of John's Prologue*, JSNTSup 89 (Sheffield: JSOT, 1993), 80–1. To add to this, there are some minor verbal parallels between Jn 1:17–18 and Exod. 24:10–12: Μωϋσῆς; ὁ νομος; δίδωμι are mentioned in both Jn 1:17 and Exod. 24:12 LXX. Moses and his companions see (ὁράω) the place where God stood (Exod. 24:10 LXX), and John claims no one has ever seen (ὁράω) God (1:18).

[48] On the literary device of "alternating parallelism" in ancient Jewish as well as Hellenistic texts, see Bruce W. Longenecker, *Rhetoric at the Boundaries: The Art and Theology of New Testament Chain-Link Transitions* (Waco, TX: Baylor University Press, 2005), 24–8.

[49] Similarly, Thompson, *John: A Commentary*, 35–6.

Interestingly, the "grace and truth" (ἡ χάρις καὶ ἡ ἀλήθεια) that comes through Jesus also appears to be an allusion to Sinai—not to the giving of the Law, but to Moses's entreaty for the grace of God's self-disclosure (χαρίς, Exod. 33:12–16 LXX), or perhaps the realization of that self-disclosure when the Lord passes by Moses and calls himself "merciful and truthful" (πολυέλεος καὶ ἀληθινός, וְרַב־חֶסֶד וֶאֱמֶת, Exod. 34:6).[50] If this is the case, then the juxtaposition between what comes through Moses and Jesus cannot be read as a contrast between old and new, such that the law is superseded by grace.[51] Rather, it is a contrast between two events at Sinai and what kind of perception was given or withheld. By Law God was revealed to Israel apart from visual perception, and by grace God's back was seen by Moses. The implication is that the arrival of Jesus is less like the giving of the Law and more like Moses's vision of the back of God. God's self-disclosure has come in Jesus Christ, who is in the Father's bosom, and who makes God known (1:18).[52] The effect of the alternating parallelism is to entangle and interpret the coming of Jesus in the flesh with reference to the revelation(s) at Sinai, and this entanglement is intertwined with matters of revelation and perception.

These glimmers of Sinai at the end of the Prologue are carried forward into the witness of John (the Baptist) by an ancient rhetorical device for transitions between textual units that Bruce Longenecker calls "chain-link interlock," based on Lucian of Samosata's second-century work *How to Write History*.[53] Lucian writes:

> After the preface, long or short in proportion to its subject matter, let the transition to the narrative be gentle and easy. … When he has finished the first topic he will introduce the second, fastened to it and linked with it like a chain, to avoid breaks and a multiplicity of disjointed narratives; no, always the first and second topics must not merely be neighbours but have common matter and overlap." (*How to Write History* 55 [Kilburn])

Longenecker explains that chain-link interlock is a transitional device between two independent textual units with a "back-and-forth pattern (A-b-a-B)" in which the content at the end of a textual unit anticipates the following textual unit, and the following textual unit looks back to the previous one, just like overlapping links in a chain.[54]

This is precisely how the Fourth Gospel transitions between the Prologue (1:1–18) and the witness of John (1:19–34). The two passages are interlinked in such a way that

---

[50] So, for example, Evans, *Word and Glory*, 81 fn.2.

[51] So Hays, *Echoes of Scripture in the Gospels*, 296–8; Thompson, *John: A Commentary*, 35. I am aware that this is a controversial claim, which touches on debates about the role of the Law in the Fourth Gospel. See the erudite discussion in William R. G. Loader, "The Law and Ethics in John's Gospel," in *Rethinking the Ethics of John: "Implicit Ethics" in the Johannine Writings*, ed. Jan G. van der Watt and Ruben Zimmermann, WUNT 291 (Tübingen: Mohr Siebeck, 2012), 143–58.

[52] Evans offers the intriguing suggestion that there is a deliberate contrast between Moses's vision of God's back and Jesus who is at the Father's chest, that is, God's front (*Word and Glory*, 81).

[53] Longenecker's name for this rhetorical device comes from Lucian, but he also draws on Quintillian's work on the same device (*Rhetoric at the Boundaries*, 11–20).

[54] Longenecker, *Rhetoric at the Boundaries*, 44.

neither can be understood apart from the other. The "A-a" chain regards John's witness. Toward the end of the Prologue the account of John's witness is anticipated:

> [A] John testified [Ἰωάννης μαρτυρεῖ] to him and cried out, "This was he of whom I said, 'He who comes after me ranks ahead of me because he was before me.'" (1:15)

The following textual unit begins with verbal repetition of John's witness (1:19).

> [a] And this is the witness of John.
> καὶ αὕτη ἐστὶν ἡ μαρτυρία τοῦ Ἰωάννου. (1:19)

This sentence introduces the account of John's witness (1:19–34) and resembles other sentences in the Fourth Gospel where a concept previously discussed is resumed with the demonstrative (in this case, αὕτη) and then explicated (cf. 3:19; 6:39; 15:12; 17:3).[55] So the "A-a" chain is formed by reference to John's witness, which was first introduced in the Prologue (1:15), then resumed and explicated in the following textual unit (1:19–28).

The "B-b" chain is formed by the allusions to the revelation at Sinai discussed earlier (1:16–18) and John's visual perception of Jesus when he first appears (1:29–34). The most direct verbal connections are made with the language of sight (ὁράω, 1:18, 1:34) and the Gospel's first two uses of the name Jesus (Ἰησοῦς, 1:17, 1:29). There are also thematic connections, since both textual units deal with matters of divine revelation and human perception. To try to visualize the chain link all together then:

> [A] John bore witness (1:15)
> [b] Jesus and the revelation(s) at Sinai (1:16–18)
> [/] [transition between textual units]
> [a] This is the witness of John (1:19–28)
> [B] The revelation of Jesus through John's ablutions (1:29–34)

This chain-link transition works to illuminate John's witness to Jesus with the light of the revelation at Sinai.

Through this chain-link transition, the arrival and revelation of Jesus to Israel through John's ablutions are related both to Jesus's identity as the Word and to the revelation at Sinai. A typology emerges between Moses and John (the Baptist). Whereas God commissions Moses to purify Israel three days before the Law is revealed at Sinai (Exod. 19:10–11), God commissions John to ablute with water before the revealing of Jesus across the Jordan, which he does for at least a few days before Jesus appears (Jn 1:28–29). The Fourth Gospel's reference to Israel as the recipient of God's revelation (Ἰσραήλ, 1:31)—one of only four mentions of Israel in the Fourth Gospel—occurs in the context of John's ablutions and resonates with the corporate purification of all

---

[55] So Bultmann, *The Gospel of John*, 85, fn. 2.

Israel at Sinai. Even the location of John's ablutions in the wilderness across the Jordan resembles with the giving of the Law in the wilderness and the early Jewish traditions that conceptualize the wilderness as a place of both revelation and purification.[56]

The revealing of Jesus to Israel through John's ablutions both recapitulates and retells the revelation of God in the giving of the Law. In the Fourth Gospel, Jesus claims that Israel's Scripture bears witness about him (5:39) and that Moses wrote of him (5:43; cf. 1:45). What is given in the Law is a witness to Jesus, so that when Jesus appears in the flesh, the one of whom the Law speaks arrives. That is, the Law is to reveal Jesus, and when Jesus appears, the God who gave the Law is revealed by a Word that can be seen. It is as though Israel, purified by John's ablutions with water for the coming of Jesus, does not now remain at the foot of the mountain, but ascends with Moses to see what can be seen of God. If, then, God provided ritual purity for Israel to prepare them to receive what is revealed of God in the Law, how much more will God purify Israel to prepare them to perceive Jesus, the word of God made flesh (1:14) and the Son of God (1:34)? At least, that seems to be the intertextual logic at work. Through careful intertextual signals, the Fourth Gospel represents the arrival of Jesus as the word made flesh, the visible voice from Sinai, and the revelation of God.

The Fourth Gospel adopts a biblical tradition about ritual purification derived from the giving of the Law at Sinai and adapts it to serve its Christology. Early Jewish writings in which purification precedes divine disclosure tell of those who are pure being prepared to perceive the glory of God, the knowledge of God, the wisdom of God, or the vision of God's dwelling place. In no instance is one to be pure for the appearance of an only mortal being. By narrating John's ablutions with water as ritual purification that prepares Israel to perceive what God reveals of God, the Fourth Gospel presents Jesus as none less than the revelation of God (cf. 1:14–18; 14:9). For John, the medium is the message. The theology embedded in ablutions with water comes to serve the revealing of the embodied word of God, which is perceived visually rather than aurally. That is, ritual purification becomes a hermeneutic for interpreting Jesus as the Word made flesh at the beginning of the Fourth Gospel's narrative. The Fourth Gospel employs ritual purification in service of the Christology of the Prologue.

In the Fourth Gospel, John (the Baptist) anticipates that the one to come after him is no ordinary mortal. Only the Fourth Gospel places the words of Isaiah on the lips of John, who says, "I am the voice of one crying out in the wilderness, 'Make straight the way of the Lord'" (Jn 1:23; cf. Isa. 40:3). In the text from Isaiah, after the voice cries out the wilderness and the way of the Lord is straightened, "then the glory of the Lord shall appear [ὀφθήσεται ἡ δόξα κυρίου], and all flesh shall see the salvation of God, because the Lord has spoken" (Isa. 40:5, NETS). John had expected that the one to come after him would bring the appearance of God's glory. As the Fourth Gospel's narrator puts it, "the Word became flesh and lived among us, and we have seen his glory" (ἐθεασάμεθα

---

[56] Philo, for instance, explains that the Law was given in the wilderness (ἔρημος) because one "must first cleanse his soul and purge away the deepest stains which it has contracted [ἐκκαθήρασθαι τὰς δυσεκπλύτους κηλῖδας]" (*Decalogue* 10 [Colson]). For other early Jewish associations between wilderness, purification, and revelation see Najman, "Towards a Study of the Uses of the Concept of Wilderness in Ancient Judaism," 105–13.

τὴν δόξαν αὐτοῦ, 1:14). John enacts his witness to Jesus by abluting with water because it provides what purity Israel needs if it is to see the glory of God in the face of Jesus Christ, as John's disciples who followed Jesus would come to see at Cana (2:11; cf. 12:41; 17:1–5). Israel is supposed to receive from Jesus grace in place of grace (1:16) and to perceive in Jesus what God reveals of God (1:18).

The interpretation of John's ablutions as a purification that prepares for the revelation of Jesus explains why John's witness is invoked by Jesus in a controversy with the *Ioudaioi* about his claim that God is his Father. The *Ioudaioi* perceive this claim as Jesus "making himself equal to God" (5:18). In response, Jesus claims that "just as the Father has life in himself, so he has granted the Son also to have life in himself" (5:26). About this remarkable claim, Thompson writes that "the formulation assumes the unity of the life-giving *work* of Father and Son, but it also predicates a remarkable status of the Son, one that is not made of any other mediator figure."[57] To put it differently, the work of Jesus in giving life and rendering judgment (5:25–27) is the work of the Father, and he is able to do this because of the divine life he shares uniquely with the Father.[58] After making one of the most stunning theological and christological claims in the Fourth Gospel, Jesus appeals to the witness of John to attest to the truth of what he has said about himself:

> If I testify about myself, my testimony is not true. There is another who testifies on my behalf, and I know that his testimony to me is true. You sent messengers to John, and he testified to the truth. Not that I accept such human testimony, but I say these things so that you may be saved. He was a burning and shining lamp, and you were willing to rejoice for a while in his light. (5:31–35)

In speaking of John as a burning and shining lamp that gives light, Jesus speaks of John as one whose ablutionary witness might have prepared the *Ioudaioi* to perceive what God was revealing to Israel in the sending of Jesus. But instead, Jesus speaks of a deficiency in the perception of God's revelation on the part of the *Ioudaioi*. He tells them, "You have never heard [the Father's] voice or seen his form" (5:37). In saying that, Jesus identifies them with the wilderness generation that "heard the sound of words but … did not notice a likeness, only a voice" (ὁμοίωμα οὐκ εἴδετε, ἀλλ᾽ ἢ φωνήν, Deut. 4:12 NETS).[59] But Jesus also denies that they heard the Father's voice, a possible allusion to Israel's request for Moses to speak to them on God's behalf (Exod. 20:19; cf. 24:3). John's witness, like Moses's ablutions, might have helped prepare the *Ioudaioi* to perceive the truth about Jesus so that they "may be saved" (5:34). Through

---

[57] Marianne Meye Thompson, *The God of the Gospel of John* (Grand Rapids, MI: Eerdmans, 2001), 78–9.

[58] Richard Bauckham argues that the unique identity of God is characterized in early Jewish writings in God's giving life in creation, rule and judgment over all things, and reception of worship, which are, one notices, all works that are predicated of Jesus in Jn 5:19-30; see *Jesus and the God of Israel: God Crucified and Other Studies on the New Testament's Christology of Divine Identity* (Grand Rapids: Eerdmans, 2009), 7–13.

[59] On this connection to Deuteronomy, see Thompson, *John: A Commentary*, 134–5.

the ablutions of John, ritual purification is transformed into a site of christological controversy and development.[60]

2.3 Ritual Purification in the Fourth Gospel

The Fourth Gospel's orientation toward ritual purification reflected in John's ablutions is maintained elsewhere in the Fourth Gospel, especially in the scenes at Cana (2:1–11) and Siloam (9:1–7). In the Fourth Gospel, then, one finds not a replacement of early Jewish purification, but an appeal to one particular stream of early Jewish discourse about ritual purification related to the revelation at Sinai that is developed to serve the Fourth Gospel's Christology.

The sign at Cana carries forward the constellation of purity, perception, and revelation reflected in John's ablutions and early Jewish writings on God's self-disclosure. Jesus's first sign is the last link in a succession of days that begins with the witness of John, each marked by the phrase "the next day" (ἐπαυριον, (1:29, 35, 43; cf. 1:19), until one arrives at Cana, which is on "the third day" (2:1). Some interpreters have found an echo of Sinai in the phrase "on the third day" (τῇ ἡμέρᾳ τῇ τρίτῃ, 2:1), since on the third day after Moses purified Israel at Sinai the Lord was to be revealed (τὴν ἡμέραν τὴν τρίτην, Exod. 19:10–11 LXX).[61] What is more, the sign at Cana marks the sixth day in the temporal sequence, which is the number of days that "the glory of God" covered Mount Sinai before Moses entered that glory and received the two tablets of the covenant (ἡ δόξα τοῦ θεοῦ, 24:16–17; cf. 31:18).[62] This would make John 1:19–2:11 a six-day long glimpse of Jesus's glory before the beginning of his public ministry at the temple.[63] But these echoes are rather faint. More plainly, both the temporal sequence and repetition of the term *reveal* (φανερόω, 1:31; 2:11) connect the sign at Cana to the revelation of Jesus that John's ablutionary witness had anticipated.

---

[60] Larry Hurtado has argued that early high Christology developed within an early Jewish context through the offering of devotion to Jesus; see his outline of this argument in Larry W. Hurtado, *How on Earth Did Jesus Become a God? Historical Questions about Earliest Devotion to Jesus* (Grand Rapids, MI: Eerdmans, 2005) or its expanded presentation in Larry W. Hurtado, *Lord Jesus Christ: Devotion to Jesus in Earliest Christianity* (Grand Rapids, MI: Eerdmans, 2005). Jörg Frey has recently assessed how John's Christology is a Jewish development of the kind of early high Christology Hurtado described; see "Between Jewish Monotheism and Proto-Trinitarian Relations: The Making and Character of Johannine Christology," in *Monotheism and Christology in Greco-Roman Antiquity*, ed. Matthew V. Novenson, NovTSup 180 (Leiden: Brill, 2020), 189–221. The argument I have set forward about John's concept of ritual purity, taken in historical perspective, supports these contentions of Hurtado and Frey, as it reflects a novel christological development that draws from early Jewish tradition and directs early Jewish devotional practice toward Jesus.

[61] See, for example, Lincoln, *The Gospel according to Saint John*, 126, although he does not connect the sequence of days in Exod. 19:11 to the purification of the people.

[62] The enumeration of days is debated. Richard Bauckham reasonably argues that the passage of a day is implied in 1:40–42, making for seven days, but the explicit repetition of ἐπαύριον suggests to me a six-day sequence; see *Gospel of Glory: Major Themes in Johannine Theology* (Grand Rapids, MI: Baker Academic, 2015), 132–5.

[63] Bauckham refers to this week and the six days before Passover at the end of the Fourth Gospel the "Gospel's two momentous weeks," and helpfully coordinates them structurally and thematically (*Gospel of Glory*, 132–5).

At Cana, Jesus's glory is first revealed to his disciples, some of whom were formerly John's disciples (cf. 1:7, 47). Among the first to perceive the glory of God in Jesus Christ were those in Israel who had been ritually purified by John's ablutions with water.

Jesus and his disciples evidently arrive late to the wedding, since the wine had already run out when they got there (2:2–3).[64] The six stone vessels for the purpose of ritual purification are in need of being filled with water (2:6–7). Jesus asks the servants to draw water from the vessels and to bring it to the chief steward (2:7–8). Only when the chief steward tastes what is brought to him does one discover it has become wine (2:9). The story ends with the chief steward's judgment about the superior quality of the wine over that which was first served, as well as the unexpected order in which it was served (2:10). As both Bauckham and Thompson have suggested, the chief steward's judgment ought to help give focus to the significance of the sign at Cana. The chief steward contrasts good wine with the best wine. It is not a contrast between water and wine, or between emptiness and abundance, or between the old and the new. In other words, it is not a contrast that signals the replacement of one thing with another. Instead, it is a comparison of the relative quality of the wine served at the wedding.[65]

In Israel's Scripture, the image of abundant wine conjures expectations of abundant joy and life at the time that God was to restore Israel (cf., e.g., Jer. 31:10–14; Amos 9:13–15).[66] Significantly for the interpretation of the sign at Cana, only Isaiah's vision of cosmic restoration refers to the quality of the wine in the restoration of Israel and the world:[67]

> On this mountain the LORD of hosts will make for all peoples a feast of rich food, a feast of well-aged wines, of rich food filled with marrow, of well-aged wines strained clear [שְׁמָרִים מְזֻקָּקִים]. And he will destroy on this mountain the shroud that is cast over all peoples, the sheet that is spread over all nations; he will swallow up death forever. (Isa. 25:6)

Three aspects of this passage make it particularly harmonious with Jesus's sign at Cana. First, and most importantly, the phrase translated "well-aged wines strained clear" employs the metallurgical term זקק, which is used to describe the process of removing impurities and adulterations from gold and silver, which is sometimes employed metaphorically as a term for purification (cf. Mal. 3:3; Ps. 12:6; Job 28:1; 1 Chron. 28:18; 29:4).[68] That is, what makes the eschatological wine of such surpassing quality is

[64] Busse, "Reinigung und Heiligung," 145–6.
[65] Thompson, *John: A Commentary*, 62; Bauckham, *Gospel of Glory*, 181.
[66] So, for example, Thompson, *John: A Commentary*, 62–3; Brown, *The Gospel according to John*, 1:105.
[67] Bauckham relates this text to Jn 2:1–11, rightly noting that the Fourth Gospel has more resonance here with the MT than with the LXX (*Gospel of Glory*, 182). For example, whereas the MT refers to the quality of the wine, the LXX simply reads, "they will drink joy; they will drink wine" (Isa. 25:6), and where the MT envisions death being swallowed up, the LXX suggests that death prevails and consumes the nations (25:7–8).
[68] For example, the purity of the word of the Lord is described by the Psalmist as "silver refined in a furnace on the ground, purified [מְזֻקָּק] seven times" (Ps. 12:6), which the LXX translates with a term often used of purification (καθαρίζω, Ps. 11:7 LXX). The lexical relationship between the language of purity and metallurgy in Hebrew is not limited only to metallurgic terms or contexts,

its purity. In this sense, the use of stone vessels for purification to hold the water that became wine suggests it is the purest wine, and, for that reason, the best. Second, as the signs in the Fourth Gospel bear witness to the Father's work of giving life through Jesus, it is surely significant that the Lord's banquet with food and wine in Isaiah's vision of restoration marks the removal of death's veil from the peoples and the consumption of death itself.[69] Third, the Lord's banquet for all peoples is located on "this mountain," which is a reference back to Mount Zion in its co-text: "for the LORD of hosts will reign on Mount Zion and in Jerusalem, and before his elders he will manifest his glory" (Isa. 24:23). The banquet of the Lord, full of rich food and pure wine, then, is the revealing of God's glory on earth (cf. Isa. 40:3). The Fourth Gospel's narrator interprets the whole episode at Cana as a revelatory sign: "Jesus did this, the first of his signs, in Cana of Galilee, and revealed his glory; and his disciples believed in him" (2:11). If the wine at Cana is to be interpreted symbolically with recourse to Israel's Scripture, Isaiah's reference to the quality of wine in connection to God's work of consuming death and revealing glory makes it a particularly apt comparison.[70]

That being said, the role that the stone vessels for the ritual purification of the *Ioudaioi* play in the sign at Cana may now be better understood. Busse's suggestion that the stone vessels were empty because the guests had already used the water to ritually purify themselves—implicitly contrasting their piety with the impurity of the temple in the next episode (2:12–22)—is possible, but since the narrator does not make the connection it is difficult to derive such significance from it.[71] Somewhat differently, Bauckham adduces that the stone vessels for purification are mentioned only to explain how much wine was produced and how it was contained, so that purification has no significance in the episode except to allow the plot to move forward.[72] But the Fourth Gospel need not have specified that these six large vessels were for purification for the sake of the plot, and the intertextual echo of Isaiah suggests purity is important to the wine's quality. The stone vessels for the purification of the *Ioudaioi* and the water that filled them became the surprising resource that Jesus uses to disclose his glory to his disciples. The wine that signifies the arrival of the age to come and the surpassing abundance of life that it brings is contained by pure vessels. There is even a suggestion, reminiscent of Isa. 25:6, that the wine is the best wine because it is the purest. This does not intimate the replacement of ritual purity so much as it demonstrates its indispensability and usefulness. The messianic wine needs containment, and the vessels for Jewish ritual purification are those from which one may draw and taste

---

   on which see Feder, "The Semantics of Purity in the Ancient Near East," 106–11; Lam, *Patterns of Sin*, 191–4.

[69] The connection between the banquet's fine wine and the abolition of death is made by Bauckham, *Gospel of Glory*, 182. On what the Fourth Gospel's signs signify, see Thompson, *John: A Commentary*, 65–8. On the "shroud cast over all peoples" as the veil that one might wear while mourning, see Brevard S. Childs, *Isaiah*, OTL (Louisville, KY: Westminster John Knox, 2001), 185.

[70] Isaiah 25 is both alluded to and quoted elsewhere in the NT (Mk 14:25; Lk. 22:18; 1 Cor. 15:54; Rev. 7:17; 21:4), which suggests that some early readers would have been able to grasp echoes of the text such as I am proposing here, especially because John's Gospel encloses the public ministry of Jesus with quotations attributed to Isaiah (1:23; 12:38–41).

[71] Busse, "Reinigung und Heiligung," 145–7.

[72] Bauckham, *Gospel of Glory*, 181.

the abundance and extravagance of the messianic age. At Cana, then, vessels for ritual purification facilitate the revelation of Jesus's glory, and only the disciples of Jesus— presumably, having been abluted by John and thus ritually pure themselves—are able to perceive that glory (2:11).

One finds that ritual purification is bound up with revelation and perception also in the giving of sight to the man born blind (9:1–10:21) and in Jesus's washing of his disciples' feet (13:1–11). As these two passages will be analyzed in more depth in subsequent chapters, only a few remarks are here necessary. After smearing mud on the eyes of a man born blind, Jesus commands him to wash in the pool of Siloam. When the man does so, he receives his eyesight (9:1–7). Archeologists have recently discovered that the pool of Siloam was one of the two largest pools in Jerusalem built for ritual purification.[73] This suggests that the washing by which this man born blind received his eyesight was a ritual purification. Even before the man confesses his trust in Jesus and worships him (9:37–38), he perceives that Jesus is from God (9:30–33). The ritual purity of the man born blind, as will be seen, corresponds to the moral purification that takes place through his encounter with Jesus, evident in the removal of the judgment that he is a sinner and his inclusion among those sheep who have seen and entered life.

Later, when Peter resists the washing of his feet, Jesus answers him, "You do not know now what I am doing, but later you will understand" (13:7). Within its early Jewish context, the washing of only the feet can, at most, be considered as supplementary to an otherwise complete state of ritual purity, which the disciples must have had in preparation for Passover (cf. 11:55; 13:10a).[74] Even so, Jesus's strange manner of washing his disciples' feet will later help them perceive that his death was a lowly act of love.[75] The disciples, that is, were ritually pure in preparation for the Passover during which the disciples would see the glory of Jesus in his glorification in cross and resurrection (17:24). In these two passages, as will be seen, ritual purification points to the moral purification brought into effect by Jesus's word and work. Nevertheless, ritual purification still figures as that by which one perceives what God reveals in Jesus, not least, the work of moral purification that Jesus brings into effect, which is the subject of the next chapter of this book.

2.4 Conclusion

At least with respect to ritual purity, the Fourth Gospel is most christological when it is most characteristically Jewish. The Fourth Gospel participates in an early Jewish tradition of purity derived from the biblical account of the giving of the Law at Sinai

---

[73] Urban C. von Wahlde, "The Gospel of John and Archeology," in *The Oxford Handbook of Johannine Studies*, ed. Judith Lieu and Martinus C. de Boer, Oxford Handbooks (Oxford: Oxford University Press, 2018), 102–6.

[74] So argues John Christopher Thomas, *Footwashing in John 13 and the Johannine Community*, 2nd ed. (Cleveland, TN: CPT Press, 2014), 114.

[75] On the footwashing as an act that shows the love of Jesus in laying down his life, see Jan G. van der Watt, "The Meaning of Jesus Washing the Feet of His Disciples (John 13)," *Neot* 51.1 (2017): 25–39.

in which (ritual) purification is related to human perception and divine revelation. In this tradition, ritual purity cannot be defined as the mere absence of impurity; it is a bodily preparation necessary to perceive what God reveals.[76] In early Jewish writings, ritual purification was to prepare people only for what God reveals of God, whether knowledge of God, wisdom from God, or the vision of God. In the Fourth Gospel, John's ablutions are interpreted as a ritual purification in preparation for the revealing of Jesus to Israel, and the relation between ritual purity and the revelation of Jesus is retained throughout the narrative. That is, the Fourth Gospel employs an early Jewish concept of ritual purification as a hermeneutic for interpreting who Jesus is in relation to God. Its strategy is not to replace purity with Jesus, so much as it is to illuminate who Jesus is through a particular biblical and early Jewish concept of ritual purity. In so doing, ritual purification becomes a site of christological controversy.

Whereas early Jewish writings conceptualize both ritual and moral purity as necessary preparation for revelation, in the Fourth Gospel ritual purity and moral purity remain conceptually distinct from one another, and it is only ritual purification that prepares for the revealing of Jesus. John's ablutions with water are not for the removal of sin, and there is no indication that the *Ioudaioi* supposed that purification with water removed sin. As will be explored in the next two chapters, moral purification is the work of God through Jesus, is effected for (most of) the disciples through the word of Jesus, and is concerned with both salvation and ethics.

---

[76] On ritual purity as the absence of impurity, see, for example, Hannah K. Harrington, *The Purity Texts*, Companion to the Qumran Scrolls (London: T&T Clark International, 2004), 9.

3

Born from Above: Jesus, Moral Purity, and Restoration

In Chapter 2, I concluded that in the Fourth Gospel, the purpose of ritual purification is to prepare Israel to perceive the revelation of God in Jesus. The Fourth Gospel draws from a vibrant, if marginal, biblical and early Jewish tradition about ritual purification as that which prepares a person to encounter God and perceive what God reveals. Since ritual purification prepares a person to perceive what is *from God*, John's ablutions with water for the revealing of Jesus work to identify Jesus with God. So the Fourth Gospel employs an early Jewish discourse about the significance of ritual purity to narrate how Israel is prepared for the coming of Jesus, the Word made flesh. The Fourth Gospel maintains a distinction between ritual and moral purity in its representation of John's witness. Ritual purity is a bodily condition that results from washing with water, which does not remove sin, and which prepares one to perceive divine revelation. John denied that his ablutions with water accomplished the moral purification that some ancient Jews expected the Messiah, Elijah, or the Prophet to bring (Jn 1:25). The focus of this chapter is on the work of God in Jesus to make God's people morally pure.

In this chapter, I will argue that the Fourth Gospel employs biblical and early Jewish traditions of moral purification associated with Israel's restoration in order to represent Jesus as the one through whom God morally purifies Israel and so enables them to see and enter life (Jn 1:19–34; 3:1–4:3; 9:1–10:21; cf., e.g., Ezek. 36:25–27; Jer. 33:7–11; *Jub.* 1.25–29). I will demonstrate that the Major Prophets related the divine work of moral purification to Israel's restoration, and this association between moral purification and Israel's restoration was carried forward with different emphases in early Jewish writings, the Fourth Gospel among them. John the Baptist's introduction of Jesus as "the lamb of God who takes away the sin of the world" (1:29) and "the one who ablutes with the Holy Spirit" (1:33) focuses ancient Jewish expectations for moral purification and Israel's restoration onto Jesus. The diptych formed between the accounts of the dialogue with Nicodemus and the overlapping ablutionary ministries of John and Jesus further conceptualizes Jesus's work as that of moral purification, and does so with recourse to Isaiah's figure of Israel's restoration as a birth (Jn 3:1–12; Isa. 44:3–4; 46:1–4; 65–66) and Jeremiah's image of a joyous marriage as a sign that God had purified Israel from sin (Jn 3:22–4:3; Jer. 33:7–11). In light of this, the phrase "born of water and Spirit" is to be interpreted as "birth resulting from the purification from above," and the result of this birth is a restored ability to see and enter the kingdom of

God. This "birth resulting from purification from above" is instantiated in the giving of sight to a man born blind through washing (9:1–10:21), a work of Jesus that removes the judgment that the man is a sinner, reverses his congenital blindness, and makes him able to see and enter life.

It should be noted that the focus of this chapter is on Jesus as the one through whom God enacts Israel's moral purification. Chapter 4 will focus on the beneficiaries of this work of purification, namely, the disciples of Jesus, as well as how their purity relates to the moral quality of their lives and their ability to love one another as Jesus loved them. The focus of this chapter is soteriological, and the focus of the next is ethical, but conceptually they belong together.

3.1 The Baptizing Messiah? Moral Purity and Israel's Restoration

In this section, I will argue that the Fourth Gospel locates Jesus within early Jewish expectation for God to make Israel pure from sin in its restoration, and does so in its opening scene (1:19–34). This expectation is evident in the interrogation between John (the Baptist) and the delegation sent from Jerusalem (1:19–28). After learning that John does not claim to be the Messiah, the delegation asks if he is Elijah or the Prophet, which John also denies (1:20–21). These three figures may simply reflect the diversity of eschatological expectation among ancient Jews, each being in some way associated with Israel's restoration.[1] Or, as Bauckham suggests, the three figures together may "represent the three roles of king, high priest, and prophet," which are "the three human leaders that a properly restored Jewish theocracy would require."[2] In any case, after John denies being the Messiah, Elijah, and the Prophet, the Pharisees pose a question that associates all of them with ablutions: "Why then are you abluting (βαπτίζω) if you are neither the Messiah, nor Elijah, nor the prophet?" (1:25 NRSV, trans. mod.; cf. 1:20–21). Apparently, claiming to be any one of these eschatological figures would be enough to explain why *John* was abluting. But no passages in Israel's Scripture or extant early Jewish writings associate any of these figures with ablutions as such. What grounds are there for the association, then? There is expectation in Scripture and early Jewish tradition that in the restoration of Israel God would purify Israel from sin, and, as will be seen, sometimes this purification from sin is described with imagery from ritual purification.[3] John's ablutions provoked the Pharisees' eschatological

---

[1] On the role of these figures in the restoration of Israel—the Davidic Messiah, the Prophet like Moses (Deut. 18:18), and Elijah (Sir. 48:4–12)—particularly as they might relate to the Johannine Jesus, see Thompson, *John: A Commentary*, 43–5; see also Richard Bauckham, "Messianism according to the Gospel of John," in *Challenging Perspectives on the Gospel of John*, ed. John Lierman, WUNT 2/219 (Tübingen: Mohr Siebeck, 2006), 34–68.

[2] Bauckham, on the basis of the identification of Aaron's grandson Phinehas as Elijah in Tg. Ps.-J., suggests that Elijah's role in the restoration could be priestly, and finds a similar "eschatological trio" in 1QS 9.11 and 4Q175.5–10 ("Messianism According to the Gospel of John," 37).

[3] Brown (*The Gospel according to John*, 1:51), Bultmann (*The Gospel of John*, 88), Thompson (*John: A Commentary*, 46, 48), and Michaels (*The Gospel of John*, 88) interpret the Pharisees' question about ablution in terms of the sort of purification expected by the Prophets (cf., e.g., Ezek. 36:25–27; Zech.

speculation, and John (the Baptist)'s identification of Jesus as "the one who ablutes with the Holy Spirit" (1:33) suggests that the presuppositions of the Pharisees were correct, only misplaced. In other words, it is not John whose ablutions are explained by his eschatological significance, but Jesus. Through the work of Jesus, God would purify Israel from sin and so enable them to live fully in the presence of God.

The hope for Israel's restoration involved a complex of themes that repeat through the prophetic texts of Israel's Scripture. The hopes for restoration included deliverance from foreign oppression, the return of the Lord to Jerusalem, the restoration and repopulation of the land of Israel, the reestablishment of David's throne, the renewal of Israel's humanity, the rebuilding of the temple, the reinstatement of right worship, the inclusion of the nations in Israel's salvation, and the purification of the people from sin.[4] This prophetic vision suggests that Israel's hope for restoration exceeded any of its past conditions. Israel's golden age was not a return to the past so much as a yet unrealized future. As has been recognized, the Fourth Gospel may be included among those early Jewish texts that imagine and envision Israel's eschatological restoration by God.[5] Christopher Blumhofer has recently contended that the Fourth Gospel functions as a "narrative argument," the thesis of which is that "in his own person Jesus provides continuity between the biblical past and the prophesied future of Israel for the Jewish tradition."[6] Blumhofer's work shows that the Fourth Gospel has a thoroughgoing concern for Israel's future, and sets forth its christological vision for that future in conversation with Israel's Scripture and early Jewish traditions. In the

---

13:1) and some ancient Jews (e.g., 1QS 3–4). Barrett resists this implication without indicating a reason (*The Gospel according to St. John*, 174). Brant points out that evidence for the connection between these particular figures and ablution is scarce, but that ablutions with water were interpreted eschatologically in 1 QS 3–4 (*John*, 48).

[4] For this summary of themes related to Israel's restoration in the Prophets I am dependent on the canonical analysis of the Prophets by Konrad Schmid and Odil Hannes Steck, "Restoration Expectations in the Prophetic Tradition of the Old Testament," in *Restoration: Old Testament, Jewish, and Christian Perspectives*, ed. James M. Scott, JSJSup 72 (Leiden: Brill, 2001), 49–61. For similar conclusions, but with more focus on moral purification, see the treatment of Zion theology in the Prophets in Frederik Poulsen, *Representing Zion: Judgement and Salvation in the Old Testament*, Copenhagen International Seminar (London: Routledge, 2015).

[5] John A. Dennis attends to how the Fourth Gospel appeals to early Jewish restoration theology in its conceptualization of the death of Jesus as that by which Israel is regathered (*Jesus' Death and the Gathering of True Israel: The Johannine Appropriation of Restoration Theology in the Light of John 11.47–52*, WUNT 2/217 (Tübingen: Mohr Siebeck, 2006). Stephen Motyer argues that even the Fourth Gospel's most severe polemic against the *Ioudaioi* may be understood as a call to repentance and faith in Jesus (Jn 8:31–59), and does so by locating the Fourth Gospel among other early Jewish documents (cf., e.g., 2 Bar.; 4 Ezra; Apoc. Abr.; T. 12 Patr.) that offer ways to work through the crisis of the Jerusalem temple's destruction in 70 CE (*Your Father the Devil?: A New Approach to John and "the Jews,"* Paternoster Biblical and Theological Studies [Carlisle: Paternoster, 1997]). On the Fourth Gospel as a response to the destruction of the Jerusalem temple see also, Andreas J. Köstenberger, "The Destruction of the Second Temple and the Composition of the Fourth Gospel," in *Challenging Perspectives on the Gospel of John*, ed. John Lierman, WUNT 2/219 (Tübingen: Mohr Siebeck, 2006), 69–108; but cf. Marianne Meye Thompson who rightly observes that the destruction and restoration of the temple envisioned in Jn 2:19–22 is a reference to Jesus's body "Jesus and the Victory of God Meets the Gospel of John," in *Jesus, Paul, and the People of God: A Theological Dialogue with N. T. Wright*, ed. Nicholas Perrin, Richard B. Hays, and N. T. Wright (Downers Grove, IL: IVP Academic, 2011), 33–7.

[6] Christopher Blumhofer, *The Gospel of John and the Future of Israel*, SNTSMS 177 (Cambridge: Cambridge University Press, 2020), 40; cf. 2–3.

words of Thompson, it may be said that in the Fourth Gospel "Jesus both bestows and embodies the fullness of what Israel's various institutions, feasts, and central figures commemorate, promise or signify."[7] As will be seen, God's purification of Israel from sin—moral purification, that is—was a biblical tradition carried forward in early Jewish expectation for Israel's restoration, which the Fourth Gospel adapts to its narrative about the work of God in Jesus. That is, the Fourth Gospel employs biblical and early Jewish traditions of moral purity related to Israel's restoration in order to represent Jesus as the one through whom God brings moral purification and so enables Israel to participate in salvation.

3.1.1 Defilement Desolates, Purity Populates: Moral Purity and Restoration in the Major Prophets

In the major Prophets, Israel's moral purification from sin was entailed in its return to and repopulation of the land of Israel.[8] Moral purification must remedy the defiling sins for which the prophets indicted Israel—sins such as bloodshed, sexual misdeeds, and idolatry—in order to make possible the return of Israel to the land, as is seen in Ezekiel, Jeremiah, and Isaiah.[9] As will be argued, John's Gospel draws on such texts to construct its vision of the work of Jesus in terms of moral purification. The Fourth Gospel adapts the prophetic connection between moral purification and the repopulation of the land by emphasizing the relation of purity to life and neglecting the promise of return to the land.

Ezekiel's vision of God's purification of Israel from sin is the most vivid, visualizing the Lord removing the people's idols by sprinkling pure water on them (Ezek. 36:25–27). This is the second of Ezekiel's four prophecies about Israel's restoration after the fall of Jerusalem.[10] The prophecy begins with an indictment of Israel for defiling both the land and themselves with their idolatry and bloodshed (Ezek. 36:16–18). Their judgment is exile among the nations (36:19). God is to reverse this judgment by gathering Israel from the nations and reverse the cause of judgment by purifying Israel from its sins and idols. The language of this oracle became the basis for much early Jewish expectation for an eschatological, moral purification:

> And I will take you from the nations and gather you from all the lands and bring you into your own land. And I will sprinkle pure water upon you [ῥανῶ ἐφ᾽ ὑμᾶς ὕδωρ καθαρόν], and you shall be purified from all your impure acts and from all your idols [καθαρισθήσεσθε ἀπὸ πασῶν τῶν ἀκαθαρσιῶν ὑμῶν καὶ ἀπὸ πάντων

---

[7] Thompson, *John: A Commentary*, 15.
[8] So also, Poulsen, *Representing Zion*, 164–9.
[9] See the discussion of moral (im)purity and defiling sins in § 1.3.
[10] Tova Ganzel argues that the four, post-fall prophecies of Ezekiel about Israel's restoration follow a coherent progression. It begins with the institution of a shepherd-leader for Israel (Ezek. 34), then with the purification of Israel by the Lord, which will prepare the people for regathering (36:16–38), then the restoration of the temple in Jerusalem (37:15–28), and finally the outpouring of the Spirit on Israel (39:21–29) ("The Descriptions of the Restoration of Israel in Ezekiel," *VT* 60 [2010]: 205–10). This suggests that in Ezekiel's view, moral purification is an indispensable element in Israel's restoration.

τῶν εἰδώλων ὑμῶν], and I will purify you [καθαριῶ ὑμᾶς]. And I will give you a new heart, and a new spirit I will give in you, and I will remove the stone heart from your flesh and give you a heart of flesh. And I will give my spirit in you and will act so that you walk in my statutes and keep my judgments and perform them. (Ezek. 36:24–27, NETS, trans. mod.)[11]

What is the kind of purification in view in this oracle of Ezekiel? Although the visualization of God's purification of Israel draws from water rites typically associated with ritual purification, moral purification is in view, which is evident in that Israel's lawlessness and idolatry is removed by this purification.[12] Furthermore, God is the one who is envisioned as bringing this purification from sin and is represented as the only one who can bring moral purification.

In Ezekiel, the result of this divine, moral purification is a transformation of the inner person for the people of Israel. Stone hearts will become flesh, God's Spirit will come to dwell in them, they will become capable of observing God's commandments, and human life will be abundant.[13] Moral purification was also to bring the transformation of the land through the life of its inhabitants. Ezekiel taught that Jerusalem was destroyed and its land made desolate because of the defiling sins of the people (33:25–29; cf. 24:13). In this oracle of restoration, the rebuilding and repopulation of the land is a result of God's moral purification of the people from the sin that had once caused the land to be desolate: "In the day I will purify you from all your lawless acts [καθαριῶ ὑμᾶς ἐκ πασῶν τῶν ἀνομιῶν ὑμῶν]; I will also settle the cities, and the deserts shall be built" (36:33 NETS, trans. mod.). God's purification of Israel from sin, then, involves the transformation of humanity and the transformation of the land of Israel, making both hospitable to God's life.

Several passages in the Fourth Gospel have verbal affinity with Ezek. 36, but not enough to establish direct dependence (Jn 1:29–34; 3:1–4:3).[14] Ezekiel prophesied that God would sprinkle Israel with pure water (ὕδωρ), give them a new Spirit (πνεῦμα), and would purify (καθαρίζω) them (Ezek. 36:25–26). The terms ὕδωρ and πνεῦμα play a significant role in the Fourth Gospel's account of John's witness to Jesus (1:26, 31, 33), and John's announcement of Jesus's ablution with the Holy Spirit (βαπτίζω) has a close match in Ezekiel's vision of moral purification (καθαρίζω, Ezek. 36:25; cf. Jn 1:33; καθαρισμός, 3:25). Repeated together in the account of John's and Jesus's

---

[11] Throughout this book the LXX is often quoted, because it seems to have been the textual tradition on which the author(s) of John's Gospel relied, even though many of John's quotations do not exactly correspond to the Septuagintal text. See Bruce G. Schuchard, "Form versus Function: Citation Technique and Authorial Intention in the Gospel of John," in *Abiding Words: The Use of Scripture in the Gospel of John*, ed. Alicia D. Myers and Bruce G. Schuchard, Resources for Biblical Study 81 (Atlanta, GA: SBL Press, 2015), 23–45.

[12] See also, Tova Ganzel, "The Defilement and Desecration of the Temple in Ezekiel," *Bib* 89 (2008): 274, fn. 28.

[13] On the relationship between moral purification and the keeping of the commandments, see §§ 4.3–4.

[14] See the discussion of water symbolism in the Fourth Gospel and Ezekiel in Gary T. Manning, *Echoes of a Prophet: The Use of Ezekiel in the Gospel of John and in Literature of the Second Temple Period*, JSNTSup 270 (London: T&T Clark, 2004). 172–89.

ablutions are the terms water (ὕδωρ 3:22; cf. 3:5), Spirit (πνεῦμα, 3:34; cf. 3:5), and baptism (βαπτίζω, 3:22–23). The prophetic focus on the transformation of the land is left behind in the Fourth Gospel, but the focus on the transformation of humanity is carried forward with particular reference to human capacity to see and enter the life of God, as will be argued with reference especially to Jesus's dialogue with Nicodemus (Jn 3:1–21) and his giving of sight to the man born blind (9:1–10:21). Even so, the Fourth Gospel's appeal to the expectation that God was to purify Israel from sin seems to be more diffuse than it is derived from a single text.

Jeremiah's vision of God's moral purification of Israel is more cursory than that of Ezekiel, but it is no less important. Its compactness, in fact, may illustrate how closely the moral purification of Israel and new life in the desolated land were held together in the prophetic imagination:

> I will return the exile of Iouda and the exile of Israel and build them as they were before. And I will purify them from all their injustices which they sinned against me, [καθαριῶ αὐτοὺς ἀπὸ πασῶν τῶν ἀδικιῶν αὐτῶν, ὧν ἡμάρτοσάν μοι] and I will not remember their sins which they sinned against me and they withdrew from me … Thus did the Lord say: There shall yet be heard in this place of which you say, "It is a wilderness apart from human beings and animals," in the cities of Iouda and outside of Ierousalem, that are desolate, to the point that there are no human being or animal, a voice of gladness and a voice of joy, a voice of bridegroom and a voice of bride, a voice of people saying, "Acknowledge the Lord Almighty, because the Lord is kind, because his mercy is forever!" And they will bring gifts into the house of the Lord, because I will return the exile of that land as before, said the Lord. (Jer. 40:7–8, 10–11 NETS, trans. mod., cf. 33:7–11 MT)

This singular promise of moral purification in Jeremiah is bound by an *inclusio* in which God will act to restore the exiled Judah and Israel to the land that they had once defiled with their sin (cf. 2:7; 3:2). Within the *inclusio* is a reversal of an earlier judgment on Judah. Judah had "arrayed their abominations in the house where my name is called on it, to defile it" (μιαίνω, 7:30 LXX), with the result that God would "abolish a sound of people making mirth and a sound of people rejoicing, a voice of bridegroom and a voice of bride from the cities of Iouda and from the streets of Ierousalem, because all the land shall become a desolation" (7:34 LXX; cf. 6:8; 9:11). As the land's defilement by Israel's sin caused its desolation, so would God's purification of Israel from sin cause the land's repopulation. The land would become inhabited not only through the return of the dispersed, but also from births resulting from the consummate joy of new marriage (33:7–11; cf. 31:7–9). As will be seen, this text underlies John (the Baptist)'s response to his disciples about why Jesus's ministry of ablution must increase in relation to John's own (Jn 3:28–30).[15] While the repopulation of the land falls into the background, John sees in Jesus's ablutions and words the possibility of God's life for those who believe in him (3:36).

---

[15] On which, see Jocelyn McWhirter, *The Bridegroom Messiah and the People of God: Marriage in the Fourth Gospel*, SNTSMS 138 (Cambridge: Cambridge University Press, 2006), 50–8.

Isaiah's vision of God's purification of Israel from sin is multifaceted. Frederik Poulsen has argued that there are two primary visions of Zion theology in Isaiah that can also be found in other prophetic writings.[16] Poulsen summarizes that there is "first, the classical Zion motif designating the inviolable city and YHWH's defeat of the city's enemies (cf. the Zion tradition); second, the dynamic Zion motif designating the dynamic development and transformation of Zion: it is destroyed and abandoned, yet eventually rebuilt and repopulated."[17] Whereas in Jeremiah and Ezekiel the hope for moral purification belongs to the "dynamic Zion motif," God's purification of Israel from sin has a place in each of Isaiah's Zion motifs. In the first, Zion is portrayed as a city that suffered a devastating attack, but that has a remnant of survivors whom God will purify from their former impurity and bloodshed:[18]

> And what is left behind in Sion and remains in Ierousalem will be called holy [ἅγιοι], all who have been recorded for life in Ierousalem [οἱ γραφέντες εἰς ζωὴν], because the Lord will wash away the filth of the sons and daughters of Sion [ἐκπλυνεῖ κύριος τὸν ῥύπον τῶν υἱῶν καὶ τῶν θυγατέρων Σιων] and will purify the blood from their midst by a spirit of judgment and a spirit of burning [τὸ αἷμα ἐκκαθαριεῖ ἐκ μέσου αὐτῶν ἐν πνεύματι κρίσεως καὶ πνεύματι καύσεως]. (Isa. 4:3-4 NETS, trans. mod.)

The language of purification (ἐκκαθαρίζω) and washing (ἐκπλύνω) is employed to describe God's removal of the sins for which the daughters and sons of Zion were earlier judged, which among other things included bloodshed (1:15, 21), idolatry in the land (2:8, 20-21), and sexual misdeeds (3:16-17). This moral purification transforms both the people and Zion itself. The people who lived through the devastation, who were earlier called "sinful nation, people full of sins, evil offspring, lawless sons" (1:4 LXX), would now simply be called "holy" (ἅγιοι, 4:3). This is perhaps the clearest example in Israel's Scripture of moral purification from sin causing the holiness of the people. The return of the Lord would transform Zion as well, which was earlier forsaken by the Lord (1:8, 15). The Lord's return to Zion would be actualized in a glory that would cover it like a canopy and become its refuge (4:5-6). In this vision, God's purification of Israel from sin is integral to the restoration that would make possible Israel's life in the shade of God's glory.

Isaiah also speaks of the transformation of the exiles as they are returning to Zion on a pure and holy way. This belongs to the second Zion motif that Poulsen identified, namely, the restoration of Zion after its destruction and the exile of the people. In this instance, the purification of the people precedes and makes possible their return to the land.

---

[16] In contrast to older approaches to Zion theology, Poulsen's approach is synchronic and literary, with a focus on the Prophets rather than the Psalms (*Representing Zion*, 1-35).

[17] Poulsen, *Representing Zion*, 189.

[18] Poulsen locates the account of the surviving remnant in Isa. 4 alongside other texts in Isa. 1-39 in which God both judges Israel through foreign nations and saves a remnant of Israel from that attack, based in part on Israel's decision to repent (*Representing Zion*, 26-8, 99-100; cf. Isa. 1:27-28).

A pure way shall be there, and it shall be called a holy way [ὁδὸς καθαρὰ καὶ ὁδὸς ἁγία]; and the impure [ἀκάθαρτος] shall not pass by there, nor shall be there an impure way [ὁδὸς ἀκάθαρτος], but those who have been dispersed shall walk on it, and they shall not go astray. ... And those gathered together because of the Lord shall return [ἀποστρέφω; שׁוּב] and come to Sion with joy; everlasting joy shall be above their head, for upon their head shall be praise and gladness, and joy shall take hold of them—pain and sorrow and sighing have fled away. (Isa. 35:8, 10 NETS, trans. mod.)

Among those returning to Zion on this pure way are the lame, blind, deaf, and mute, except that all have been healed and made able to walk, see, hear, and speak (35:5–6; cf. Jer. 31:8–9). What is more, all of those who were dispersed are now able to walk in the pure and holy way to Zion, on which no impure person may travel (35:8). They have, apparently, become pure from sin in their exile.[19] Poulsen has rightly suggested that the term *return* (שׁוּב) has a double meaning, referring both to physical return and to repentance.[20] So, the moral purity of the people enables them to travel on the pure way as they return to Zion.

The return to Zion is sometimes figured in Isa. 40–66 in terms of a woman giving birth (cf., e.g., Isa. 42:10–17; 46:1–7; 49:9–26; 54:1; 66:7–9).[21] Zion, barren and bereaved, is astonished to discover a crowd of children and asks, "Who has begotten [γεννάω] me these? But I was childless and a widow, so who has reared these for me?" (49:21 LXX). The implicit answer to this question is that the Lord has begotten them, which is followed by the announcement that the sons and daughters of Zion would soon be saved from the nations (49:22–26).[22] At the end of Isaiah, the people of Israel are called a "disobedient and contrary people, who did not walk in a true way [ὁδῷ ἀληθινῇ] but after their own sins" (Isa. 65:2 LXX). In contrast to those who traveled on a pure way back to Zion (35:8), their ways are described by appeal to the most impure acts of worship imaginable: making sacrifices to demons, sleeping in tombs, and eating swine's flesh (65:3–4 LXX). Even as God threatens to repay Israel for these defiling sins, God promises to beget a remnant: "I will bring forth the offspring [σπέρμα] that comes from Iakob and from Ioudas, and it will inherit my holy mountain, and my chosen ones and my slaves shall inherit it and dwell there" (65:9). Those of Israel not defiled by sin, in other words, will be begotten by God, becoming children who receive an inheritance in the land.

---

[19] Interestingly, septuagintal Jeremiah also writes of a way that Israel travels on that could purify them: "see what the good way is, and walk in it, and you will find purification for your souls [εὑρήσετε ἁγνισμὸν ταῖς ψυχαῖς ὑμῶν]. And they said, 'We will not walk in it'" (6:11 LXX).

[20] Poulsen, *Representing Zion*, 146. I would add that the double meaning of the term *return* (שׁוּב) is most evident in the oracle in which the Lord says to those who were just called "a rebellious people, faithless children" (Isa. 30:9) that "in returning (בְּשׁוּבָה) and rest you shall be saved" (30:15).

[21] On birth as a figure of return in these Isaianic texts, see Maggie Low, *Mother Zion in Deutero-Isaiah. A Metaphor for Zion Theology*, StBibLit 155 (New York: Peter Lang, 2013), 111–44.

[22] Low argues that the metaphor of the Lord as a mother giving birth coheres with that of a warrior gathering Israel from the nations, the latter interpreting the former as an act of power (*Mother Zion in Deutero-Isaiah*, 112–17).

At the very end of Isaiah, the moral impurity of the people of Israel (66:3–5, 17) is again met with a vision of a birth, although this time it is Mother Zion who gives birth to children, having before been barren:

> Before she who was in labor gave birth, before the pain of her pangs came, she escaped and gave birth to a male. Who has heard of such a thing? And who has seen thus? Did the earth give birth in one day? Was also a nation born all at once? Because Sion was in labor and she gave birth to her children. But I am the one who gave you this expectation, and you did not remember me, said the Lord; see, was it not I who made the woman who gives birth and the one who is barren? said God. (Isa. 66:7–10 LXX)

This vision of birth makes for a division in Israel between those who are still captive to sin's defilement and those who are the servants of the Lord, born of mother Zion to joy and life.[23] In other words, those who are born of Zion by God's creative act are those of Israel delivered from moral impurity, and made able to "delight from the entrance to her glory" (66:11 LXX) and to see comfort in Jerusalem and rejoice (66:14 LXX). As the servants of the Lord—in contrast to those defiled by sin—the children of Israel will come to participate in the new heavens and new earth and to worship the Lord (66:22–23). As will be argued, the dialogue between Nicodemus and Jesus may be read as a fast-paced, highly allusive debate over Israel's restoration, with recourse to Isaiah's metaphors of Israel's election and restoration as birth.

Four points may be made in to summarize this discussion of moral purification in Ezekiel, Jeremiah, and Isaiah. First, God's purification of Israel from sin enables the people to participate in Israel's restoration. Insofar as the desolation and destruction that followed Israel's defiling sins were God's judgment, the moral purification of the people is a transformation that makes possible Israel's restoration, which includes Israel's return to life in the land. However, Isaiah holds out that there are those who are not purified from sin and cannot participate in God's salvation. Only those whom God purifies from sin and makes holy will be restored to the land, so that bloodshed, sexual misdeeds, and idolatry will pollute the land no more. Second, moral purification entails a transformation in Israel so that they are able to enter the land with joy, bring the land to a fullness of life, and see the glory of God. Isaiah alone envisions this return and proliferation of life in the land as a kind of birth from God, but this is related to purification only by contrast to the moral impurity of those not so born. Third, God's moral purification of the people is eschatological not only in the sense that it is yet unrealized, but also in the sense that when it happens Israel's future will have arrived. Ezekiel envisions the land inhabited by a purified people becoming a new garden of Eden (Ezek. 36:35; cf. Isa. 35:2) and Isaiah imagines that those who return to Zion on a pure way "shall see the glory of the LORD" (Isa. 35:2; cf. 4:5–6). Indeed, Israel is to be born in a single day, and its birth is to accompany the renewal of the whole heavens and earth (Isa. 66). Fourth, the moral purification is enacted by God. This work not only

---

[23] On the division between the servants of the Lord and those still faltering in Israel in Isa. 65–66 see Childs, *Isaiah*, 526–48.

makes possible Israel's participation in salvation, it is integral to God's saving work. The vision of moral purification by God is most vivid when the language of washing is used, but even then it is unclear what exactly this action may have looked like.

The Fourth Gospel can be located in the same theological stream as the Prophets when it comes to moral purity. The Messiah, Elijah, and the Prophet—all figures connected with Israel's restoration in early Jewish writings—were rightly associated with ablutions by the Pharisees in the Fourth Gospel because of the way that the Prophets associate Israel's restoration with God's work of moral purification.[24] John the Baptist calls Jesus, among other things, the lamb of God who removes sin (1:29) and the one who ablutes with the Holy Spirit (1:33), predications about Jesus that focus onto him the prophetic expectation that God would purify Israel from sin in its restoration. As will be seen, Jesus does remove the judgment of sin from the man born blind by giving him sight (9:2, 34). Even more so, the Fourth Gospel appeals to a positive vision of moral purity in its connection to Israel's ability to enter life. The necessity of birth from above is connected to the ability to see and enter the kingdom of God in such a way that reminds one of Isaiah's pure way to Jerusalem, and the ablutionary ministry of Jesus is associated with the proliferation of life that Jeremiah imagined would come through joyful new marriages (3:1–4:3; cf. Isa. 35:8–10; Jer. 33:7–11). Unlike the Prophets, the Fourth Gospel neglects both the restoration of God's people to the land of promise and the transformation of that land after the people are purified. Another point of departure is the way that the Fourth Gospel envisions Jesus as an agent through whom God effects moral purification. The involvement of a human agent in God's work of moral purification, however, is anticipated by early Jewish writings that carry forward the prophetic expectation that God would morally purify Israel when it was being restored. As the Fourth Gospel was not written in a cultural vacuum, it is illuminating to consider how prophetic hopes for a divine work of eschatological, moral purification are reflected in early Jewish writings.

3.1.2 Pregnant Expectation: Moral Purity and Restoration in Early Jewish Writings

Not surprisingly, the expectation that God would enact moral purification in the restoration of Israel is evident across a spectrum of early Jewish writings, but not all. Although Josephus speaks of moral purification in his writings, he interprets it neither eschatologically nor in terms of divine action.[25] Similarly, Philo speaks at length about the moral purification of individuals from vice, but nowhere interprets moral

---

[24] Bauckham finds eschatological expectations associated with the prophet like Moses (primarily in Josephus's accounts of contemporary wilderness prophets, cf., e.g., *Ant.* 20.97–99; 20:169–172; 188), Elijah (cf., e.g., Sir. 48.10–11; 1 En. 90.31) and the Messiah (cf., e.g., Pss. Sol. 17, 18); see "Messianism according to the Gospel of John," 36–67.

[25] Josephus conceives of Israel's restoration as a pattern of deliverance from sin and impurity by righteous and holy persons, such as the kings Asa, Hezekiah, Manasseh, and Josiah, by whom Israel's temple was purified after its defilement by idols (see, e.g., *Ant.* 8.290; 9.252–276; 10.41–46; 10.68–72).

purification as a divine, eschatological work that God completes on Israel's behalf.[26] Instead, this section will focus on 2 Macc, 1 QS, *Jub.*, and Pss. Sol., which all anticipate that Israel's restoration will follow God's work of moral purification. These writings reflect the complex variety of early Jewish expectation that God would purify Israel from sin in its restoration. The Fourth Gospel may be located somewhere within that complex variety of expectation, particularly because it alludes to the prophetic traditions that inspired the hope that God would purify Israel from sin. This hope was fluid. There is variety as to whether God acts directly to bring about moral purification (as in 1 QS 3–4; *Jub.* 1:23–25) or calls a human agent to do so, such as Judas (as in 2 Macc. 10.1–7) or the Davidic Messiah (as in Ps. Sol. 17.30–31). Furthermore, different emphases are given to the object of moral purification—whether the temple (2 Macc.; Pss. Sol.), the people of Israel (*Jub.*; Pss. Sol.), or individual human beings (1 QS). Interestingly, several of these writings link together moral purification with Israel's becoming God's children. In some instances, early Jewish hope for God's moral purification was a kind of pregnant expectation.

The purification of the temple in Jerusalem by Judas is interpreted by 2 Maccabees as an act of God that signaled the beginning of Israel's restoration. The narrator frames the work as an account of, among other things, "the purification of the greatest temple" (τὸν τοῦ ἱεροῦ τοῦ μεγίστου καθαρισμὸν, 2 Macc. 2:19). Furthermore, a letter is appended to the account that commends the observance of a festival celebrating "the purification of the temple" (τὸν καθαρισμὸν τοῦ ἱεροῦ, 1:18; cf. 2:16). The historical narration speaks of how Judas and his soldiers "purified the sanctuary" (τὸν νεὼ καθαρίσαντες, 10:1; cf. 10:5, 7). This purification consisted in removing the foreign altars made for the worship of idols (10:2–3), after which they offered sacrifice followed by a prayer. Their prayer for mercy if Israel should sin in the future was that God would not "hand them over to blasphemous and barbarous nations" (10:4), echoing the earlier words of one who was killed for his refusal to disobey the Law of Moses, that "we are suffering because of our own sins" (7:32). Second Maccabees imagines that God granted the nations power over Israel as judgment on its sin, but gives assurance that God would show mercy again to Israel (7:37). This mercy was realized in the temple's purification on the twenty-fifth of Chislev, the same day it was profaned (10:5). That calendrical coincidence helped interpret Judas's act as God's own act of purifying the temple (10:7), so that Judas was regarded as one used by God to bring about this divine purification. God's purification of the temple became the basis of Israel's hope for imminent regathering: "We have hope in God that he will soon have mercy on us and will gather us from everywhere under heaven into his holy place, for he has rescued us from great evils and has purified the place" (τὸν τόπον ἐκαθάρισεν, 2:18 NRSV).[27]

---

[26] On personal, national, and cosmic eschatology in both Philo and Josephus, neither of whom have strong interest in national nor cosmic eschatology of the kind found in prophetic and apocalyptic Jewish traditions, see Lester L. Grabbe, "Eschatology in Philo and Josephus," in *Judaism in Late Antiquity 4. Death, Life-after-Death, Resurrection and the World-to-Come in the Judaisms of Antiquity*, ed. Alan Avery-Peck and Jacob Neusner, Handbook of Oriental Studies. Section 1 The Near and Middle East 49 (Leiden: Brill, 2000), 163–85.

[27] Robert Doran observes that the hope of regathering is logically dependent on the rescue and purification, and that this hope takes the form of a new exodus (*2 Maccabees*, ed. Harold W. Attridge, Hermeneia [Minneapolis, MN: Fortress, 2012], 61–3; cf. Deut. 30:1–5; Ps. 105:47 LXX).

The book ends with a priestly prayer that God will "keep undefiled forever [εἰς αἰῶνα ἀμίαντον] this house that has been so recently purified" (κεκαθαρισμένον οἶκον; 14:36 NRSV).[28] The moral purification of the temple may be a past event for the author of 2 Maccabees, but it is one that evokes confidence that Israel's final restoration and return will soon arrive.

The Psalms of Solomon, likely written sometime after 2 Maccabees, lament the defilement of the Jerusalem temple by the sin of the people (see, e.g., Pss. Sol. 2:3, 13; 8:22–23).[29] The prayers also express hope that God will finally purify Israel from sin (9:6–7; 10:1–2; 18:5).[30] At least in the case of individuals, God's purification from sin is predicated on repentance and the acceptance of discipline: "You will purify a soul from sins [καθαριεῖς ἐν ἁμαρτίαις ψυχὴν] when he will confess, … for shame is upon us and our faces on account of all these things" (9:6 NETS, trans. mod.; cf. 10:1–2). God's work of moral purification is at once a judgment and a mercy. God will purify (καθαρίζω) the one "who prepares his back for lashes" (10:2). The military removal of the nations' oppressing Jerusalem is described as a purification (17:22). But God's purification of Israel also entails mercy, including the removal of sin (9:6–7; 10:1), the restoration of Jerusalem (17:30), and the bestowal of blessing (18:5).

In Ps. Sol. 17, the prayerful hope for purification is joined with the expected arrival of a messianic king, who would be the agent of Jerusalem's purification. The Messiah was to "gather a holy people" (συνάξει λαὸν ἅγιον, 17:26) and to acknowledge that "all are their God's sons" (πάντες υἱοὶ θεοῦ, 17:27), a phrase that suggests a kind of divine begetting. Not unlike the remnant theology of Isa. 4:2–6, the holy people gathered by the Messiah are presumably those who were left after the Messiah expelled "sinners from the inheritance" (17:23). This Messiah would purify Jerusalem (and, presumably, the remnant of Israel in it) to make it holy:

And he [their king, the son of Dauid, 17:21] shall have the peoples of the nations to be subject to him under his yoke, and he shall glorify the Lord in the mark of all the earth, and he shall purify Ierousalem in holiness as it was at the beginning [καθαριει Ιερουσαλημ εν αγιασμω ως και το απ αρχης], so that nations may come

---

[28] Similarly, as Mermelstein argues, Sirach's portrayal of the rebuilding of a holy temple under Zerubbabel and Joshua and the worship of Simon the son of Onias commends an understanding of the rebuilt temple as pure, holy, and glory-filled (Sir. 49:6, 11–12; 50:1–19); see *Creation, Covenant, and the Beginnings of Judaism*, 52–87.

[29] Kenneth Atkinson argues that while Pss. Sol. 2, 8 speak of Pompey's sack of Jerusalem in 63 BCE, Pss. Sol. 17 refers to Herod's murder of Antigonus II, Aristobulus III, and Hyrcanus II, as well as the siege of Jerusalem by Herod and Sosius in 37 BCE, which places the events to which it refers between 37 and 30 BCE ("Herod the Great, Sosius, and the Siege of Jerusalem (37 BCE) in Psalm of Solomon 17," *NovT* 38.4 [1996]: 313–22). Scholars typically date 2 Macc. to sometime in the second or first century BCE. Its rosy view of relation with Rome suggests that it predates the Pompey's invasion in 63 BCE (see, e.g., 2 Macc. 4:11; 8:17). On the dating of 2 Macc., see Doran, *2 Maccabees*, 14–15; David A. DeSilva, *Introducing the Apocrypha: Message, Context, and Significance* (Grand Rapids, MI: Baker Academic, 2004), 268–70.

[30] Bradley Embry points out that NT scholars overlook the emphasis on purity in Psalms of Solomon, and suggests this is because of the methodological decision to approach these psalms from the perspective of their interest in the NT, rather than reading them on their own terms and as a collection ("The Psalms of Solomon and the New Testament," 106–10).

from the end of the earth to see his glory, ... and to see the glory of the Lord with which God has glorified her. (17:30–31 NETS)

Unlike the rulers of Israel who "were in every sin" (ἐν πάσῃ ἁμαρτίᾳ, 17:20), this messianic king would "be pure from sin [καθαρὸς ἀπὸ ἁμαρτίας] so that he may rule a great people" (17:36). The purification effected by this pure Messiah consists in the transformation of Jerusalem. It will once again be holy and all the nations will be gathered to it, no longer as enemies but as worshipers. Significantly, the purification of Jerusalem enables Israel and the nations to see the glory of the Lord (cf. Isa. 40:5; 66:18–21). In this prayer, the moral purification effected by the Messiah inaugurates Israel's restoration.[31]

God's purification of a remnant of Israel from sin is also what one finds in the Rule of the Community (1 QS). Eyal Regev locates 1 QS among those sectarian texts in which most people in Israel are regarded as defiled by sin, and the temple in Jerusalem is considered desecrated and defunct.[32] Thus, whoever does not join the community:

will not become clean by the acts of atonement [לוא יזכה בכפורים], nor shall he be purified by the cleansing waters [ולוא יטהר במי נדה], nor shall he be made holy by the seas or rivers, nor shall he be purified by all the water of the ablutions [ולוא יטהר בכול מי רחץ]. Defiled, defiled shall he be all the days [טמא טמא יהיה כול יומי] he spurns the decrees of God, without allowing himself to be taught by the Community of his counsel. (1 QS 3:4–5)

It is worth bearing in mind that in 1 QS there is what Jonathan Klawans refers to as the "full integration of ritual and moral impurity into a single conception of defilement."[33] In other words, to become pure through washing with water, one must also be pure from sin, and to be pure from sin, one must also be ritually pure.[34] In 1 QS, purity requires *both* acts of atonement for sin *and* washing with water to remove (ritual) impurities.

---

[31] Ps. Sol. 18 also associates purification with a messianic figure, except that there God purifies Israel directly in advance of the anointed one's coming: "may God purify Israel for the day of mercy with blessing, for the day of election when he brings up his anointed one" (18:5, NETS, trans. mod.).

[32] Eyal Regev connects 1 QS to the *pesherim* and to the Damascus Document, and sees reflected in these texts the tendency toward social division on account of the perceived moral impurity of outsiders ("Abominated Temple and a Holy Community: The Formation of the Notions of Purity and Impurity in Qumran," *DSD* 10.2 [2003]: 256–60). On pessimistic attitudes toward the purity of the temple in Jerusalem held by the Qumran community, see Jonathan Klawans, *Purity, Sacrifice, and the Temple*, 145–61. Against the idea that the Qumran Community regarded itself as an alternative temple through which purity could be found, see idem, "Purity in the Dead Sea Scrolls," in *The Oxford Handbook of the Dead Sea Scrolls*, ed. Timothy H. Lim and John J. Collins, Oxford Handbooks in Religion and Theology (Oxford: Oxford University Press, 2010), 388–98.

[33] Klawans, *Impurity and Sin*, 90.

[34] On this conflation of ritual and moral impurity, which is apparent especially in 1 QS, 1 QM, and 1 QH, see Klawans, *Impurity and Sin*, 85–91; see also, Gudrun Holtz, "Purity Conceptions in the Dead Sea Scrolls: 'Ritual-Physical' and 'Moral' Purity in a Diachronic Perspective," in *Purity and the Forming of Religious Traditions in the Ancient Mediterranean World and Ancient Judaism*, ed. Christian Frevel and Christophe Nihan, Dynamics in the History of Religions 3 (Leiden: Brill, 2013), 519–36.

In contrast to those of Israel who are defiled all their days, the moral purification anticipated by the community may be understood in two stages, the first being a rite of entry performed within the community (1 QS 3.6–8) and the second being an eschatological work of God for those who had been initiated into the community (4.19–26).[35] Those who join the community are imagined to receive the spirit of truth as they live with exacting obedience to the law (3.6–8). Their entrance into the community locates them within that division of humanity that God will purify on the day of eschatological visitation (4.19, 25). On that day of God's visitation, the Rule of the Community envisions that

> [God] will purify [יברר אל] for himself the configuration of man, ripping out all spirit of deceit [רוח עולה] from the innermost part of his flesh, and cleansing him with the spirit of holiness [ולטהרו ברוח קודש] from every irreverent deed. He will sprinkle over him the spirit of truth like lustral water [ויז עליו רוח אמת כמי נדה] (in order to cleanse him) from all the abhorrences of deceit and from the defilement of the unclean spirit [ברוח נדה]. In this way the upright will understand knowledge of the Most High ... For these are those selected by God for an everlasting covenant [לברית עולמים] and to them shall belong all the glory of Adam. (1 QS 4:20–23)

In this eschatological visitation, no human mediators are involved in God's purification of human beings from sin. God does not purify from sin with water, but the spirit of holiness and spirit of truth are poured out like water to purify humanity, thereby undoing the defilement and sin caused by the unclean spirit and the spirit of deceit. This work of restoration is not universal. Only the elect ones are to be purified by God, but those whose share is with the spirit of deceit will be in "darkness until their destruction, without there being a remnant or survivor among them" (4.13–14). Within this anthropological dualism, there may be a suggestion that the "birthright" (נחלה) of the elect is their moral purification by God (4.16, 24). The moral purification of human beings involves an anthropological transformation, a change in the inner person. Whatever part of the deceitful spirit is lodged in within humanity will be removed, with the result that only righteousness remains. Their moral purification enables them to receive all of Adam's glory.

Jubilees ascribes singular importance to God's purification of Israel from sin, because that divine act brings Israel's history to its promised end and finally ends the cycle of sin in which Israel is entrapped. At the beginning of *Jubilees*, God warns Moses that Israel will give itself to the nations' idols and abominations, which, as has been observed, is one of the classic, defiling sins (1.9).[36] At Sinai, Moses intercedes for Israel,

---

[35] Anja Klein has argued that the final eschatological purification by God completes the initial purification of entering the community, and her work informs my reading of this text ("From the 'Right Spirit' to the 'Spirit of Truth': Observations on Psalm 51 and 1QS," in *The Dynamics of Language and Exegesis at Qumran*, ed. Devorah Dimant and Reinhard Gregor Kratz, FAT 2.35 [Tübingen: Mohr Siebeck, 2009], 182).

[36] Eibert Tigchelaar reconstructs the Hebrew of *Jub.* 1.9 by recourse to 1Q22, which results in the reading that Israel became like the nations, worshipping "their idols" (גלוליהם) and practicing "their abominations" (תועבתם), as opposed to the usual translation "their defilements and their shame" ("A

asking God not to abandon Israel, but to "create a pure heart and a holy spirit for them" (*Jub.* 1.21; cf. Ps. 51:10).[37] God assures Moses that a time will come after Israel acknowledges its sin when:

> I shall create for them a holy spirit, and I shall purify them so that they will not turn away from following me from that day and forever. And their souls will cleave to me and to all my commandments. And they will do my commandments. And I shall be a father to them, and they will be sons to me. And they will all be called "sons of the living God." (*Jub.* 1.23–25)

God's purification of Israel from sin entails a transformation of the inner person: a holy spirit will be imparted to them, they will be capable of keeping God's commandments always (cf. Ezek. 36:25–27), and God will become their father, begetting them as sons (cf. Jer. 31:8–10).[38] But until that time, Israel will find itself in a cycle of sin and idolatry. *Jubilees* ends where it begins, in a way, with a reference to God's work of moral purification. The moment that Israel will finally be freed from its faltering is the moment that God purifies Israel from its sin forever: "And jubilees will pass until Israel is purified from all the sin of fornication, and defilement, and uncleanness, and sin and error. ... And the land will be purified from that time and forever" (50.5; cf. Dan. 12:6 LXX). As has been argued by Ari Mermelstein, the message of *Jubilees* that God has not abandoned Israel on account of its sin and breach of the Sinai covenant is served by its strategy of locating Israel's election in creation rather than in the exodus. This inspires confidence that God has not abandoned Israel for its sin, and will finally redeem Israel from sin and judgment when creation's end arrives.[39] It also suggests that all Israel, rather than just a remnant, will be redeemed. Strikingly, the language given by *Jubilees* to this eschatological restoration of all Israel is that of moral purification.

These biblical and early Jewish writings are a window into a rich and varied hope that God would purify Israel from sin in the restoration of Israel. While each of these writings associate divine moral purification with Israel's restoration, differences emerge as to whether it is all Israel or only a remnant that is to be purified. Furthermore, whereas some writings envision God's direct agency in purification, others imagine human mediators employed by God in Israel's purification. The Fourth Gospel stakes its place in this complex of expectations in the first scene after the Prologue. The

---

Cave 4 Fragment of Divre Mosheh (4QDM) and the Text of 1Q22 1:7–10 and *Jubilees* 1:9, 14," *DSD* 12.3 [2005], 306–8).

37 Unless otherwise noted, the translation and versification of *Jubilees* follows O. S. Wintermute, *OTP* 2:52–142.

38 Marianne Meye Thompson argues that Israel's Scripture appropriates the social role of human fathers to speak of God's election of Israel, God's merciful care and redemption of Israel, and God's worthiness for honor from Israel; she finds that early Jewish literature invokes God as Father in similar ways, sometimes universalizing or individualizing its significance (*The Promise of the Father: Jesus and God in the New Testament* [Louisville, KY: Westminster John Knox, 2000], 35–55).

39 Mermelstein, *Creation, Covenant, and the Beginnings of Judaism*, 88–132. See also, James L. Kugel, who similarly argues that locating the election of Israel on the seventh day and depicting the patriarchs celebrating Israel's feasts was a strategy to create a sense of continuity between post-exilic Jews and the biblical past (*A Walk through Jubilees: Studies in the Book of Jubilees and the World of Its Creation*, JSJSup 156 [Leiden: Brill, 2012], 5–9).

Pharisees' eschatologically charged inquiry that connects ablutions to the Messiah, Elijah, and the Prophet works to frame Jesus's ministry in terms of the eschatological, moral purification that makes possible the restoration of Israel (Jn 1:25). This is why John (the Baptist) vehemently denies that he is any one of the figures that the Pharisees inquire about. His ablutions with water are meant only to reveal the one who was to effect the moral purification of Israel. In John's ablutionary witness, Jesus, the lamb of God, is figured as the pure one whose ablutions with the Holy Spirit would purify Israel from sin and inaugurate its restoration.

3.2 Jesus: the Pure and Purifying One

In this section, closer attention will be given to how this weight of expectation for God to purify Israel from sin bears on the interpretation of two phrases by which John (the Baptist) identifies Jesus when he first meets him. John calls Jesus "the lamb of God who takes away the sin of the world" (ὁ ἀμνὸς τοῦ θεοῦ ὁ αἴρων τὴν ἁμαρτίαν τοῦ κόσμου, 1:29) and "the one who baptizes with the Holy Spirit" (ὁ βαπτίζων ἐν πνεύματι ἁγίῳ, 1:33). It will be argued that these two phrases identify Jesus as one who is pure and who purifies those who come to trust through John's witness.

3.2.1 Pure as a Lamb

John introduces Jesus as "the lamb of God who takes away the sin of the world" (1:29). The definite article has suggested to some interpreters that ὁ ἀμνὸς τοῦ θεοῦ is a title that would have been recognized by original audiences. It is not clear what the referent of this title would have been. Jesper Tang Nielsen compiles twelve scholarly arguments for different referents for the appellation *lamb of God* and observes scholarly movement toward regarding it as polysemous.[40] Nielsen attempts to break through the impasse by using the conceptual blending theory of Gilles Fauconnier. Conceptual blending theory is a cognitive approach to metaphor that explicates how metaphors produce meaning by understanding one mental space in terms of another, with mental space understood as the cognitive structure to which language refers.[41] Nielsen summarizes conceptual blending theory with four observations: (1) the blended metaphor cannot be reduced to one or the other mental space; (2) the blended metaphor can be elaborated in multiple ways; (3) metaphors evoke many potential meanings, only some of which are activated in the narrative context; and (4) only certain elements of each mental space can be projected to produce a blended metaphor.[42]

To illustrate how conceptual blending theory works for the metaphor of Jesus as the lamb of God, consider the metaphor that men are dogs. This metaphor could be

---

[40]   See Jesper Tang Nielsen, "The Lamb of God: The Cognitive Structure of a Johannine Metaphor," in *Imagery in the Gospel of John: Terms, Forms, Themes, and Theology of Johannine Figurative Language*, ed. Jörg Frey et al., WUNT 1/200 (Tübingen: Mohr Siebeck, 2006), 217–58.

[41]   Nielsen, "Lamb of God," 220.

[42]   Nielsen, "Lamb of God," 224.

interpreted in many ways, but its narrative context constrains its meaning. In a western context, dogs are often characterized as loyal and faithful companions. Does saying that men are dogs mean that men are loyal and faithful companions? Of course not. The narrative context of this metaphor activates the opposite meaning. When a man is unfaithful to a woman with whom he is in a romantic relationship, someone might wryly remark that men are dogs. The narrative context indicates that the metaphor characterizes men as unfaithful opportunists. In the same way, the narrative context of the metaphor that Jesus is the lamb of God constrains some potential meanings and activates others. Identifying the background of the lamb of God, therefore, is helpful only insofar as it is inscribed into the Fourth Gospel's narrative.

Because Nielsen understands John's declaration identifying Jesus as the lamb of God to be a programmatic statement for Jesus's ministry, he takes the whole Fourth Gospel as the narrative context of the metaphor. Nielsen argues that the Fourth Gospel blends concepts associated with both the Passover lamb and the Isaianic lamb (Isa. 53:7), and activates these concepts when it speaks of Jesus's death as apotropaic, protective, and a passageway from death to life (Jn 8), also as the moment of glorification, revelation, and vicarious atonement (Jn 19).[43] Nielsen's approach to metaphor using conceptual blending theory is helpful, but in his analysis he too quickly bypasses the immediate narrative context in which the metaphor occurs. Jesus is called the lamb of God in the context of John's ministry of ablution, replete with eschatological expectation for the moral purification of Israel. What meanings are activated by John's identification of Jesus as the lamb of God within such a narrative context?

John's identification of Jesus as the lamb of God while he was abluting people activates the association of lambs with purity. Calling Jesus the lamb of God does not identify him with a single known figure as much as it reveals what Jesus is like: he is pure from sin.[44] The association of purity with a lamb is suggested by the requirements that the lamb for the daily sacrifice be without blemish (ἀμνοὺς ... ἀμώμους, Exod. 29:38, LXX), that the sheep for the paschal sacrifice be perfect (πρόβατον τέλειον, 12:5), and also that the Isaianic servant who suffered silently like a lamb led to slaughter (ἀμνός, Isa. 53:7) would be purified by God from the wound (κύριος βούλεται καθαρίσαι αὐτὸν τῆς πληγῆς, 53:10). The Psalms of Solomon compare the "holy ones of God" (οἱ ὅσιοι τοῦ θεοῦ) to innocent lambs (ὡς ἀρνία ἐν ἀκακίᾳ, Pss. Sol. 8:23). And the phrase ἀμνός τοῦ θεοῦ is interpreted in T. 12 Patr. as a reference to the blameless character of "the unspotted one" (ἄμωμος), who "will be betrayed by lawless men" (T. Benj. 3:8 [Kee, OTP 1:826]). In 1 John the capacity of Jesus to take away (αἴρω) sins is predicated on Jesus having no sin in him (3:5). In the words of J. Ramsey Michaels, "the One who purifies the world is himself pure."[45] The problem with purification is that those who have aspired to purify the world are not themselves pure from sin, so that what ought

[43] Nielsen, "Lamb of God," 240–1.
[44] Michaels argues that the phrase ὁ ἀμνὸς τοῦ θεοῦ was originally a scriptural metaphor that the Fourth Gospel made into a title, much like other Johannine appellations for Jesus, such as " 'the Holy One of God' (6:69), 'the gift of God' (4:10), 'the bread of God' (6:33)" (*The Gospel of John*, 109). Although the purity of lambs could activate the concept of ritual purity or acceptability for sacrifice, I will argue in the following paragraphs that the moral purity of Jesus is in view.
[45] Michaels, *The Gospel of John*, 110.

to have been cleansing becomes horrific violence that stains the earth with blood. Or else, as happened with the Hasmonean dynasty, the crises of the past from which people desired to be delivered are recapitulated by their deliverers. Thus, the Psalms of Solomon speak of the coming messianic king as one who "shall be pure from sin [καθαρὸς ἀπὸ ἁμαρτίας] so that he may rule a great people, … and remove sinners by the strength of his word" (Pss. Sol. 17.36 NETS). John (the Baptist) bears witness that Jesus is the lamb of God, which means that Jesus is morally pure. Because Jesus is pure from sin, he is able to take away sin.

The Fourth Gospel interprets the appellation *lamb of God* with the phrase *who takes away the sin of the world* (ὁ αἴρων τὴν ἁμαρτίαν τοῦ κόσμου, 1:29). The difficulty with this interpretation of the lamb of God is, in the words of Rudolf Bultmann, that the evangelist "nowhere else attaches the gift of the forgiveness of sins specifically to Jesus' death, but understands it as the effect of his Word."[46] The phrase *takes away sin* seems to conceptualize sin as a burden to be lifted and carried away by another, which is a pervasive metaphorical pattern for speaking of sin in Israel's Scripture.[47] But, as Bultmann and others have noticed, the Fourth Gospel rarely speaks of sin in these terms (but cf. Jn 19:11; 20:23), and nowhere else speaks of these sins being forgiven or borne away by God. Perhaps it does not do so here either. In the LXX, αἴρω (I take away) is never used to translate נָשָׂא (he bears; he forgives) when it is used in the sense of bearing sin, but instead φέρω (I carry) is used in its various forms.[48] The Fourth Gospel employs *takes away* (αἴρω) for a concept different than forgiveness. Given the way the metaphor of Jesus as the lamb of God characterizes Jesus as one who is pure, it is likely that *takes away sin* refers not to forgiveness, but to moral purification from sin.[49] That is, the pure lamb of God removes sin through moral purification. In this sentence, sin is neither a weight to be lifted away, nor a trespass to be forgiven. Sin is a defilement, pollution, or stain to be removed. The impurity of sin will be purified by the lamb of God, by the one who ablutes with the Holy Spirit (1:33).

3.2.2 Purifying with the Holy Spirit

There is an analogy evident between John's identification of Jesus as "the lamb of God who takes away the sin of the world" (ὁ αἴρων τὴν ἁμαρτίαν τοῦ κόσμου, 1:29) and as "the one who ablutes with the Holy Spirit" (ὁ βαπτίζων ἐν πνεύματι ἁγίῳ, 1:33).[50] In addition to both phrases using a present-participle form, they also mirror each other

---

[46] Bultmann, *The Gospel of John*, 96–7. Haenchen also interprets "takes away the sin of the world" in terms of expiatory sacrifice, and for that reason finds it at odds with John's Christology and interposed from other sources (Jn 1:153).

[47] On the pervasiveness of the metaphor of sin as a weight in the Hebrew Bible, see the helpful work of Lam, *Patterns of Sin*, 18–21.

[48] The Hebrew term נָשָׂא used in relation to sin conceptualizes sin as a weight either to be borne by the sinner or borne by another, most often God, hence rightly lexicalized in English as "he forgives" (see Lam, *Patterns of Sin*, 21–40).

[49] Thompson argues that "to 'take away sin' means to remove sin, to purify from sin" (*John: A Commentary*, 46). So too, Michaels, *The Gospel of John*, 110–11.

[50] I am indebted to Michaels for his work on the relationship between these two phrases (*The Gospel of John*, 116–17).

structurally. Just as Jesus's capacity to take away sin is contingent on his purity as lamb of God (1:29; cf. 1 Jn 3:5), so his capacity to ablute with the Holy Spirit is contingent on his having had the Spirit descend and remain on him (1:32–33). This, moreover, is one of only three times in the Fourth Gospel that the Spirit is called holy (ἅγιος; 1:33; 14:26; 20:22), which makes explicit its antonym, sin (ἁμαρτία), in the corresponding phrase (1:29). Thus, the first identification of Jesus is interpreted by the second: the sin of the world is taken away through ablution with the Holy Spirit.[51] This is not unlike what one finds in 1 QS, which envisions that God, in his eschatological visitation, will purify humanity "with the spirit of holiness from every irreverent deed" (4.21). That is, God removes sin through purification with the Holy Spirit. Whereas the phrase *taking away sin* describes the intended result of Jesus's moral purification of Israel, *abluting with the Holy Spirit* sets forth the means by which such purification happens. Jesus purifies with the Holy Spirit. The lamb of God taking away sin is not about the death of Jesus as an expiatory sacrifice as much as it is about the moral purification effected by ablution with the Holy Spirit.[52] Admittedly, ablution with the Spirit is referentially ambiguous in the Fourth Gospel, since the phrase is used only here. This will be discussed in due course, but for now it is enough to see the connection drawn between Jesus's ablution with the Holy Spirit and the removal of sin.[53]

For the sake of clarity, it is worth repeating that John (the Baptist) emphatically differentiates between his own practice of abluting with water and the ablution with the Holy Spirit to be administered by the one to come after him (1:32–33). John's ablutions with water were a practice in ritual purification, which the Fourth Gospel interprets in relation to the revelation of Jesus to Israel (1:31). With the exception of those represented by some of the sectarian literature at Qumran, ancient Jews did not usually associate ritual purification with the removal of sin, but rather, with the removal of bodily conditions that inhibited one from coming into the presence of God's holiness (see, e.g., Lev. 7:20; 15:31; *Spec. Laws* 1.261; *J.W.* 5.193–99, 227–29, 236). By contrast, Jesus's ablution with the Holy Spirit is a moral purification, which is clear in that Jesus is spoken of as taking away sin. This contrast between ablutions with water and Spirit does not indicate that early Jewish rites of ritual purification are replaced with God's purification from sin, since ritual and moral purity were not mutually exclusive in biblical or early Jewish tradition.[54] The context against which one ought to read Jesus's work of purification is that of early Jewish expectation for God to remove Israel's sin, restore them to holiness, and give them abundant life. So the contrast between Jesus and John functions to locate Jesus within that complex of early Jewish expectation, derived from prophets like Isaiah, Jeremiah, and Ezekiel. Jesus in the Fourth Gospel is

---

[51] So also Stare, "Die Reinheitsthematik," 85.

[52] Of course, the purity of a lamb was usually related to its acceptability as a sacrifice to God, whether for the daily offering or the paschal lamb. The text leaves open the possibility that this purity qualifies Jesus also to be a sacrifice for the people of God, a theme that receives a more robust treatment in 1 Jn 1:7–9; 4:10, where the blood of Jesus is said to purify from sin (so argues Michaels, "By Water and Blood," 149–62). On sacrifice as an underdeveloped soteriological theme in the Fourth Gospel, see also Jan G. van der Watt, "Salvation in the Gospel According to John," in *Salvation in the New Testament: Perspectives on Soteriology*, ed. Jan G. van der Watt (Leiden: Brill, 2005), 114–17.

[53] On Jesus's ablution with the Spirit as the speech of Jesus, see § 3.3.3.

[54] On the correspondence between ritual and moral purity in some early Jewish writings, see § 4.1.

one as pure as a lamb of God, who will bring moral purity to Israel through the Spirit that rests on him.

All this to say, in the first scene after the Prologue, the Fourth Gospel locates Jesus within early Jewish expectation for the moral purification that would begin the restoration of Israel. It represents Jesus as having both assumed and exceeded expectations for Israel's moral purification. These eschatological expectations were first introduced into the narrative through the Pharisees' association between moral purification and the Messiah, Elijah, and the Prophet, and are confirmed in John's witness that Jesus is the pure and purifying one to come: the lamb of God who takes away the sin of the world and who ablutes with the Holy Spirit.

3.3 Moral Purification, Birth from Above, and Restoration

In this section, we will turn our attention to Jesus's dialogue with Nicodemus (3:1–15) and the account of Jesus and John (the Baptist) that follows it (3:22–4:3). It will be argued that this text carries forward the expectation that Jesus would purify Israel, and develops that expectation with the figure of birth, the language of water and Spirit, and the witness of John (the Baptist) to Jesus in a conflict over purification.

The reason Jn 3:1–4:3 is the focus of this section is that it forms a sequel to the first encounter between John and the *Ioudaioi* (1:19–34). In that encounter, the issue of moral purity was first introduced into the Fourth Gospel, through reference to Jesus as one who removes sin and ablutes with the Holy Spirit. The close relationship between Jn 1:19–34 and 3:1–4:3 is signaled by linguistic resonance, particularly with respect to setting, characters, and subject matter. The dialogue is set in Jerusalem (2:23), which is origin of the delegation that was sent to inquire of John's identity (1:19). Nicodemus is identified as a Pharisee and a ruler of the *Ioudaioi* (3:1), and those first sent to John are said to have been sent both from the *Ioudaioi* and from the Pharisees (1:19, 24).[55] Jesus speaks to Nicodemus about birth from water and Spirit (3:5), and at this point in the narrative water and Spirit have been mentioned together only with reference to the ablutions of John and Jesus (1:33). The term Israel (Ἰσραήλ), used only four times in the Gospel of John, appears both when Jesus refers to Nicodemus as the teacher of Israel (3:10) as well as when John interprets the reason for his ablution as the revelation of Jesus to Israel (1:33). The conflict between the disciples of John and a *Ioudaios* about purification (3:25) hearkens back to the questions raised by John's practice of abluting others (1:25). And the disciples of Jesus now ablute with water in the way that John had at the Jordan (3:22; 4:1–3; 1:28). John reminds his disciples that he said "I am not the Christ" (οὐκ εἰμὶ ἐγὼ ὁ χριστός, 3:28), which is a verbatim repetition of his earlier witness to the *Ioudaioi* (1:20). And John's disciples refer to Jesus as the one who was

---

[55]   It is somewhat unclear whether one or two groups were sent to inquire of John, one group of Levites and priests sent by the Jews in Jerusalem (1:19) and another group sent by the Pharisees (1:24). The problem is in part textual. See the discussion in C. H. Dodd, *Historical Tradition in the Fourth Gospel* (Cambridge: Cambridge University Press, 1963), 263–4.

with him across the Jordan (πέραν τοῦ Ἰορδάνου) to whom John had borne witness (3:26, cf. 1:28).[56] The similarity of setting, characters, and subject matter suggests that the questions about purification first raised in John's encounter with the Jews are now at stake in the dialogue between Jesus and Nicodemus, as well as in the following account of Jesus's and John's ablutionary ministries.[57]

3.3.1 The Possibility and Promise of Israel's Restoration

The central contention of the dialogue between Jesus and Nicodemus has often been overlooked. The argument between Jesus and Nicodemus revolves around the simple, unassuming word *can* (δύναμαι).[58] The significance of δύναμαι is signaled not only by its six-fold repetition in the span of such a short dialogue, but also by its appearance in every exchange of speech between Jesus and Nicodemus.[59] Nicodemus tells Jesus that "no one can [δύναμαι] do these signs that you do apart from the presence of God" (3:2); Jesus responds that "no one can [δύναμαι] see the kingdom of God without being born from above" (3:3); Nicodemus counters with two assertions about what is not possible when he says, "How can [δύναμαι] anyone be born after having grown old? Can [δύναμαι] one enter a second time into the mother's womb and be born?" (3:4); Jesus repeats and interprets his first statement and picks up the word *enter* (εἰσέρχομαι) from Nicodemus's second question, saying "no one can [δύναμαι] enter the kingdom of God without being born of water and Spirit" (3:5); and the final response of Nicodemus is "How can [δύναμαι] these things be?" (3:9).[60] In every exchange between Jesus and Nicodemus, the force of δύναμαι is negative. That is, the word δύναμαι repeatedly indicates exactly what is not possible.

The prevalence of the word δύναμαι reveals that the problem between Jesus and Nicodemus is the problem of potentiality.[61] The problem is not whether the kingdom of God will possibly be realized. Jesus does not speak in such a way that indicates the coming of the kingdom is dependent on Israel's action. Instead, his focus is on what capacities are needed to participate in the kingdom of God. In the Fourth Gospel, Jesus lexicalizes participation in the kingdom of God in terms of seeing (ὁράω) and entering

---

[56] Similarly, Brown notes that some have considered 3:22–30 a "doublet" of 1:19–34 (*The Gospel according to John*, 1:154).

[57] Thompson finds that there is a thoroughgoing theme of purification through Jn 1:19–4:54 (*John: A Commentary*, 41). While themes of purification are implicit in the action of Jesus in the temple and the dialogue with the Samaritan woman, I have sought to focus on what I regard as the peaks of this theme in these chapters, namely, Jn 1:19–34 and 3:1–4:3.

[58] I owe this observation to a conversation about this text with the poet James McMichael, who, incidentally, wrote a book called *Capacity*, which is not unrelated to the word δύναμις. On understanding the interaction between Jesus and Nicodemus as an argument, see below in this section.

[59] Thompson notices how Jesus's first response to Nicodemus (3:3) mirrors Nicodemus's initial statement to Jesus (3:2), but does not comment on the repetition of δύναμαι throughout the passage (*John: A Commentary*, 79).

[60] The frequency of the appearance of δύναμαι in this passage is atypical; these few sentences account for roughly 16 percent of the verb's occurrences in the Fourth Gospel.

[61] Giorgio Agamben says that the whole concept of potentiality is hidden in the word *can* (*Potentialities: Collected Essays in Philosophy*, ed. and trans. Daniel Heller-Roazen, Meridian: Crossing Aesthetics [Stanford: Stanford University Press, 2007], 177).

(εἰσέρχομαι).[62] He suggests that those like Nicodemus cannot see (οὐ δύναται ἰδεῖν) and cannot enter (οὐ δύναται εἰσελθεῖν) the kingdom of God as they are. Without birth from above, Jesus implies that Nicodemus is as one blind and lame with respect to the kingdom of God.[63] Nicodemus must be "born from above" (γεννηθῇ ἄνωθεν; 3:3), which is to say, born from water and Spirit (γεννηθῇ ἐξ ὕδατος καὶ πνεύματος; 3:5).[64] Each statement about birth is grammatically subordinate to the statement about participation in the kingdom of God (ἐὰν μή τις γεννηθῇ; 3:3, 5). At the same time, the capacities to see and to enter the kingdom of God are logically dependent on birth from above. Whatever else it does, birth from above results in the ability to see and enter God's kingdom. Interestingly, the two major healings in the Gospel of John relate to these very capacities: the restoration of mobility (5:1–9) and the giving of sight (9:1–7).[65] Nicodemus does not accept what Jesus says about birth from above. It is no more possible for him to conceive of birth from above than it is for him to imagine an old man being born a second time (3:4). From the perspective of Nicodemus, what Jesus says cannot be possible (3:9).

At stake in the dialogue between Jesus and Nicodemus is the restoration of Israel, which is indicated by the use of political language throughout the dialogue. In the Fourth Gospel, the phrase *kingdom of God* (βασιλεία τοῦ θεοῦ) is used only in the dialogue with Nicodemus (3:3, 5), and its use here accentuates the national and political focus of what they are discussing.[66] Nicodemus, moreover, is characterized as a "ruler of the *Ioudaioi*" (ἄρχων τῶν Ἰουδαίων, 3:1) and is the only named ἄρχων in the Fourth Gospel. He is also called the "teacher of Israel" (ὁ διδάσκαλος τοῦ Ἰσραήλ, 3:10). Israel is a politically-charged term in the Fourth Gospel, as Jesus is twice referred to

---

[62] Brown follows Bultmann's assertion that these verbs function synonymously and denote participation in the kingdom of God (Brown, *The Gospel according to John*, 1:130; Bultmann, *John*, 135, fn.2). That said, nothing is gained by losing the specificity of the words chosen to signal participation.

[63] In this sentence and the ones like it I am trying to follow the logic and language of the Fourth Gospel, but I do not wish to do so without recognizing that certain disabilities are here portrayed as liability and limitation. There are not simple answers to this negative representation of blindness for disciples of Jesus, and I can do no better here than refer to John Hull's stirring personal, theological essay "Open Letter from a Blind Disciple to a Sighted Saviour," in *Borders, Boundaries and the Bible*, ed. Martin O'Kane, JSOTSup 313 (London: Sheffield Academic, 2002), 154–77.

[64] The Greek term ἄνωθεν can mean either "from above" or "again" (BDAG, s.v. "ἄνωθεν"). Pierre-Marin Boucher surveys the uses of ἄνωθεν in the LXX, NT, Philo of Alexandria, and Justin Martyr and concludes that the primary meaning of ἄνωθεν in Jesus's speech was spatial, (i.e., denoting "from above"; cf. 3:31; 19:11; 19:23), was interpreted as such by the Greek fathers and Syriac versions, and only in the Latin tradition did its primary meaning begin to be taken temporally as "again" ("Jn 3,3.7: γεννηθῆναι ἄνωθεν * (IV)," *ETL* 88.1 [2012]: 71–93). As I will argue, Nicodemus's reference to second birth was not lexical misunderstanding, but logical inference (3:4).

[65] Whereas the fate of the man healed of paralysis is unknown, the man born blind comes both to see Jesus (ὁράω, 9:37) and to be included among those who enter salvation through Jesus (εἰσέρχομαι, 10:9). So the man born blind will receive attention later in this chapter, but the man healed of paralysis will not.

[66] Although the phrase βασιλεία τοῦ θεοῦ is lacking in the LXX, the concept of God's universal reign is expressed through the portrayal of God as king, and God's action in terms of rule (on which, see Joel B. Green, "Kingdom of God/Heaven," *DJG*, 2nd ed., 470–2); the disjunction between God's reign and oppression by foreign powers led to the kingdom of God being conceived eschatologically (it is in the future), spatially (it is in heaven), or spiritually (it is in human transformation), on which, see Dale C. Allison Jr., "Kingdom of God," *EDEJ*, 860–1.

as Israel's king (ὁ βασιλεὺς τοῦ Ἰσραήλ, 1:49; 12:13).[67] Although Jesus and Nicodemus are speaking about the possibility of an individual participating in the kingdom of God—in this case, Nicodemus—the literary context suggests that what is possible for this individual is indicative of what is possible for all Israel when it is born from above, namely, to see and enter the kingdom of God.

That Jesus and Nicodemus are dialoguing about the restoration of Israel is also evident in the use of figures of speech from Israel's Scripture and early Jewish tradition.[68] The metaphor of birth from above, especially when it is described as a birth from water and Spirit, echoes the same collection of prophetic expectations that were evoked by John's ablution and his identification of Jesus as the one who ablutes with the Holy Spirit. As was seen in the earlier survey of texts, God's purification of Israel from sin was to make possible Israel's restoration to fullness of life in their return to the land (Ezek. 36:18–36; Jer. 33:7–11; Ps. Sol. 17.30). The one responsible for this proliferation of life is God, who says, "I will multiply them, human beings like sheep" (Ezek. 36:37 LXX). John's Gospel downplays the prophetic emphasis on Israel's return to the land, while retaining the association between Israel's restoration and the fullness of life that would come with it. In this vein, Isaiah's use of a metaphor of birth for Israel's restoration is particularly generative in light of the Fourth Gospel's theme of eternal life (see, e.g., Isa. 42:10–17; 46:3–4; 49:9–26; 54:1; 66:7–9; cf., also, Mic. 5:3).[69] Jesus's words to Nicodemus about birth from above are not without context. They are conditioned by Israel's Scripture, which Jesus and Nicodemus shared.

Nicodemus's response to Jesus has suggested to interpreters that he fundamentally fails to understand what Jesus is saying:

> Jesus answered and said to him, "Truly, truly I say to you, unless one is born from above, one cannot see the kingdom of God." Nicodemus says to him, "How can a man be born after having grown old (ἄνθρωπος … γέρων ὤν)? Can he enter a second time into the womb (κοιλία) of his mother and be born? (3:3–4, my translation)

Nicodemus's questions have been described as "well intentioned but theologically inadequate,"[70] "crudely literal,"[71] and "foolish and grotesque."[72] However, one may read Nicodemus's response to Jesus's words about birth from above as informed and adversarial, which is seen in his appeal to Isaiah's metaphor of Israel's election as a birth. Importantly, the two images that Nicodemus introduces into the figure of birth—an

---

[67] On the significance of the term *Israel* as an "eschatological entity" in the Fourth Gospel, see Blumhofer, *The Gospel of John and the Future of Israel*, 11–27, here 23 fn. 66.

[68] So also, for example, Brown, *The Gospel according to John*, 1:140–41.

[69] In several early Jewish texts roughly contemporaneous with the Fourth Gospel, Zion is figured as a mother ready to give birth, which signals the arrival of God's salvation. Particularly striking are Gal. 4:21–31 and 4 Ezra 9:38–10:59.

[70] Brown, *The Gospel according to John*, 1:138.

[71] Michaels, *The Gospel of John*, 182.

[72] Haenchen, *John*, 1:200.

aging man (ἄνθρωπος ... γέρων ὤν) and the womb (κοιλία)—appear together with reference to Israel's election in Isa. 46:3–4 LXX:

> Hear me, O house of Iakob and everyone who is left of Israel, you who are being carried from the womb [κοιλία] and trained from the time you were a child. Until your old age, I am [ἕως γήρους ἐγώ εἰμι], and until you grow old, I am [ἕως ἂν καταγηράσητε, ἐγώ εἰμι]; I bear with you; I have made, and I will set free; I will take up and save you.

Although the exact vocabulary for old age is not shared between John and Isaiah, reference to the process of aging is common to both.[73] The coincidence between the images of old age and the womb is also striking, since these images appear together only here in the NT, and in Israel's Scripture only in Isa. 46 and Ps. 70 LXX.[74]

Furthermore, the literary context of both Isaiah and John involves the question of who is able to be saved. The dialogue with Nicodemus and the monologue that follows it are concerned with who sees and enters the kingdom of God (3:3, 5), who has eternal life (3:15, 16), and those whom God saves through the Son (3:17–18). In Isaiah, the remnant of Israel, having been carried by God from the womb to old age, has God's promise that "I will take up and save you" (46:4). In its literary context, this promise of salvation stands in deliberate contrast to the worshipers of Bel and Dagon, "who will not be able to be saved from war" (οὐ δυνήσονται σωθῆναι ἀπὸ πολέμου, Isa. 46:2 LXX). Based on this echo of Isaiah in his questions, it does appear that Nicodemus's response to Jesus was informed, even if it was adversarial.

The basis of Nicodemus's challenge to Jesus, then, is Isaiah's metaphor of Israel's election as a birth, which, in Isaiah, virtually guarantees God's restoration of Israel (Isa. 44:1–5; 46:3–4; 49:1–26; cf. Deut. 32:6–9). To take two further instances of this pattern from Isaiah:

> Thus says the Lord God who made you
>   and who formed you from the womb [κοιλία]:
> You will still be helped; do not fear, O Iakob my servant
>   and the beloved Israel whom I have chosen,
> because I will provide water in their thirst
>   to those who walk in a dry land;
> I will put my spirit on your offspring
>   and my blessings on your children. (Isa. 44:2–3 LXX)

---

[73] Based on the textual form of the explicit quotations of Israel's Scripture in John's Gospel, it would seem that, in the words of Schuchard, "The evangelist's Old Testament Bible was a Greek Bible" ("Form versus Function: Citation Technique and Authorial Intention in the Gospel of John," 23–45, here 34). For this reason, I am looking to the LXX in my comparison of Nicodemus's words to Isa. 46:3–4.

[74] The echoes of Isaiah in Jesus's initial statement about birth from above suggest that Nicodemus would respond also with reference to Isaiah. Interestingly, in Ps. 70 LXX the psalmist's reference to the faith (s)he had with God from the mother's womb (70:6) is part of the basis for the psalmist's appeal that God not abandon her or him in old age (70:9, 18).

Even more poignantly, "Will a mother forget her child so as not to have mercy on the descendants of her womb [κοιλία]? But even if a woman should forget these, yet I will not forget you, said the Lord" (49:15 LXX). Perhaps, for Nicodemus, God's election of Israel was already its birth from above.[75] Had God not chosen Israel? Had God not promised to be with Israel into old age? And, that being the case, how could one speak of the need for birth from above without repudiating God's faithfulness to Israel? As Nicodemus sees it, birth from above would be a second birth, which could not be possible given God's faithfulness. "How can a man be born after having grown old? Can a man enter a second time into the womb of his mother and be born?" (Jn 3:4). Nicodemus's questions to Jesus are not failures to understand a basic scriptural metaphor. Instead, his questions use the same scriptural metaphor of Israel's birth to form a carefully constructed, substantive theological challenge to Jesus's words about participation in the kingdom of God.[76] For Nicodemus, those whom God elected, God will save.

Nicodemus's apparent conviction that Israel's election was sufficient basis for its salvation is attested across a variety of early Jewish writings. In his book, *Creation, Covenant, and the Beginnings of Judaism,* Ari Mermelstein argues that the profound sense of covenantal disruption after the exile was addressed by retelling the history of Israel with a new beginning. He notices how Sirach, *Jubilees,* the Animal Apocalypse, and 4 Ezra all locate the election of Israel at creation rather than at Sinai. The problem with Sinai for these authors was that it was "a beginning that did not guarantee God's eternal commitment."[77] It could be broken, in other words. But if Israel's election began with creation, then the consummation of creation would bring with it Israel's restoration, regardless of sin's seemingly endless repetition.[78] So Nicodemus's appeal to Isaiah's metaphor of birth to describe Israel's election fits within this pattern of finding Israel's end in its beginning. If Israel was already carried by God from the womb, then God would be faithful to Israel to old age, and save Israel. To put it another way, Nicodemus interprets birth from above as an unthinkable disruption to Israel's covenantal history with God.

Thus, one may regard Nicodemus's questions to Jesus as only *apparently* foolish. Nicodemus feigns misunderstanding, but in truth responds to Jesus intelligently and critically with the same scriptural language of birth to challenge Jesus's words. The argument that I am advancing builds on the work of Jo-Ann Brant and Michael Whitenton, who have contended that Nicodemus resembles the type of character

---

[75] Elsewhere in John, the *Ioudaioi* speak about how they regard God as their father, emphasizing that "we are not born from a sexual misdeed" (ἐκ πορνείας οὐ γεγεννήμεθα, 8:41), which may further suggest that the *Ioudaioi* would have already considered themselves born from above. I am grateful to Christopher Blumhofer for suggesting the co-text to me. On God as the father of Israel in relationship to Israel's election, a theme found in Israel's Scripture and early Jewish writings, see Thompson, *The Promise of the Father,* 40–55.
[76] Interestingly, Jesus praises a woman who answers him in terms of the same metaphor that he first used with her (Mt. 15:26–28; Mk 7:26–30). That is, in those passages, the woman's response to Jesus in the terms with which he addressed her was a sign of understanding, not ignorance.
[77] Mermelstein, *Creation, Covenant, and the Beginnings of Judaism,* 183.
[78] Mermelstein, *Creation, Covenant, and the Beginnings of Judaism,* 6–15, 180–4.

that Theophrastus called "the dissembler" (cf. Theophrastus, *Char.* 1).[79] According to Theophrastus, dissemblers will praise their enemies (1.2), misrepresent what they hear, see, or remember (1.5), act as though they are astonished (1.5–6), and pretend to be ignorant (1.6). Theophrastus warned his readers to be more wary of dissemblers than vipers (1.7). Nothing dissemblers say can be taken at face value. Brant observes that Jesus characterizes Nicodemus's responses to him with just what qualities one would expect from a dissembler: astonishment (Jn 3:7), unacceptance (3:11), and disbelief (3:12).[80] Whitenton develops Brant's insight at length with recourse to cognitive theory and ancient rhetoric.[81] He argues that Nicodemus's absurdly foolish response is so incongruous with his role as a Pharisee, ruler of the *Ioudaioi*, and teacher of Israel that early readers would have come to understand him as a dissembler, not a fool. Furthermore, Jesus does not criticize Nicodemus for his failure to understand, but for his failure to believe and receive his testimony (3:11–12).[82] Thus, Whitenton concludes that "early listeners would have thought that Nicodemus does *not* misunderstand Jesus, but willfully rejects his teaching."[83] In other words, Nicodemus is a dissembler, and his questions about birth from above are not foolish, but adversarial.[84]

How, then, does Jesus answer Nicodemus's challenge? Jesus responds to Nicodemus with a statement that closely resembles what he first said to him: "no one can enter the kingdom of God without being born of water and Spirit" (ἐὰν μή τις γεννηθῇ ἐξ ὕδατος καὶ πνεύματος, οὐ δύναται εἰσελθεῖν εἰς τὴν βασιλείαν τοῦ θεοῦ; 3:5). This restatement suggests that Jesus does not concede Nicodemus's argument that birth from above is tantamount to a second birth of the same kind, as if birth from above was what happened when God first elected Israel, so that its repetition would be a repudiation of God's faithfulness. Instead, Jesus maintains that he speaks of a different sort of birth, not a second birth.[85] What Nicodemus cannot yet know—though readers of the Fourth Gospel do know—is that the one who spoke to him of birth from above was in the beginning with God (Jn 1:1–5, 14), and gives to all who receive and believe him the

---

[79] Jo-Ann A. Brant, *Dialogue and Drama: Elements of Greek Tragedy in the Fourth Gospel* (Peabody, MA: Hendrickson, 2004), 128–30; Brant, *John*, 74–5. My former professor Mickey Klink first referred me to Brant's insight, for which I am grateful. See also, Michael R. Whitenton, *Configuring Nicodemus: An Interdisciplinary Approach to Complex Characterization*, LNTS 549 (London: T&T Clark, 2019); Michael R. Whitenton, "The Dissembler of John 3: A Cognitive and Rhetorical Approach to the Characterization of Nicodemus," *JBL* 135.1 (2016): 141–58.

[80] Brant, *John*, 74–5.

[81] Whitenton pays particular attention to how the stock characters of the obtuse man and dissembler-shaped ancient audiences' understanding of Nicodemus (*Configuring Nicodemus*, 4–8, 55–77).

[82] Whitenton, *Configuring Nicodemus*, 88–106. For a sympathetic reading of Jesus's statement about the teacher of Israel and Nicodemus's lack of knowledge of "these things" (3:10), see Ole Jakob Filtvedt, "Revisiting Nicodemus's Question in John 3:9," *JTS* 70.1 (2019): 127–9.

[83] Whitenton, *Configuring Nicodemus*, 106, emphasis original. Whitenton argues that Nicodemus's next and final speech in the Fourth Gospel also fits the pattern of the dissembler (7:45–52), but at that point he dissembles in favor of Jesus (*Configuring Nicodemus*, 107–14).

[84] Brant understands Nicodemus's questions as his means of "rendering Jesus's assertion absurd," since Nicodemus thought he had no need for rebirth (*John*, 75).

[85] Similarly, Richard Bauckham, "Sacraments and the Gospel of John," in *The Oxford Handbook of Sacramental Theology*, ed. Hans Boersma and Matthew Levering (Oxford: Oxford University Press, 2015), 85.

power to become God's children (1:9–13).[86] If birth from above is a new beginning for Israel, it is a beginning for Israel located in *the* beginning, when the Word was with God (Jn 1:1). Perhaps this is why, in Johannine literature, there is "birth from God" (ἐκ θεοῦ γεννάω, Jn 1:13; cf. 1 Jn 2:29; 3:9; 4:7; 5:1; 5:18), but, strictly speaking, no rebirth (παλιγγενεσίας, Tit. 3:5; ἀναγεννάω, 1 Pet. 1:3). John's Gospel guards continuity with the past at the same time as it places surprising conditions on participation in Israel's future. Nicodemus need not be born again, but he must be born from above.

Jesus differentiates birth from above from a second birth by distinguishing between what is born from the flesh (τὸ γεγεννημένον ἐκ τῆς σαρκὸς) and what is born from the Spirit (τὸ γεγεννημένον ἐκ τοῦ πνεύματος, 3:6). As numerous interpreters have suggested, the focus of this statement is eschatological, not anthropological.[87] What comes from flesh is destined for death; what comes from Spirit is illimitably alive. What happens if the differentiation is interpreted within a debate about Israel's future restoration? In that case, flesh and spirit allude to God's election and restoration of Israel, respectively. Whereas God's election of Israel was inscribed in its flesh by means of circumcision and did not do away with death (see, e.g., Gen. 17:11; Lev. 12:3; cf. Jn 7:22–23), God's salvation of Israel was expected to bring an outpouring of the Spirit that causes abundant life (see, e.g., Isa. 32:15; 44:3; Ezek. 36:26–28).[88] Ezekiel, for example, supposed that Israel had to be born of flesh before being given spirit because their hearts had become stone, just like the stone idols they had worshipped (Ezek. 36:26; 20:32). Then, having become flesh, Israel had to be made alive by the Spirit (Ezek. 37:5–14). Similarly, in the Fourth Gospel, Jesus says that birth from above provides the flesh what it does not have: life from the Spirit. The problem with the flesh is its mortality. As Jesus will later say, "It is the spirit that gives life; the flesh is useless"— useless, that is, with respect to giving life (6:63).[89] Nicodemus is wrong about Israel's restoration, as Jesus sees it. It is not a return to the covenant inscribed in the flesh eight days after birth. To be born of the Spirit is to be born from above.

---

[86] Christopher W. Skinner argues that the Prologue privileges readers of the Fourth Gospel with knowledge of Jesus's identity that characters in the Fourth Gospel do not have ("Misunderstanding, Christology, and Johannine Characterization: Reading John's Characters through the Lens of the Prologue," in *Characters and Characterization in the Gospel of John*, ed. Christopher W. Skinner, LNTS 461 [London: T&T Clark, 2013], 111–18).

[87] Thompson understands σάρξ and πνεῦμα not in terms of the constitutive elements of a human person, but in terms of origin and destiny, the flesh destined for death and the Spirit spirating toward life (*John: A Commentary*, 82). So also Dodd, who draws on Origen for support (*Interpretation*, 224–7); Michaels, *The Gospel of John*, 185–6.

[88] On a reading of flesh as reference to God's covenant with Israel, see Sandra Schneiders, "Born Anew," *ThTo* 44.2 (1987): 192. Interpreting Jn 3:5, Timothy D. Foster reads "water" in terms of God's election of Israel and "Spirit" in terms of its salvation; had he made a similar interpretive move with flesh and Spirit (3:6), we would be in substantial agreement ("John 3:5: Redefining the People of God," *BBR* 27.3 [2017]: 351–60).

[89] Jesus seems to contradict himself, because only a few sentences earlier he claimed to give his own flesh (σάρξ) for the life of the world (6:51). The contradiction is only apparent. Jesus's flesh gives life because Jesus's flesh is πνεῦμα. As Dodd says, "It is only in connection with the incarnation that the idea of birth ἐκ πνεύματος makes sense (*Interpretation*, 226–7; cf. also Troels Engberg-Pedersen, *John and Philosophy: A New Reading of the Fourth Gospel* [Oxford: Oxford University Press, 2017], 153–76).

"How can these things be?" is Nicodemus's final response to Jesus in this dialogue (3:9). Suppose again that Nicodemus is a dissembler, and his question masks his knowledge with feigned ignorance. Nicodemus is not mystified by misunderstanding. His question is a morally serious one that concerns God's faithfulness to Israel. The consequence of Jesus's distinction between birth from flesh and birth from Spirit is the possibility that those born to be Israel by flesh will not be born from above into the capacities to see and enter the kingdom of God. In other words, Jesus's teaching about birth from above supposes a division in Israel between those who will see and enter what God has promised, and those who are not capable of doing so. Interestingly, the final time Isaiah uses the figure of birth it refers not to Israel's election, but to its restoration. There emerges a sharp distinction between the faithful and unfaithful within Israel (66:1–17).

But Jesus does not appeal directly to that Isaianic text in response to Nicodemus's final question, even if it was implicit earlier in the dialogue. Instead, Jesus employs a different scriptural figure, in which there is a more permeable division between those who will see and enter salvation and those who will not. After Israel's unfaithfulness in the wilderness, God judged Israel with deadly serpents, and many people are said to have died (Num. 21:4–9). As an antidote, God tells Moses "Make for yourself a snake, and set it on a sign. And it shall be that if a snake bites a person, everyone who is bitten when he looks at it shall live" (ἰδὼν αὐτὸν ζήσεται; Num. 21:8 NETS). Jesus compares himself to that serpent, that is, the object of sight that makes alive those who see it (Jn 3:14). He too will be lifted up, "that whoever believes in him may have eternal life" (πιστεύων ἐν αὐτῷ ἔχῃ ζωὴν αἰώνιον; 3:14–15). If Jesus is the serpent in the wilderness, the implication is that Nicodemus and those whom he represents are the wilderness generation. That is, Nicodemus and those whom he rules are identified with Israel born only of the flesh, still vulnerable to unfaithfulness and death. A sharp difference emerges between Jesus and Nicodemus in how Israel's present condition is imagined in relation to its future. Whereas Nicodemus appeals to the Isaianic image of Israel's election as a birth as a guarantee of God's unfailing faithfulness, Jesus appeals to Isaiah's image of restoration as a birth, with the consequence that only those who are born from above will be able to see and enter God's life when it arrives. Whereas Nicodemus sees absolute continuity between Israel's past and future, Jesus sees such continuity as made possible only with birth from above, which makes one able to see and enter the kingdom of God (3:5). This birth from above is the result of God's work of moral purification in Jesus.

3.3.2 Birth from Above, the Result of Purification

Having argued that at stake in the dialogue between Jesus and Nicodemus is how one participates in Israel's restoration, closer analysis of the controverted phrase "born from water and Spirit" (γεννηθῇ ἐξ ὕδατος καὶ πνεύματος) is needed. In this section I want to develop an interpretation of this phrase that may be paraphrased as, "birth resulting from the purification that comes from above," or, to put it less succinctly, "birth resulting from the purification that God enacts through the ablutions of John (with water) and Jesus (with Spirit)."[90] That is, water and Spirit are metonyms that allow

---

[90] This interpretation is similar to that developed by Thompson, *John: A Commentary*, 80–1, who writes that "to be 'born' or 'begotten' of God implies the Spirit's generative power in creating

the mediums with which John and Jesus each ablute to stand for their complementary ministries of ritual and moral purification. This contention is strengthened by the account of John and Jesus's overlapping ablutionary ministries that immediately follows and mirrors the dialogue between Jesus and Nicodemus (3:22–4:3).

Richard Bauckham, in his summary of the interpretation of Jn 3:5 in contemporary scholarship, finds that basically four referents for this phrase have been proposed: (1) Christian baptism; (2) some form of early Jewish purification; (3) physical and spiritual births; and (4) the gift of the life-giving Spirit.[91] Bauckham proposes the following helpful criteria for deliberating between these interpretive options: (1) the interpretation of this phrase must make sense within its narrative context; (2) the proposed interpretation must also have been accessible to Nicodemus; (3) the proposed interpretation must show how "birth from water and spirit" (3:5) helps clarify "birth from above" (3:3); and (4) "water" and "spirit" ought to be viewed as a "conceptual unity," since they are "anarthrous nouns connected by καί" and the four other instances of this grammatical construct in the Fourth Gospel imply such.[92] Bauckham himself suggests that the term *water* is introduced in response to Nicodemus's words about physical birth, in which case amniotic fluid is meant. Jesus then helps him understand that a different order of birth is intended, namely, to be born "from womb-water, that is, Spirit."[93] All five of these interpretations have something to commend them depending on one's interpretive interests and orientation. My interest is to construct, in light of the foregoing analysis of Jn 3, a reading of being born from water and Spirit as the eschatological, moral purification that God brings to bear on Israel through Jesus. A case for this can be made that meets Bauckham's criteria and answers his two primary objections to such an interpretation. Bauckham objects to the contention that "water symbolizes cleansing (from impurity or sin), not new birth" and objects to the interpretation of "water and Spirit" as a reference to purification, since "cleansing … is completely absent from Jesus' discussion with Nicodemus."[94]

Much of the argument for the interpretation of "birth from water and Spirit" as a result of purification from above has already been anticipated. Already accounted for is Bauckham's second criterion on availability of this interpretation to Nicodemus. Nicodemus's association with the Pharisees and *Ioudaioi* in Jerusalem suggests that the interpretation of water and Spirit as purification from above would have been available to him, on account of the witness of John to the delegation sent from Jerusalem (cf. 1:19,

---

children of God," then proceeds to explicate this generative power in terms of purification, drawing from Ezek. 36:25–28, *Jub.* 1.23–24, and 1 QS 4.20–22. Building on Adele Reinhartz's contention that the Fourth Gospel reflects an Aristotelian theory of procreation in which it is the man's semen that "imparts form and function to the female matter" (see Reinhartz, " 'And the Word Was Begotten': Divine Epigenesis in the Gospel of John," *Semeia* 85 [1999]: 88), Turid Karlsen Seim concludes that "there is no female principle involved in the divine begetting and birth-giving" (Turid Karlsen Seim, "Descent and Divine Paternity in the Gospel of John: Does the Mother Matter?," *NTS* 51.3 [2005]: 375). The language of birth or begetting does little to expand the Fourth Gospel's limited focus on males with respect to purity and purification.

[91] Bauckham, "Sacraments," 87–8.
[92] Bauckham, "Sacraments," 86.
[93] Bauckham, "Sacraments," 88.
[94] Bauckham, "Sacraments," 87.

24; 3:1; 5:33).[95] And while the Fourth Gospel has at this point given us the response of John's disciples to his witness (1:35–51), only in the dialogue with Nicodemus do we get any direct insight into the reception of his witness by the delegation that was sent from Jerusalem. Bauckham's objection that purification does not symbolize new birth is true only with respect to individuals.[96] However, as was already argued, God's work of moral purification was anticipated in prophetic and early Jewish traditions as that which made possible the return to the land and flourishing of life within it, a restoration that was sometimes figured in terms of birth (Isa. 66:7–9) or divine begetting (*Jub.* 1.23–25).[97] Thus, there is a basis in Israel's Scripture and early Jewish tradition for moral purification to make possible Israel's birth. What must still be answered is how the interpretation of "born from water and Spirit" as "born from the purification from above" is an answer to Nicodemus's statement in 3:4, as well as what grounds there are in this passage for interpreting this phrase with reference to purity.

Jesus explains the term from above (ἄνωθεν, 3:3) as from water and Spirit (ἐξ ὕδατος καὶ πνεύματος, 3:5). Because of its relationship to ἄνωθεν, the preposition ἐκ is best understood to indicate source, or provenance.[98] That is, the water and Spirit from which one is born come from above. It is not terribly difficult to imagine ablutions with the Spirit come from above, but in what sense do ablutions with water come from above? The origin of both ablutions with water and Spirit from above is clear in the only other point that the two terms have appeared with each other in the Fourth Gospel so far:

> And John testified, "I saw the Spirit (πνεῦμα) descending from heaven (ἐξ οὐρανοῦ) like a dove, and it remained on him. I myself did not know him, but the one who sent me to ablute with water (ὁ πέμψας με βαπτίζειν ἐν ὕδατι) said to me, 'He on whom you see the Spirit descend and remain is the one who baptizes with the Holy Spirit.' (ὁ βαπτίζων ἐν πνεύματι ἁγίῳ; 1:32–33)

Here the Spirit descends on Jesus, a downward movement that creates a spatial metaphor that locates the Spirit above. Moreover, the Spirit is said to have descended from heaven. Elsewhere heaven is made equivalent to the heights above, as demonstrated in the parallel between "the one who comes from heaven" (ὁ ἐκ τοῦ οὐρανοῦ ἐρχόμενος) and "the one who comes from above" (ὁ ἄνωθεν ἐρχόμενος, 3:31). John's ablution with water was from above in the sense that God sent John to do it (1:32; cf. 1:6). Later in the

---

[95] The close intratextual relationship between the inquiry into John (the Baptist)'s ablutions (1:19–28) and Jesus's dialogue with Nicodemus (3:1–15) has already been observed. See § 3.3.1.

[96] Keener does demonstrate that there was a relationship between ablutions for proselytes and their status as a newborn in later rabbinic literature (*The Gospel of John*, 543–4). But even if this tradition was available to the Fourth Gospel's author, Nicodemus was neither a Gentile nor a proselyte, so the analogy is doubtful.

[97] See § 3.1.

[98] Boucher makes the reverse point, namely, that because ἐκ is used in parallel to ἄνωθεν, the latter term has a spatial dimension ("Jn 3,3," 87). It is unlikely that the phrase denotes birth into the realm of the Spirit (one would expect ἐν or εἰς, *contra* Bultmann, *The Gospel of John*, 139–40, fn. 1) or birth into a mode of human existence (one would expect κατά, *contra* Dodd, *Interpretation*, 304–5).

Fourth Gospel, Jesus makes the point that Pilate's authority to release or crucify him is not absolute, but derived from above (ἄνωθεν, 19:10–11), which suggests that ἄνωθεν can also denote the place from which authority is derived for certain kinds of action.[99] Thus, it is no stretch of the imagination to suppose that John's ablution with water may be regarded as from above, since God sent him to ablute.

On this reading, water and Spirit are interpreted as metonymy, in which the mediums of ablution signify the complementary, ablutionary ministries of John and Jesus, which were each purifying in their own way.[100] John's ritual purification with water was for the purpose of revealing Jesus to Israel (1:31). Jesus later acknowledges John's witness (which must be interpreted as inclusive of his ablutions) as that which would help the *Ioudaioi* be saved (5:31–38). This explains why Jesus first tells Nicodemus that one must be born "from water and Spirit," but speaks only of being born "from Spirit" in the rest of the dialogue (3:6, 8). In other words, while John's ablution with water prepared one to perceive that Jesus is from God, the only ablution by which one would be born from above is Jesus's ablution with the Spirit. That is, the source of Israel's birth from above is the moral purification that God worked through Jesus, for whom Israel was prepared through John's revelatory, ritual purification. Only Jesus's ablutions with the Spirit, as John had said, were those that would remove sin and restore Israel. Thus, Jesus's reformulation of *birth from above* first as *birth from water and Spirit* and then simply as *birth from Spirit* may be interpreted as a claim that in Jesus's ministry God was making Israel pure from sin, so that Israel would be able to participate in God's rule and life.

That "water and Spirit" signifies the ablutionary ministries of John and Jesus is supported by Jesus's abrupt change to first-person plural later in the dialogue. Arguably, Jesus makes this change in order to include John's witness with his own witness, which he claims that Nicodemus and those he represents did not receive. Jesus says,

Very truly, I tell you, we speak of what we know [ὃ οἴδαμεν λαλοῦμεν] and testify to what we have seen [ὃ ἑωράκαμεν μαρτυροῦμεν]; yet you do not receive our testimony [τὴν μαρτυρίαν ἡμῶν]. (3:11)

This abrupt switch in number is an interpretive puzzle. It may be that for a moment the narrator allows those outside the narrative to be included with Jesus, that is, the historical hearers of the Gospel of John.[101] However, as Benjamin Reynolds has argued,

---

99 Interestingly, in the Synoptics, Jesus asks whether John's baptism was from heaven (ἐξ οὐρανοῦ) or from humanity (ἐξ ἀνθρώπων) as a riddle in response to the question of where his authority came from (Mt. 21:25; Mk 11:30; Lk. 20:4).

100 Similarly, Busse, "Reinigung und Heiligung," 148. So also Gary M. Burge, who argues that "for Jesus to refer to rebirth through water as well as Spirit must imply that Nicodemus has to submit to a feature of John's baptism as well as his own," which he interprets as purifying (*The Anointed Community: The Holy Spirit in the Johannine Tradition* [Grand Rapids, MI: Eerdmans, 1987], 163). However, Burge makes only the most general connection between "rebirth" and purification, by pointing to how the latter is viewed as transformative (p. 162). What I hope to add to arguments like Burge's is a more robust sense of moral purification as that which leads to Israel's restoration, which is sometimes spoken of as a birth.

101 Dan Nässelqvist approaches the interpretation of the Fourth Gospel in terms of its public reading in the early church and suggests its listeners would identify with the first-person plural (*Public*

every time Jesus uses the first-person plural, those included with him are indicated by the literary context, so that there is no need to appeal to potential outside audiences as referents (cf., e.g., 4:22).[102] In any case, the Fourth Gospel's narrator supposes its hearers will not have seen Jesus (20:29), which renders implausible (but not impossible) the alleged inclusion of the Fourth Gospel's readers in this particular saying about what "we have seen" (3:11).

Who, then, within the literary context might Jesus have included with him in the statement "we speak of what we know" (3:11)? Reynolds summarizes the interpretive options as the Father, the Spirit, Jesus's disciples, John (the Baptist), or Jesus alone, employing "we" only of himself in order to match Nicodemus's opening conceit "we know" (3:2).[103] In deliberating between these possible referents, preference must be accorded to one who has "borne witness to what we have seen" and whose witness was available to Nicodemus so that he might "receive our testimony" (3:11).[104] On these grounds, as Reynolds also notes, the Father is excluded because in the Fourth Gospel the Father is never once the subject of verbs of seeing, the disciples are excluded because, although they had seen Jesus's glory and believed (2:1–11), it is not yet narrated that they had borne witness that would have been available to Nicodemus, and the singular "we" is unlikely because it is used this way nowhere else in the Fourth Gospel.[105] The Spirit, also, is excluded because the Spirit's witness to Jesus begins only after the resurrection and even then is not based on sight (15:26–27). John (the Baptist) is the one character at this point in the Fourth Gospel who had borne witness to what he had seen (cf. ἑώρακα καὶ μεμαρτύρηκα, 1:34). John spoke of the one whom he admits he did not know (οὐκ ᾔδειν αὐτόν, 1:31, 33), a confession that suggests John said only as much as he did know (cf. ὃ οἴδαμεν λαλοῦμεν, 3:11). The *Ioudaioi*, moreover, were intent on giving an answer about John's witness to those who sent them from Jerusalem where Nicodemus was, which means that his witness would have been able to be received by Nicodemus (1:22). All this to say, the inclusion of John's witness with that of Jesus in this dialogue makes it more plausible to interpret the phrase "water and Spirit" with reference to the ablutions of water and Spirit enacted by John and Jesus.

Interpreted this way, one may rightly wonder how Jesus's reformulation of birth from above (3:3) as birth from water and Spirit (3:5) answers Nicodemus's objection that birth from above implies a second birth of the same kind, and is thus a repudiation of God's faithfulness to Israel (3:4).[106] That is, when "birth from water and Spirit" is

---

Reading in Early Christianity: Lectors, Manuscripts, and Sound in the Oral Delivery of John 1–4, NovTSup 163 [Leiden: Brill, 2016], 257–8).

[102] So Benjamin E. Reynolds, "The Testimony of Jesus and the Spirit: The 'We' of John 3:11 in Its Literary Context," *Neot* 41.1 (2007): 157–9.

[103] Reynolds, "The Testimony of Jesus," 162–9.

[104] Reynolds makes it an interpretive criterion that a character must speak and testify to what is seen in the manner Jesus does, to which I have added that this character's witness must have potentially been heard by Nicodemus at this point in the narrative ("The Testimony of Jesus," 160–2).

[105] Similarly, Reynolds, "The Testimony of Jesus," 162–9. However, Reynolds argues that the Spirit (and not John the Baptist) was included with Jesus in this phrase, based especially on his reflection on the Spirit's sound to Nicodemus (3:8), the association between the Spirit and Jesus's words (6:63), and the witness of the Spirit to Jesus (15:26).

[106] See §§ 3.3.1–3.3.2.

interpreted as "birth resulting from the purification from above," how might it be taken as an answer to Nicodemus's charge of discontinuity? For one thing, it would align Jesus's response to Nicodemus with Israel's past hope that God would purify Israel from sin. Jesus's response about a birth caused by God's purifying work is in keeping with the difference that was expected to come with Israel's restoration. God's faithfulness to Israel is shown forth in that Jesus gives Israel just what it needs to receive and participate in God's life: purification from above. For another thing, the purification of Israel from sin was sometimes expected to bring with it an anthropological transformation, that is, a change in human beings that would enable them to live fully in the presence of God. In Isaiah it is on the pure way to Zion that the exiles who are no longer impure would travel (Isa. 35:8–10). On that way those who were lame would leap like deer, and the eyes of the blind would be opened (35:5–6). That is, God's work of purification meant that Israel would be able to see and enter life with God, having before not had the faculties needed to do so. Similarly, birth from water and Spirit entailed anthropological transformation. Without it, Nicodemus would neither have been able to see nor enter the kingdom of God.[107] The Fourth Gospel employs this tradition of moral purity from the Prophets—that is, God's moral purification of Israel from sin that enables them to enter restored life before God—to narrate what the work of Jesus will do for God's people. In their moral purification from sin by Jesus, humanity might be born from above, and so made able to see and enter God's life.

3.3.3 Dual(ing) Purifications: John, a Ioudaios, and Jesus

The account that immediately follows Jesus's dialogue with Nicodemus narrates the overlapping ablutionary ministries of John and Jesus:

> After this Jesus and his disciples went into the Judean countryside, and he spent some time there with them and baptized [βαπτίζω]. John also was baptizing [βαπτίζω] at Aenon near Salim because water [ὕδωρ] was abundant there; and people kept coming and were being baptized [βαπτίζω]—John, of course, had not yet been thrown into prison. Now [ἐγένετο οὖν] a discussion about purification [ζήτησις … περὶ καθαρισμοῦ] arose between John's disciples and a Jew. They came to John and said to him, "Rabbi, the one who was with you across the Jordan, to whom you testified, here he is baptizing [βαπτίζω], and all are going to him." John answered, "No one can receive anything except what has been given from heaven. You yourselves are my witnesses that I said, 'I am not the Messiah, but I have been sent ahead of him.' He who has the bride is the bridegroom. The friend of the bridegroom, who stands and hears him, rejoices greatly at the bridegroom's voice. For this reason my joy has been fulfilled. He must increase, but I must decrease." (3:22–30).

---

[107] This anthropological transformation is, I will argue, instantiated in the Fourth Gospel's account of the giving of sight to a man born blind, who comes to see Jesus and enter salvation by him, having joined his flock.

In this account, a number of themes that underlie the dialogue between Jesus and Nicodemus come forth more explicitly. In particular, as will be explored in more depth, there is an explicit association between purification and the ablutions of John and Jesus (3:25–26), and the scriptural text that John (the Baptist) alludes to in his response to the controversy about purification is the one passage in Jeremiah that relates moral purification to the restoration of Israel (Jer. 33:7–11). Arguably, the account of John and Jesus is placed immediately after the highly allusive and fast-paced debate between Jesus and Nicodemus in order to help interpret it.[108] The two passages are not merely juxtaposed, but also mirror each other in certain respects. Formally speaking, each passage involves a controversy with a *Ioudaios* (3:2; 3:25) and ends with an aphoristic speech (3:16–21; 3:31–38). Key terms are also repeated in both passages. Nicodemus was supposed to be born "from water and Spirit" (ἐξ ὕδατος καὶ πνεύματος; 3:5). The terms are then associated with John and Jesus, respectively. John ablutes where he does because water is plentiful there (ὅτι ὕδατα πολλὰ ἦν ἐκεῖ, 3:23). Jesus speaks the words of God because "[God] gives the Spirit without measure" (οὐ γὰρ ἐκ μέτρου δίδωσιν τὸ πνεῦμα, 3:34). That is, as John's ministry required an abundance of waters, so Jesus's ministry required the Spirit given limitlessly by God (cf. 1:33). In both concluding speeches, Jesus is said to come "from heaven" (ἐκ τοῦ οὐρανοῦ, 3:13, 31), Jesus bears witness to what he sees and that witness is not received (3:11, 32), and contrasting futures await those who trust in the Son and those who do not (3:16, 36). The mirrored literary structure works to establish the unity of witness between John and Jesus, and suggests that purification is common subject matter in both passages.

The overlapping ablutionary ministries of John and Jesus became the subject of a controversy about purification between John's disciples and a *Ioudaios*.[109] Commentators sometimes suppose that the controversy about purification that arises between John's disciples and a *Ioudaios* has nothing to do with what immediately comes before or follows it.[110] However, the use of οὖν in 3:25 to introduce the controversy about purification signals both continuity and development of what came before, which was the account

---

[108]   Brown argues that the account of Jesus and John baptizing is deliberately misplaced (following as it does more naturally after 1:19–34) in order to bring out the baptismal motifs in the dialogue with Jesus and Nicodemus (*The Gospel according to John*, 1:154).

[109]   The term translated by the NRSV as "discussion" denotes something more like controversy or dispute, as in the case of the controversy (ζήτησις) that divided Paul and Barnabas from those who taught that Gentiles must be circumcised to be saved (Acts 15:2; cf. also, Jos. *Ant.* 14.195). See BDAG s.v. "ζήτησις."

[110]   Several commentators do not perceive the integral relation between ablutions and purification. Haenchen fails to see the connection between ablutions and purification (*John*, 210). Bultmann regards the controversy about purification as superfluous and unrelated to its literary context (*The Gospel of John*, 167). Barrett supposes the statement is unrelated to the ablutions of John and Jesus, but purification in general, of which he says that "John cares (and perhaps knows) little" (*The Gospel according to St. John*, 221). Brown comments that "the logic of the story is not clear" because of the reference to this controversy about purification (*The Gospel according to John*, 1:153). By contrast, Thompson rightly sees the controversy over purification as interpreting the ablutions of John and Jesus as purifying (*John: A Commentary*, 92–3). Michaels (following an interpretive path that Bultmann outlines and rejects) speculates that the *Ioudaios* "had come from Judea with news of Jesus' success there, perhaps even with an account of his own 'purification' by Jesus through baptism" (*The Gospel of John*, 216).

of the ablutions of John and Jesus (3:22–23).[111] That is to say, the reason these ablutions triggered a controversy about purification is that they were rightly understood to be purifying.[112] But certain aspects of their ablutions must also have been controversial, which is precisely what one expects given the varied and contested discourse that came forth in the earlier survey of early Jewish writings dealing with eschatological, moral purification. In other words, the controversy about purification is explicated by the comparison of John and Jesus that follows it. The connective καί (3:26) relates the controversy about purification (3:25) to the report John's disciples brought to him about Jesus's ablutions (3:26). John's disciples speak about Jesus not by name, but only in terms of his relation to John. They refer to Jesus as "the one who was with you" (ὃς ἦν μετὰ σοῦ), as the one "to whom you testified" (σὺ μεμαρτύρηκας), and then impersonally as "that one" (οὗτος, 3:26). Their use of second-person pronouns to address their Rabbi is emphatic. The trouble with Jesus's ablutions for John's disciples is that Jesus is not John. The disciples of John are concerned that Jesus's ablutions are displacing John's own.

Studies in ritual have shown that the agent who performs a ritual action such as ablution is an integral part of the ritual and its meaning, particularly when that agent is understood as divinely sanctioned.[113] As was argued in the last chapter, the Fourth Gospel ascribes a peculiar prominence to John's agency in abluting others. In fact, the subject of inquiry in relation to John's ablutions was not the ablutions themselves, but how John's identity authorized him to act in such a way (1:19–28). *Who* was abluting mattered, in other words. Therefore, the subject of the argument between the disciples of John and a *Ioudaios* about purification is explicated by the rest of the passage: *who* could administer the ablutions that purify, and what did their purifications do? Ritual agency was exactly what was at stake in the conflict over purification. If the question to John from the *Ioudaioi* was "Why are *you* abluting" (1:25), John's disciples seem to wonder about Jesus, "Why is *he* abluting?"

Thus, John (the Baptist)'s following response, in which he diminishes himself in relation to Jesus, may be taken as a resolution to the argument about purification between his disciples and a *Ioudaios*. John seeks to persuade his disciples that because of who Jesus is it is right for Jesus to increase and John to decrease (3:30). John reiterates to his disciples that he said "I am not the Messiah, but I have been sent (ἀποστέλλω) ahead of him" (3:28; cf. 1:15, 20, 23, 26–27, 30). John's positive statement about himself—that God sent him ahead of the Messiah—reminds the disciples that his ablutions with water were for the purpose of revealing Jesus (1:31, 33). John's negative confession that he is not the Messiah implies that the one who was with him across the Jordan *is* the Messiah. Because Jesus is the Messiah, an eschatological figure who was earlier associated with ablutions (1:25), the ablutions of Jesus are those that will purify Israel in a way that John's do not.

---

[111] So Stephen E. Runge, who notes that "οὖν differs from other development markers by adding the constraint of close continuity with what precedes" (*Discourse Grammar of the Greek New Testament: A Practical Introduction for Teaching and Exegesis*, Lexham Bible Reference [Peabody, MA: Hendrickson, 2010], 30). Similarly, BDAG s.v. "οὖν."

[112] On ablutions with water as an act of ritual purification, see § 2.2.1.

[113] So argues Risto Uro about John the Baptist, drawing from cognitive approaches to ritual studies (*Ritual and Christian Beginnings*, 85–7).

The metaphor that follows John's self-identification in relationship to Jesus more closely associates Jesus with moral purification and Israel's restoration. John identifies Jesus as the bridegroom who has the bride, whose voice completes John's joy (3:29). As Jocelyn McWhirter has argued, John's figure of marriage alludes to Jer. 40:10–11 LXX:

> He who has the bride [νύμφη] is the bridegroom. The friend of the bridegroom, who stands and hears [ἀκούω] him, rejoices greatly [χαρᾷ χαίρει] at the bridegroom's voice [τὴν φωνὴν τοῦ νυμφίου]. (John 3:29)
>
>   There shall yet be heard [ἀκούω] in this place of which you say, "It is a wilderness apart from human beings and animals," in the cities of Iouda and outside of Ierousalem, that are desolate, to the point that there are no human being or animal, a voice of gladness and a voice of joy [φωνὴ χαρμοσύνης], a voice of bridegroom [φωνὴ νυμφίου] and a voice of bride [φωνὴ νύμφης]. (Jer. 40:10–11 LXX; cf. 33:10–11 MT)

McWhirter observes the preponderance of unique verbal correspondences between these texts, such as the setting in Judah, the reference to the bridegroom's voice, the presence of the bride, the fact that one is there who hears their voice, and the sound of joy.[114] Moreover, whereas other prophetic oracles anticipate the absence of such joy on account of God's judgment, this text alone celebrates the presence of the bridegroom and the bride (e.g., Jer. 7:34; 16:9).[115] Not coincidentally, John (the Baptist) has alluded to the only one of Jeremiah's oracles of restoration that refers to God's purification of Israel from sin: "I will purify them from all their injustices which they sinned against me" (καθαριῶ αὐτοὺς ἀπὸ πασῶν τῶν ἀδικιῶν αὐτῶν, ὧν ἡμάρτοσάν μοι; Jer. 40:8 LXX). So John (the Baptist) responds to a controversy about purification with Jeremiah's only oracle about the result of God's purification of Israel from sin (καθαρισμός, Jn 3:25). John's use of this scriptural figure assumes that Israel's restoration is now being actualized in the land of Judah, because Jesus—the bridegroom Messiah—is abluting there and many are going to him. Since Jesus's ablutions are those that remove sin and restore Israel's life and joy, it is Jesus who must increase and not John.[116]

The account of Jesus's ablutions gives only the vaguest impression as to what exactly he was doing. All throughout the Fourth Gospel, the precise way that Jesus ablutes with the Holy Spirit is left opaque, as is the birth from above that results from that purification. No action of Jesus is explicitly identified as ablution with the Holy Spirit—not even when Jesus ablutes alongside John (3:22–4:3) or when he breathes the Spirit on his disciples (20:22–23). The narrator's statement that the Spirit "was not yet" because Jesus was not yet glorified suggests that no ablution with the Spirit could have happened prior to the crucifixion and resurrection (7:38–39). But the Spirit had already descended and remained on Jesus (1:33), and abluting with the Spirit is not

---

[114] See McWhirter, *The Bridegroom Messiah*, 50–8, esp. 56. She convincingly shows that a much stronger case can be made for the relation of Jn 3:28 to Jer. 40:10–11 LXX on the grounds of verbal correspondence than can be made for Song 2:8–14; 5:2–6.

[115] McWhirter, *The Bridegroom Messiah*, 53–4.

[116] The lovely phrase "bridegroom Messiah" I have borrowed from McWhirter, *The Bridegroom Messiah and the People of God*.

quite the same as sending the Spirit (cf., e.g., 14:16).[117] Were Jesus's ablutions different than John's? Whereas John (the Baptist) needed abundant water with which to ablute (3:23), it is not stated that Jesus's ablutions used water (3:22).[118] To muddy matters more, at the end of the passage the narrator adds the qualification that Jesus did actually not ablute at all, but only his disciples, some of whom were formerly disciples of John (4:2). So, if there was ablution with water, which the term βαπτίζω seems to imply, it was administered only by Jesus's disciples. In a sense, John bequeaths his ablution of water to the disciples of Jesus, laying the groundwork for a fusion of ablutions.[119] At some point (and perhaps this account is something like an etiology for Christian baptism) ablution with water and ablution with the Spirit would be conceived as a single act.[120]

If, then, Jesus's ablution with water is ruled out as the ablution with the Spirit in the Fourth Gospel's narrative (4:2), readers might identify a different action of Jesus with that purifying work. Jesus speaks often in the Fourth Gospel, and the speech of Jesus is an act that is intelligible as an ablution with the Holy Spirit. Interestingly, the action of Jesus that receives the most focus in the account of his and John's ablutionary ministries is Jesus's speech: the bridegroom's voice (φωνή) brings joy (3:29), Jesus bears witness (μαρτυρέω) "to what he has seen and heard" (3:32), and Jesus "speaks the words of God" (τὰ ῥήματα τοῦ θεοῦ λαλεῖ), having been given the Spirit (πνεῦμα) without measure (3:34). The text suggests that Jesus speaks in the way that he does because he has come from above (3:31). Furthermore, Jesus's speech is retrospectively interpreted as morally purifying in the Farewell Discourse, when Jesus tells his disciples that "you are pure because of the word that I have spoken to you" (καθαροί ἐστε διὰ τὸν λόγον ὃν λελάληκα ὑμῖν, 15:3).[121] Since ablution with the Spirit was supposed to be a means of (moral) purification, and the Spirit is sometimes closely identified with the words of Jesus (6:63; cf. 3:34), it seems that Jesus's ablutions with the Spirit are performed not by washing with water but by speaking God's word.[122] That is, the ablution with the Spirit that removes sin and restores Israel is enacted in the words that Jesus speaks. One is able to see and enter God's life, having been purified by Jesus's words.

To summarize, the dialogue between Jesus and Nicodemus as well as the controversy about purification immediately following develop the identification of Jesus as the one who brings the moral purity that will enable Israel to see and enter God's life. It was argued that at stake in the debate between Jesus and Nicodemus was participation in Israel's restoration. Reading Nicodemus's first response as an intelligent rebuttal to Jesus suggests that Nicodemus objects to birth from above on account of the discontinuity it creates between Israel's election and restoration. Jesus's counterargument can be paraphrased in terms of Nicodemus's need to be born from the purification from above,

---

[117] Bennema, "Spirit-Baptism in the Fourth Gospel," 36–40.

[118] I am indebted to Busse for this insight ("Reinigung und Heiligung," 148).

[119] The reference to John's arrest foreshadows the cessation of his ablutions with water (Jn 3:24), and, after this account in John 3:22–4:3, John's ablutions are recounted only in retrospect (10:40–42).

[120] On which see Busse, "Reinigung und Heiligung," 148.

[121] So also Busse, "Reinigung und Heiligung," 154. On the word of Jesus as purifying, see § 4.4.2.

[122] The identity between ablutions with the Spirit and the speaking of God's word is rendered more likely in the close relation between the Spirit and Jesus's word in the Fourth Gospel (e.g., 3:34; 6:63) as well as the morally purifying effect accorded to both actions, to the former implicitly (1:33; 3:5; 3:22–4:3) and to the latter explicitly (15:3).

that is, from the purifying ablutions of John and Jesus. Such purification would cause Nicodemus and those he rules to be born from above. The dialogue between Jesus and Nicodemus revolves around the word *can* (δύναμαι), which shows that purification from above is about possibility, that is, the potential for a person to see and enter the kingdom of God (3:3, 5). However, if persons are not born from such purification, then they will be incapable of perceiving and coming into Israel's restoration, creating a division within Israel for which there is precedent in Scripture (Isa. 65–66). Following this dialogue, John (the Baptist) again bears witness to Jesus, this time to his disciples in response to a controversy over purification. I suggested that the controversy over purification was a matter of *who* was authorized by God to ablute, as ritual agents are to be considered integral to purification. John's identification of Jesus as the Messiah and the bridegroom intratextually and intertextually expresses that Jesus is the one whose ablutions enable the restoration of Israel and their participation in the life of God. What remains to be seen is what action of Jesus in the Fourth Gospel (if any!) may be understood as causing "birth from the purification from above" that enables one to see and enter the kingdom of God.

3.4 "Washing I Received Sight": The Man Born Blind, Born from Above

In this section, I argue that the giving of sight to the man born blind shows that Jesus's work of moral purification enables a person to see and enter life (9:1–10:21).[123] I will first suggest that this purifying work of Jesus must be recognizable prior to the conclusion of his public ministry, since a crowd believes in him on account of John's witness to Jesus as one who brings into effect moral purification (10:40–42). Then attention will be given to how the account of Jesus giving sight to a man born blind may be understood as a purifying work of God that enables the man to see and enter life.

Toward the end of the Fourth Gospel's account of Jesus's public ministry, John (the Baptist) is mentioned for the last time in the Gospel. The narrator reports that Jesus:

> went away again across the Jordan to the place where John had been baptizing earlier [πέραν τοῦ Ἰορδάνου εἰς τὸν τόπον ὅπου ἦν Ἰωάννης τὸ πρῶτον βαπτίζων], and he remained there. Many came [ἔρχομαι] to him, and they were saying, "John performed no sign, but everything that John said about this man was true [πάντα

---

[123]   Although the focus of this section will be on 9:1–10:21, Jan A. Du Rand advances a compelling, narratological argument that 9:1–10:42 is a literary unity; see "A Syntactical and Narratological Reading of John 10 in Coherence with Chapter 9," in *The Shepherd Discourse of John 10 and Its Context: Studies*, ed. Johannes Beutler and Robert Tomson Fortna, SNTSMS 67 (Cambridge: Cambridge University Press, 1991), 94–115. See also, Brant, *John*, 152; Troels Engberg-Pedersen, "Philosophy and Ideology in John 9–10," in *"The One Who Sows Bountifully": Essays in Honor of Stanley K. Stowers*, ed. Caroline E. Johnson Hodge et al., BJS 356 (Providence, RI: Brown Judaic Studies, 2013), 296–8. Against J. W. Holleran, "Seeing the Light: A Narrative Reading of John 9," *ETL* 69.1 (1993): 11–12, who argues that 9:1–41 is organized as a chiasm and bound together by an *inclusio*, making 10:1–21 its own literary unit with its own structure.

δὲ ὅσα εἶπεν Ἰωάννης περὶ τούτου ἀληθῆ ἦν]." And many believed [πίστευω] in him there. (Jn 10:40–42)

Given what John said about Jesus, the crowd's judgment that "everything that John said about this man was true" is arresting, particularly since John said that Jesus was "the lamb of God who takes away the sin of the world" (1:29) and "the one who ablutes with the Holy Spirit" (1:33). The reliability of the crowd's judgment is validated by their response to Jesus, since they come to Jesus (ἔρχομαι) and believe in him there (πίστευω), orientations toward Jesus commended by the Fourth Gospel (see, e.g., 6:30–40). Is one not to suppose from this that in his public ministry Jesus had acted in such a way that such predications of him became recognizably true? In other words, even if the work of removing sin and abluting with the Holy Spirit was not yet complete, the crowd could acknowledge the truth of John's witness to Jesus because Jesus had acted in such a way that made these claims credible. Jesus's work of eschatological, moral purification of which John spoke was already initiated in his public ministry.

Two features of the giving of sight to the man born blind resonate with the Fourth Gospel's representation of Jesus as the one who brings God's eschatological, moral purification to bear on the world. First, the man receives sight from Jesus by washing in a pool built for ritual immersion, and he does so at the command of Jesus. The reception of eyesight by washing with water suggests the reception of insight by ablution with the Spirit. That is, the ritual purification with water is a material witness to the moral purification effected in Jesus' word. Second, the work of God enables the man born blind to see Jesus (ὁράω, 9:37) and enter through him into salvation (εἰσέρχομαι, 10:9). These are the very abilities imparted by birth from above, or, as I paraphrased it earlier, birth resulting from the purification from above (3:3, 5).

After smearing mud on the eyes of a blind man, Jesus tells him to wash (νίπτω) in the pool of Siloam (9:7). The narrator reports that the man "washed (νίπτω) and came back able to see (βλέπω)" (9:7). The story is repeated twice by the man born blind to those who inquire about how he received sight (9:11, 15). The second time he tells the story, he does not reiterate the words of Jesus or the place he went (9:11). Nevertheless, he continues to narrate his newfound faculty of sight as a direct result of washing: "Then I washed (νίπτω), and now I see (βλέπω)" (9:15). The pool of Siloam where the man washed was almost certainly a pool built for the purpose of ritual purification.[124] Massive in size and located to the south of Jerusalem, it is likely that many ancient Jews who traveled to Jerusalem for feasts such as Tabernacles would have purified themselves in that very pool.[125] To be sure, the narrator does not make explicit that washing in the pool of Siloam was for ritual purification. Nevertheless, receiving sight through washing with water is congruent with the Fourth Gospel's

---

[124] The purpose of the pool of Siloam has been controverted by archeologists, but like other pools built for ritual immersion, it was stepped and its source of water was what later rabbinic sources would consider fitting for purificatory purposes, on which see Burge, "Siloam, Bethesda, and the Johannine Water Motif," 259–65; Urban C. von Wahlde, "The Gospel of John and Archeology," 102–6. On the basis of such archeological findings, both Burge and von Wahlde urge scholars to consider that ritual purification is a matter the Fourth Gospel takes up and addresses.

[125] So von Wahlde, "The Gospel of John and Archeology," 106.

earlier associations between ritual purification, perception, and revelation. The ablutions of John with water prepared for the revealing of Jesus (φανερόω; 1:31) and the use of stone vessels for purification occasioned the revealing of Jesus's glory at Cana to his disciples (φανερόω; 2:11). In the case of Jesus giving a man sight, washing with water was the means by which God's works were revealed through the man born blind (φανερόω; 9:3).[126] That said, ritual purification does not adequately account for how sin is removed from the man born blind, how his reception of sight amounts to a birth from above, or how he comes to be included among those who see and enter God's life. In his encounter with Jesus, the man born blind became morally pure. He was born of water and Spirit.[127] Having been born from the purification from above, the man's receiving sight is the Fourth Gospel's actualization of Isaiah's oracle about moral purification in Israel's restoration: the blind whose eyes were opened would return to the Lord on a pure way, and God's glory would be revealed (Isa. 35:1–10 LXX).

The first indication that the giving of sight to the man born blind involves moral purification is Jesus's reversal of the judgment that the affliction of the man born blind was caused by sin.[128] This judgment is made both by Jesus's disciples, who ask, "Rabbi, who sinned, this man or his parents, that he was born blind?" (τίς ἥμαρτεν, ... ἵνα τυφλὸς γεννηθῇ, 9:2), and the Pharisees, who immediately before casting him out said to him: "You were born entirely in sins [ἐν ἁμαρτίαις σὺ ἐγεννήθης ὅλος], and are you trying to teach us?" (9:34). The story leads to a surprising reversal. Whereas the man's blindness was presumed to be caused by sin, Jesus tells the Pharisees that "if you were blind, you would not have sin" (εἰ τυφλοὶ ἦτε, οὐκ ἂν εἴχετε ἁμαρτίαν, 9:41). This is not unlike Jesus's earlier admonition, "Do not judge by appearances [κατ ὄψιν], but judge with right judgment" (7:24).[129] In other words, it is not the blindness of the Pharisees that is the problem, but their particular way of seeing. The way of seeing which was for them darkness was a particular relation to the law, because instead of seeing Jesus's work of healing on Sabbath as God's work, they judged it to be sin and Jesus to be a sinner (7:19–23; 9:16). But the man born blind saw that Jesus was

---

[126] This reading assumes that the clause ἵνα φανερωθῇ τὰ ἔργα τοῦ θεοῦ ἐν αὐτῷ is dependent on what follows, which would render the whole sentence as "Neither this man sinned, nor his parents. But, in order that the works of God might be displayed in him, we must carry out the works of the one who sent me while it is day" (Jn 9:3–4a; cf. the ἵνα-clause in 1:31). For an argument to this effect, see John C. Poirier, " 'Day and Night' and the Punctuation of John 9.3," *NTS* 42.2 (1996): 288–94.

[127] The Spirit is nowhere mentioned in Jn 9:1–10:21. Perhaps this is to be expected in light of what Jesus says about those born of the Spirit to Nicodemus, namely, that birth from the Spirit is like the movement of the wind, which is beyond human knowing. As the giving of sight to the man born blind is set at Tabernacles, the identification of living water that proceeds out of the belly of Jesus as the Spirit (7:38–39) may also attune readers to an otherwise imperceptible ablution of the Spirit that happens to this man. The possessive pronoun αὐτοῦ in the sentence ὁ πιστεύων εἰς ἐμέ, καθὼς εἶπεν ἡ γραφή, ποταμοὶ ἐκ τῆς κοιλίας αὐτοῦ ῥεύσουσιν ὕδατος ζῶντος may be interpreted either as referring to "the one who trusts" or the object of trust, namely, Jesus (7:38). For discussion, see Thompson, *John: A Commentary*, 175–6; Blumhofer, *The Gospel of John and the Future of Israel*, 137–40.

[128] Among those who alerted me to the importance of sin and judgment in Jn 9 are L. Anne Jervis, "Worlds of Judgment: John 9," in *Conception, Reception and the Spirit: Essays in Honour of Andrew T. Lincoln*, ed. J. Gordon McConville and Lloyd K. Pietersen (Cambridge: James Clarke, 2015), 48–57; and Holleran, "Seeing the Light: A Narrative Reading of John 9," 354–82.

[129] On the importance of this sentence in Jn 7–10, see Thompson, *John: A Commentary*, 228.

from God. Because of this, the judgment of sin is removed from the man born blind by the judgment of Jesus, a judgment by which "those who do not see may see, and those who do see may become blind" (9:39). So, the giving of sight to the man born blind may be interpreted, as L. Ann Jervis suggests, as a "narrative embodiment" of the identification of Jesus as "the lamb of God who takes away the sin of the world" (1:29).[130] The man born blind began as one judged to be completely in sin (9:2, 34), and, after encountering Jesus, was judged to be without sin, and made to be without blindness.

The man's birth is referred to six times as the narrative unfolds—twice in connection to his sin (9:2, 34), and always in connection to his blindness (9:1, 2, 19, 20, 32, 34). Jesus's giving of sight to a man so born cannot be anything less for him than a birth from above, as his congenital blindness was determinative for his situation in life to that point. Furthermore, for the man born blind, Jesus' work of giving sight could not be understood as anything other than having come from God (9:31–33). The only place where the language of birth is more densely concentrated in the Fourth Gospel is in the dialogue between Jesus and Nicodemus, where γεννάω is repeated eight times in just a few sentences (3:3–8). There Jesus said that one must be born of water and Spirit in order to enter the kingdom of God. The man is born from above when he is born from washing in the water of Siloam and from the Spirit that rested on Jesus when he commanded the man to wash, and disclosed himself to the man as the Son of Man.

Crucially, the work of God that Jesus does for the man born blind enables him both to see and enter salvation, which is what Jesus earlier told Nicodemus became possible when one was born from above. The recovery of the man's sight is referred to twenty times by a variety of voices, including that of the narrator (9:7, 13, 14, 18, 24), the man born blind (9:11, 15, 25, 30, 32), the man's neighbors (9:10), the man's parents (9:20–21), the *Ioudaioi* (9:15, 17, 19, 26; 10:21; 11:37), and Jesus (9:37). The man born blind deduces from the remarkable nature of his recovery of sight that Jesus is "from God" (παρὰ θεοῦ, 9:32–33; cf. 3:2; 9:16; 10:21), which suggests that the man received not eyesight only, but insight into the identity of Jesus and origin of his power.[131] The reference to the man's sight that is most consequential comes when Jesus finds the man and addresses him:

[Jesus] said, "Do you believe in the Son of Man?" He answered, "And who is he, sir? Tell me, so that I may believe in him." Jesus said to him, "You have seen him, and the one speaking with you is he" [καὶ ἑώρακας αὐτὸν καὶ ὁ λαλῶν μετὰ σοῦ ἐκεῖνός ἐστιν]. He said, "Lord, I believe" [πιστεύω, κύριε]. And he worshiped him. (9:35–38)

---

[130] Jervis, "Worlds of Judgment," 55. However, it must be noted that Jesus also retains sin (9:41).

[131] The claim that the man receives both sensory perception (eyesight) and true understanding of the identity of Jesus (insight) is made by a number of interpreters. See, for example, the reading of Dorothy A. Lee, who attends to the interplay between literal (eye)sight and symbolic (in)sight in Jn 9, with more attention than I can give to the Pharisees as a counterpoint to the man born blind (*The Symbolic Narratives of the Fourth Gospel: The Interplay of Form and Meaning*, JSNTSup 95 [Sheffield: JSOT Press, 1994], 161–87).

Jesus's address to the man shows that he does not only have the capacity to see, but that he has in truth seen the Son of Man, a term Jesus previously used of himself with reference to his ascent and descent from heaven (see, e.g., 1:51; 3:13; 6:62).[132] The man has rightly apprehended what the sign of his recovered sight signifies, namely, the origin of Jesus with God. So he addresses Jesus as Lord, confesses his trust in him, and worships him (9:38).

Jesus's discourse on the good shepherd is a continuation of the controversy occasioned by Jesus giving sight to the man born blind (10:1–18). There is no change in speaker, addressee, time, or place, and the response of the *Ioudaioi* to the shepherd discourse includes a reference to Jesus's ability to give sight to the blind (10:19–21).[133] The narrator explains that the image of the shepherd, thieves, gate, and sheep was Jesus's response to the Pharisees, who had previously asked him if he considered them blind (10:6; cf. 9:39–41). The man born blind, now seeing (ὁράω, 9:37), is included among those sheep who will enter (εἰσέρχομαι) salvation through the gate, which is Jesus (10:7, 9). The man born blind, having heard and heeded Jesus's voice in his blindness, now sees in such a way that he participates in God's life. Having come to trust in Jesus, the man comes to have life abundantly (10:10).

In the discourse on the good shepherd, the man born blind ought to be regarded as one of the sheep about which Jesus speaks. The sheep are characterized by their relation to Jesus and to other would-be shepherds. The sheep hear the voice of the shepherd and follow him (10:3–4, 16), they enter the fold through the gate (10:7, 9), they come to have life because of the shepherd (10:10–11), and they are gathered together into one flock under one shepherd (10:16). At the same time, the sheep are vulnerable to thieves who would steal, kill, and destroy (10:1, 10); wolves who would snatch them or scatter them (10:12); and hired hands who would abandon them (10:13).[134] Jesus's speech makes profound soteriological and christological claims: salvation (10:9), the abundant life involved in finding pasture (10:10), and the gathering of many sheep into one flock (10:16) are works of God brought to fullness in the coming of Jesus and the laying down of his life.[135] No other presumed leader of God's people would bring this good future into effect.

---

[132]   On the interpretation of the enormously difficult phrase "son of man" in the Fourth Gospel (υἱὸς τοῦ ἀνθρώπου) see the summary of evidence and issues in Benjamin E. Reynolds, "The Use of the Son of Man Idiom in the Gospel of John," in *"Who Is This Son of Man?": The Latest Scholarship on a Puzzling Expression of the Historical Jesus*, ed. Larry W. Hurtado and Paul Owen, LNTS 390 (London: T&T Clark, 2011), 101–29; see also Thompson, *John: A Commentary*, 55–8. Whereas Reynolds associates the son of man with Jesus's heavenly origin, Thompson finds that the phrase emphasizes the peculiar humanness of Jesus. Mediating between them, I would suppose that Jesus's humanity is itself apocalyptic, insofar as seeing Jesus is seeing the Father (Jn 14:9).

[133]   As observed by Du Rand, "A Syntactical and Narratological Reading," 94.

[134]   Thompson interprets the shepherd discourse as "Jesus' indictment of the Pharisees for their sin and blindness" (*John: A Commentary*, 222) and thus reads the words about thieves who kill and destroy as a reference to the Pharisees' severe treatment of the man born blind (224).

[135]   This christological emphasis echoes the christological emphasis in the giving of sight to the man born blind, namely, that the works of God are worked through Jesus (9:3–4) which reveal that he is from God (9:16, 32–33; cf. 3:2). Holleran suggests that "what it means to acknowledge Jesus as the Christ" is the thematic core of 9:1–41 (Holleran, "Seeing the Light," 18).

Jesus's speech in the shepherd discourse is also ecclesiological in its focus, because what is said of any single sheep ought to characterize all of them, namely, that they would know the good shepherd, listen to his voice, and follow him (10:14, 16, 27). In its literary context, is one not to consider the man born blind as an exemplary sheep? Before the man could see, he heard the voice of Jesus and obeyed it, going to wash in the pool of Siloam (9:7, 11; cf. 10:3–4, 14, 16). Then, when the man finally did see Jesus and hear his voice, he trusted in him (9:35–38; cf. 10:25–27). By contrast, his situation with respect to others was dire. He was economically destitute and subsisted on begging (9:8), his neighbors did not know him well enough to recognize him (9:9), his parents dissociated themselves from him (9:18–23), and the *Ioudaioi* cast him out because of his words about Jesus (9:34).[136] In his initial explanation of the figure of the shepherd and sheep, Jesus identifies himself as "the gate for the sheep" (10:7), explaining that "whoever enters by me will be saved (δι ἐμοῦ ἐάν τις εἰσέλθῃ σωθήσεται), and will come in (εἰσέρχομαι) and go out and find pasture" (10:9). Having been cast out by the *Ioudaioi* (9:22, 34), the man born blind enters by Jesus into salvation. To the extent that this man born blind is exemplary, his story shows that all sheep who hear Jesus's voice have been purified by Jesus, to the effect that they may see and enter life. Thus, the purification from above that enabled the man to see Jesus also enables him to enter that pasture where one may have life in abundance (10:10), and this becomes true of all who are included in the good shepherd's flock.

Jesus told Nicodemus that he must be born from above, born from water and Spirit, if he would be able to see and to enter the kingdom of God. The opening of the eyes of this man born blind is like a purification from above that makes possible his birth into God's life. He recognizes that Jesus must have come from God in order to be able to give him sight. And, by unmaking the man's congenital blindness, Jesus supplies what is in effect a birth for him. The man comes to trust Jesus, to see, and to enter life through him, which suggests that his receiving sight from Jesus results in his birth from above. The man born blind received sight by washing with water in the pool of Siloam. Although the Spirit is nowhere mentioned in this account, Jesus earlier described birth from the Spirit as an act outside of human comprehension (3:8). Even so, the word of Jesus is determinative for the man coming to see Jesus. Without the word of Jesus to wash in the pool of Siloam, the man's washing would not have given him sight. More significantly, Jesus discloses himself to the man as the Son of Man who *speaks* to him (9:35–38). If it is true that Jesus enacts ablution with the Spirit in the words that he speaks, then the man born blind's reception of Jesus's words may be understood as his reception of Jesus's ablution with the Holy Spirit. The birth from above of this man, who was blind from birth, enables him to see Jesus and enter through him into an abundant life. All of this resonates with the Fourth Gospel's appeal to the moral purification that was expected as part of Israel's restoration, that is, that act of God that would enable Israel to see and enter salvation, having before been unable to see or enter on account of sin. Thus, one aspect of the works of God revealed in the man born

---

[136] For a sensitive treatment on the social and economic consequences of blindness, including the suggestion that the man's parents had dissociated from him, see Brant, *John*, 164–6.

blind (9:3–4) is the moral purification through which humanity is enabled to perceive and receive the light and life of God.

3.5 Conclusion

The Fourth Gospel was written in an early Jewish context, charged with the hope that God would restore Israel. As the survey of the Prophets and a number of early Jewish writings demonstrated, this hope included the expectation that God's purification of Israel from sin was connected to the restoration of Israel's life in the land. It is in light of this imagined future for Israel that a number of difficult passages in the Fourth Gospel may be read, even if the Fourth Gospel does not take up the land promise in the same way that it takes up the promise of *life* for Israel. John identifies Jesus as "the lamb of God who takes away the sin of the world" (1:29) and "the one who ablutes with the Holy Spirit" (1:33). I argued that these statements identify Jesus as one who is pure, and for that reason able to purify Israel from sin. This portrayal of Jesus and his work is further developed in conflict with Nicodemus. Jesus tells Nicodemus that one must be "born from above" or "born from water and Spirit" in order to see and enter the kingdom of God (3:3, 5). When one regards Nicodemus as a competent interlocutor, the subject matter of his dialogue with Jesus comes into clearer focus. The repetition of *can* (δύναμαι) and the intertextual relation to Isaiah's metaphors of Israel's election and restoration in terms of birth shows that Jesus and Nicodemus were debating how it was possible for one to participate in God's restoration of Israel. In this text, moral purification—figured as birth from above or birth from Spirit—is that which comes from God through Jesus and enables Israel to see and enter the life of God. The account of the overlapping ablutionary ministries of John and Jesus secures such a reading, as John (the Baptist) alludes to the only text in Jeremiah that speaks of God's moral purification of Israel and uses it to interpret the significance of Jesus and his ablutions. The interpretive puzzle posed by John (the Baptist)'s words about Jesus is that they must have been recognizably true in the public ministry of Jesus, for a crowd trusts in Jesus on account of John's words about him before Jesus is glorified (10:40–42). That is, it must have already been able to be perceived that Jesus was removing sin and abluting with the Holy Spirit. For this reason, the giving of sight to the man born blind comes into focus as the instance in which Jesus's work of moral purification leading to birth from above is actualized in the public ministry of Jesus—the ablution with water, the reversal of judgment, the language of birth, and the enabling of the man to see and enter salvation—all these suggest that Jesus is indeed the pure and purifying one.

To synthesize some of the conclusions of this chapter in terms of moral purity in the Fourth Gospel, four things may be said: (1) God is the one from whom moral purification comes, and this purification is brought to bear on the world in the word of Jesus. For this reason, birth from water and Spirit may be understood as birth from the purification that comes from above. That God would act to bring moral purification was not a distinctively Christian idea. It is precedented in Israel's Prophets and was hoped for by ancient Jews. (2) The Fourth Gospel echoes and alludes to passages in the Prophets related to God's work of moral purification in the restoration of Israel such as

Isa. 35; 46:3–4, Ezek. 36:25–27, and Jer. 40:7–11 LXX. In so doing, the Fourth Gospel represents Jesus as the one through whom God enacts moral purification for Israel and so enables them to enter life. (3) Moral purification in the Fourth Gospel entails the removal of sin (1:29) and is oriented toward the restored ability to participate in the life of God. In other words, moral purification makes possible what otherwise would be imperceptible or out of reach: to see and enter the kingdom of God. (4) Moral purification is distinguished from ritual purification, but these differing kinds of purity were not compartmentalized from each other. Instead, there is a correspondence between them. The waters of John's ablutions are a witness to Jesus's work of moral purification with the Holy Spirit. And washing with water in the pool of Siloam testifies to that moral purification that makes possible insight and entrance into God's life. In the next chapter, moral purification will be explored in relation to its result in the lives of Jesus's disciples, whom he calls pure. As will be seen, their moral purity is related to their capacity to keep the commandment of Jesus, such that the love he has for them is replicated in their love toward one another.

4

Already You Are Pure: The Disciples, Moral Purity, and Ethics

As Jesus anticipates his death, he gives the disciples a vision for how in his absence their lives are to be patterned after his own life, particularly in their imitation of his love for them toward one another (Jn 13:1–17:26).[1] The Farewell Discourse is introduced with an action. Jesus washes his disciples' feet and interprets the action as a paradigm for how his disciples are to live and act. He tells them, "I have set you an example (ὑπόδειγμα), that you also should do as I have done to you" (13:15). In the long discourse that follows, Jesus twice commands his disciples to love one another just as he has loved them:

> I give you a new commandment, that you love one another. Just as I have loved you, you also should love one another [καθὼς ἠγάπησα ὑμᾶς ἵνα καὶ ὑμεῖς ἀγαπᾶτε ἀλλήλους]. (13:34)
> This is my commandment, that you love one another as I have loved you [ἵνα ἀγαπᾶτε ἀλλήλους καθὼς ἠγάπησα ὑμᾶς]. (15:12)

In Jesus's absence, his disciples are to receive and replicate his love toward one another, and in so doing they will enter blessedness (13:17), abide in love (15:10), and have complete joy (15:11). It is not without reason that in his study on the ethics of the Fourth Gospel, Sookgoo Shin argues that the weight of material dealing with the imitation of Christ and moral progress is to be found in the Farewell Discourse.[2]

The words of Jesus about the purity of his disciples are deliberately placed in this Farewell Discourse (13:10–11; 15:2–3). On the one hand, purity is a particularly timely subject, as the Farewell Discourse is located just before the only Passover that the

---

[1] On this reading of the Farewell Discourse, see Thompson, *John: A Commentary*, 279–80.
[2] Sookgoo Shin, *Ethics in the Gospel of John: Discipleship as Moral Progress*, Biblical Interpretation Series 168 (Leiden: Brill, 2019), 48–50. Similarly, Andreas J. Köstenberger, *A Theology of John's Gospel and Letters*, Biblical Theology of the New Testament (Grand Rapids, MI: Zondervan, 2009), 516–18. This ought not to suggest, however, that the first half of the Fourth Gospel is not "ethical" in the sense of making room for reflection on how one is to act toward certain others and for what reasons, on which see Michael Labahn, "'It's Only Love'—Is That All? Limits and Potentials of Johannine 'Ethic'—A Critical Evaluation of Research," in *Rethinking the Ethics of John: "Implicit Ethics" in the Johannine Writings*, ed. Jan G. van der Watt and Ruben Zimmermann, WUNT 291 (Tübingen: Mohr Siebeck, 2012), 7.

Fourth Gospel connects explicitly (and repeatedly) to purity (11:55; 13:1–11; 18:28). This Passover is first reported in connection to the *Ioudaioi* who had gone early to Jerusalem to (ritually) purify themselves for the feast, and there is no indication that Jesus and his disciples were not ritually pure also.[3] As will be seen in connection to the footwashing, the ritual purity of Jesus's disciples occasioned his evaluation of their moral purity. On the other hand, Jesus's predication of the disciples' purity is retrospective. This is particularly clear when Jesus tells his disciples "*already* you are pure" (ἤδη ὑμεῖς καθαροί ἐστε) and explains that the cause of their purity is "the word that I have spoken to you" (διὰ τὸν λόγον ὃν λελάληκα, 15:3). As was argued in Chapter 3, Jesus had already initiated his work of eschatological, moral purification through his word. However, the Fourth Gospel nowhere narrates a single moment in which the disciples who were with him at the footwashing were morally purified. They are pure already when Jesus addresses them in the Farewell Discourse.

Not coincidentally, Jesus tells his disciples, "you are pure" (ὑμεῖς καθαροί ἐστε) in each of the places that he commands them to love one another (13:1–38; 15:1–17). In this chapter, I will argue that the disciples' moral purity is what enables them to keep Jesus's commandment to love one another. As will be seen, their moral purity consists in both a moral quality and a moral capacity. The language of purity in early Jewish ethical discourse often denotes particular moral qualities. The morally pure life is unsullied by bloodshed, sexual misdeeds, and idolatry, and is characterized by the love and worship of Israel's God. Moral purity is also deeply connected to human capacity to keep God's commandments. This chapter will move back and forth between the Fourth Gospel's early Jewish context and the two passages in the Fourth Gospel in which Jesus calls his disciples pure. First, it will be shown that in early Jewish ethical discourse, human conduct was sometimes evaluated with the language of (im)purity. Acts of bloodshed, sexual misdeeds, idolatry, and theft from the poor were conceptualized as sins that defile. This analysis of how early Jewish ethical discourse employs language of purity in the evaluation of human conduct and moral character will then illuminate what Jesus predicates of his disciples in calling them pure during the footwashing, as well as why Judas is not considered to be among the pure (13:10–11). Next, we will return to a selection of early Jewish writings to consider how moral purification is conjoined with the restored human ability to keep God's commandments. This connection helps bring into focus how the disciples' purity in the discourse on the vine is what enables them to produce the fruit of love (15:1–17).

Focus on the moral qualities denoted by purity goes against the grain of Johannine interpretation, in which the disciples' purity in the Farewell Discourse is often understood only in terms of the means by which Jesus atones for his disciples, with disagreement about whether it is the word of Jesus or his death by which the disciples are purified.[4] These divergent interpretations of the cause of the disciples' purity over

---

[3]   As rightly observed by Martin Vahrenhorst, "Johannes und die Tora: Überlegungen zur Bedeutung der Tora im Johannesevangelium," *KD* 54.1 (2008): 18–20. On the likelihood that the historical Jesus had ritually purified himself for feasts in Jerusalem, see Haber, *"They Shall Purify Themselves,"* 181–206.

[4]   On the view that the disciples' purity is indicative of the salvation that comes from the word, see, for example, Bultmann, *The Gospel of John*, 470–1; Barrett, *The Gospel according to St. John*, 442, 474. On the disciples' purity as the result of the cross, see, for example, Bruce H. Grigsby, "The Cross as

the last sixty years may be understood as a function of the controversial arguments of Bultmann and Käsemann that the Fourth Gospel presents the death of Jesus not as saving, but simply as the departure that completes his revelatory mission.[5] As was argued in Chapter 3, moral purification does have a soteriological dimension, which is found in relation to the birth from above about which Jesus spoke to Nicodemus (Jn 3:3–5) and which the man born blind experienced when Jesus gave him sight through an act of washing (9:1–10:21). That said, the metaphoric density of language for purity in early Jewish writings means that interpreters need not choose between a soteriological or ethical interpretation of purity. The focus of the present chapter is on the disciples of Jesus, and just what is predicated of them when Jesus calls them pure. In other words, instead of focusing on the work of God through Jesus as in Chapter 3, in the present chapter attention is given to the effect of that work in the lives of the disciples, insofar as that effect is represented in the Fourth Gospel. The disciples are called pure by Jesus, and the cultural and literary contexts of these predications suggest that the disciples' purity is morally oriented, even as it is entirely given by God in the work of Jesus.

4.1 Pure from Bloodshed, Pure for Love: Moral Purity in Early Jewish Writings

Before discussing moral (im)purity early Jewish writings, it will be helpful to recall that, in the major Prophets, the language of impurity as it is used in ethical contexts is reserved for those sins that rupture the relation between God and Israel, particularly bloodshed, idolatry, sexual misdeeds, and theft.[6] This relational rupture is described in terms of defilement. The sins of Israel defile the land, defile the temple, and defile the people, so that even if the people seek to appear in God's presence, God will not be found by them. The indictment with which Isaiah begins captures how the language of (im)purity is used for theological ethics.

> I will no longer forgive your sins [οὐκέτι ἀνήσω τὰς ἁμαρτίας ὑμῶν]. When you stretch out your hands to me, I will turn away my eyes from you; even if you make

---

an Expiatory Sacrifice in the Fourth Gospel," *JSNT* 15 (1982): 62; Frank J. Matera, "'On Behalf of Others,' 'Cleansing,' and 'Return': Johannine Images for Jesus' Death," *LS* 13.2 (1988): 170–2. More than a few commentators have adopted a mediating position, which does not assume the word of Jesus and his action in the cross are mutually exclusive; see, for example, Brown, *The Gospel according to John*, 2:676–7; Thompson, *John: A Commentary*, 286–8.

[5] See Rudolf Bultmann, who appeals to the disciples' purity in Jn 13:10 and 15:3 in support of his argument that the death of Jesus is not particularly important for the Fourth Gospel's concept of salvation (*Theology of the New Testament*, trans. Kendrick Grobel, vol. 2 [New York: Charles Scribner's Sons, 1955], 52–9); see also Ernst Käsemann, *The Testament of Jesus: A Study of the Gospel of John in the Light of Chapter 17*, trans. Gerhard Krodel, The Johannine Monograph Series 6 (Eugene, OR: Wipf & Stock, 2017), 4–20. For a range of scholarly responses to their arguments, see John A. Dennis, "Jesus' Death in John's Gospel: A Survey of Research from Bultmann to the Present with Special Reference to the Johannine Hyper-Texts," *CBR* 4.3 (2006): 331–63.

[6] See the discussion on ritual and moral purity in § 1.3.

many petitions, I will not listen to you, for your hands are full of blood. Wash yourselves; become pure [λούσασθε, καθαροὶ γένεσθε]; remove the evil deeds from your souls before my eyes; cease from your evil deeds; learn to do good. (Isa. 1:14b–17a NETS, trans. mod.)

Because the hands stretched out to God in worship are stained with blood, God turns away from the people.[7] What is more, forgiveness would not remove the sins that defiled Israel. Instead, the stain of blood would be removed only by washing, which Isaiah employs as a metaphor for ceasing to do evil and learning to do good. Israel must become morally pure. Although Isaiah tells Israel "wash *yourselves*," it ends up that God's judgment and not Israel's own reformation purifies them (Isa. 4:2–6). Only after God's judgment purifies Israel from bloodshed does God come and dwell among them (4:4–5). The language of (im)purity at once describes the moral life of Israel and the possibility of God's presence with them. The language of moral (im)purity weaves together ethics with life before God.[8] The people are to become pure *from* bloodshed and other defiling sins, so that they may be pure *for* the worship and obedience to God.

Centuries later, Jesus is said to have told his disciples, "You are pure, but not all of you" as he washed their feet and prepared to depart from them (Jn 13:10). Unlike God's desolation of Israel on account of their defiling sin, Jesus departs from the disciples whom he called morally pure. In his departure, Jesus assures his disciples that they are pure, and would keep his commandments and that God's Spirit would come to dwell with them (14:15–17). As will become more clear, Jesus's statement about his disciples' purity at the footwashing is a moral judgment, which indicates who among the disciples will replicate the pattern of lowly love Jesus practiced in washing their feet, and who would not. The disciples' moral purity consists in their conformity to the pattern of Jesus's love for them and assures them of God's presence with them (13:15, 34–35). By contrast, Judas is excluded from among the pure on account of his complicity in a sin that ancient Jews widely regarded as defiling, namely, bloodshed, and perhaps also theft from the poor (12:5–6).

One cannot quite hear an allusion to or echo of Israel's Scripture in Jesus's statement about his disciples' purity at the footwashing. Nevertheless, Jesus's judgment that his disciples are pure has affinity with the moral use of the language of (im)purity in biblical tradition (as in the case of Isaiah above) as well as early Jewish tradition. I will explore how the language of purity is employed for moral evaluation in early Jewish writings—particularly in Philo, Josephus, and testamentary literature—in order to explicate what Jesus predicates of his disciples in calling them pure. I am trying to recover the "ethos" that the term *pure* calls forth in the Fourth Gospel by examining how the language of purity is used to evaluate human character and conduct in early

---

[7]   On the ethics involved in cultic practices in Isa. 1:10–17, see the insightful work of Hrobon, *Ethical Dimension*, 75–115.

[8]   See also Zimmermann's provocative claim that "the separation of theology and ethics does not correspond to ancient thinking, but instead reflects a structure of perception that was introduced by Rudolf Bultmann in order to describe Pauline ethics as an indicative-imperative schema" ("Is there Ethics in the Gospel of John?" 62). Shin demonstrates that ancient Greco-Roman ethics also had a theological dimension (*Ethics in the Gospel of John*, 28–32).

Jewish writings that are roughly contemporaneous with the Fourth Gospel.[9] To put it another way, I want to articulate how an "encyclopedia of reception" consisting in biblical traditions of purity from the Prophets and carried forward in early Jewish writings might illuminate the purity of Jesus's disciples at the footwashing.[10] After considering how moral purity is used in ethical discourse in selected early Jewish writings, I will focus on the language of purity in John's account of Jesus's washing of his disciples' feet.

Philo of Alexandria writes about moral purity in such a way that relates human life in the world to life with God. Philo develops his conception of purity at greatest length in *Spec. Laws*, a work in which each commandment of the Decalogue is used to categorize the disparate stipulations of the Pentateuch as a whole (*Spec. Laws* 1.1).[11] For Philo, the whole work of Jewish worship—involving instructions about the temple, priesthood, sacrifice, and purity—is a function of the first two commandments, for only through proper worship can a person rightly honor the "one truly existing God" (1.65 [Colson]).[12] This schematization of Israel's laws regarding cultic worship underneath the commandments of the Decalogue intimates his presumption that the right worship of God is a matter of moral seriousness.

In *Spec. Laws*, Philo recognizes that both the ritual purification of the body with water and the moral purification of the soul from vice are needed prior to worshiping God in the temple.[13] About one who is going to offer sacrifices in the temple, Philo writes:

the law would have such a person pure [καθαρὸν] in body [σῶμα] and soul [ψυχή], the soul purged of its passions [παθῶν] and distempers and infirmities and every viciousness of word and deed, the body of the defilements [μιαίνεσθαι] which commonly beset it. (1.257 [Colson])

---

[9] Ruben Zimmermann speaks of ethos as the morals that were assumed and practiced by a community (Ruben Zimmermann, "Is There Ethics in the Gospel of John?," in *Rethinking the Ethics of John: "Implicit Ethics" in the Johannine Writings*, ed. Jan G. van der Watt and Ruben Zimmermann, WUNT 291 (Tübingen: Mohr Siebeck, 2012), 58–60.

[10] On the use of Umberto Eco's construal of extratextual relationships as "encyclopedic" in biblical studies, see Stefan Alkier, "Intertextuality and the Semiotics of Biblical Texts," in *Reading the Bible Intertextually*, ed. Richard B. Hays, Stefan Alkier, and Leroy A. Huizenga (Waco, TX: Baylor University Press, 2009), 3–22.

[11] On the organization of *Spec. Laws*, see, for example, James R. Royse and Adam Kamesar, "The Works of Philo," in *The Cambridge Companion to Philo*, ed. Adam Kamesar, Cambridge Companions to Philosophy (Cambridge: Cambridge University Press, 2009), 48–50.

[12] Leonhardt observes that although worship in Philo is sometimes imagined to happen outside of Jewish cultic contexts and is often related to one's inner life, nevertheless, the dominant use of λατρεία and its cognates in Philo either demarcate Jewish worship as happening within the temple, or as directed toward the temple (*Jewish Worship in Philo*, 14–15). Particularly important for Leonhardt is the list of rites that Philo associates with Sabbath worship in *Decalogue* 158, namely, lustrations, prayers, and sacrifices.

[13] See Leonhardt's discussion of purity and purification in Philo, arranged according to his vocabulary for purification and washing (e.g., ἁγνεία, περιρραίνω, λούω), where she recognizes how Philo "strongly associates moral behavior with cultic and ritual purity. ... Thus he links purity, morality, and worship" (*Jewish Worship in Philo*, 257–72; here, 271).

Philo teaches that the ritual purification of the body is a kind of sanctified abasement of pride, for washing oneself with water and ash (as one did to remove corpse impurity, cf. Num. 19:9) reminds one of the lowly elements of human composition and motivates one to please God and depend on God's power (1.265; cf. *Dreams* 1.211–12). He does not suggest that washing with water removes sin, but that its repeated practice forms one's sense of lowliness before God. Thus, ritual purification is taken by Philo to generate reflection about what a human being is and how one must act toward God as a result. But for Philo, the purification of the body with water—ritual purification— is woefully inadequate unless it is matched with the purification of the soul—moral purification.[14]

Philo's understanding of moral purity—what he calls being pure in soul— is more complex than his understanding of ritual purity because of the way it interfaces both with sacrifice and moral life (see *Spec. Laws* 1.270–284). Its complexity lends to it a conceptual richness in relating the moral life to cultic worship. Philo speaks of how passions defile the soul, to the effect that one's worship becomes worth little to God (1.275). For Philo, among those defilements (μιάσματα) of life that make offerings to God unholy are "wine-bibbing and gluttony, … the love of money [φιλαργυρία], of reputation, of pleasure, and numberless other forms of passion and soul-sickness and vice" (1.281). Philo identified one such vice—the love of money (φιλαργυρία)— as idolatry (1.23–6). This identification of vice as idolatry suggests that human life is polluted by those vices that make the observance of the first two commandments impossible, so that sacrifice could not possibly be a thanks to God, as Philo thought it should be (cf., 1.283).[15] Passions such as these betray the truth about a person's life: they have rendered honor due to the Creator to created things (1.20). Thus, moral impurity makes it impossible to fulfill the first two commandments, and moral purity is what is needed for one to rightly worship God alone.

In contrast to the moral impurity that defiles one's worship, the moral purity of one's life makes even the smallest sacrifice precious in God's sight (1.275). For Philo, "what is precious in the sight of God is not the number of victims immolated but the true purity [τὸ καθαρώτατον] of a rational spirit in [the one] who makes the sacrifice" (1.277). Philo's warrant for this judgment is found in his identification of the one giving the offering with the sacrificial offering itself. The inspection of the sacrificial victim that is meant to ensure its integrity (ὁλόκληρον), perfection (παντελῶς) and freedom from blemish (μώμων ἀμέτοχον, 1.259). But the sacrificial victim is an allegory for the one bringing the sacrifice. Philo writes that the sacrificial victim:

> is a symbol representing in a figure the reformation of your own conduct … [The Law] is anxious not that the victims [τῶν θυομένων] should be without flaw but

---

[14]   On the way that Philo's purity of the body and purity of the soul roughly correspond to ritual and moral purity, see Klawans, *Impurity and Sin*, 64–6.

[15]   On Philo's view of sacrifice as ultimately and ideally motivated by thanksgiving to God, see Jean Laporte, *Eucharistia in Philo*, Studies in the Bible and Early Christianity 3 (New York: Edwin Mellen, 1983).

that those who offer them [τῶν θυόντων] should not suffer from any corroding passion. [πάθος κηραίνωσι] (1.259–60)

The moral purity required for sacrifice involves self-examination. Philo would have those bringing offerings search (σκέπτομαι, διερευνάω) their motivations for worship and ensure that their minds, like their sacrifices, are perfect (παντελῶς) and whole (ὁλόκληρον, 1.283). By identifying the one bringing the offering with the sacrificial offering, one's pure way of life in the world is drawn into the act of worship and honor of God. One's purity makes one's worship precious to God. Moreover, in the examination of one's motivations and life in the preparation for worship, the process of moral purification comes to involve the practice of moral reflection and formation. For Philo, the interface between one's life in the world and one's worship of God in the temple is moral purity.

Not unlike Philo, Josephus employs the language of purity to evaluate human conduct and character.[16] In *Against Apion*, Josephus articulates the reasons for his conviction that Jewish law—including its laws of purity—effectively cultivates moral formation (*Ag. Ap.* 2.145–219). He seeks to answer the charge that "the laws are our teachers in vice and not a single virtue" (τοὺς νόμους δὲ κακίας ἡμῖν καὶ οὐδεμιᾶς ἀρετῆς, 2.145) by laboring to show how the laws given by Moses to the Jews are "extremely well designed with a view to piety [εὐσέβεια], fellowship with one another, and universal benevolence, as well as justice, endurance in labors, and contempt for death" (2.146).[17] According to Josephus, Jewish law inculcates virtue in those who observe it, and its capacity for moral formation of a people is superlatively better than that of other codes of life (2.145–89). Among Josephus's arguments for the most excellent design of the law in promoting such virtues is that Moses:

> did not make piety [εὐσέβεια] a part of virtue [ἀρετή], but recognized and established the others as parts of it—that is, justice, moderation, endurance, and harmony among citizens in relation to one another in all matters. For all practices and occupations, and all speech, have reference to our piety towards God [ἐπὶ τὴν πρὸς τὸν θεὸν ἡμῖν εὐσέβειαν]. (2.170–1)

In other words, piety toward God is the center and goal of life and practice for Josephus, a sensibility that becomes clearer in his outline of Jewish law (2.193–219).

Josephus's explication of purity in *Against Apion* demonstrates how he regarded purity as having a human moral dimension, even as purity regulated the relation between humanity and God. Géza Vermès writes of Josephus's concise summary of Jewish law that "in this carefully conceived and simplified presentation of the Torah

---

[16] Although purity is not a major theme in Josephus's writings, it is not unimportant. The relative lack of attention to purity may be explained by the genre of his works not lending well to legal exegesis, and also his unfulfilled desire to write on the legal aspects of Jewish law (cf., e.g., *Ant.* 3.223; 20:268). On these two points, see the helpful excursus on purity in the writings of Josephus in F. M. Colautti, *Passover in the Works of Josephus*, JSJSup 75 (Leiden: Brill, 2002), 133–43.

[17] All translations of *Against Apion* in this book are from John M. G. Barclay, *Flavius Josephus: Translation and Commentary. Against Apion*, ed. Steve Mason, BJP 10 (Leiden: Brill, 2007).

we are confronted with what is probably the earliest Jewish theological synthesis."[18] He notes how Josephus structures his outline of Jewish law, first with discourse on God (*Ag. Ap.* 2.190–2), then with humanity's relation to God (2.193–205), then with humanity's relation to other creatures, including plants and animals (2.206–14), and finally with punishment on impiety and resurrection for persons who are good (2.215–19).[19] Josephus locates his discussion on purification within the section on humanity's relation to God, where he also discusses the temple and sacrifice. He alludes to the ritual purification needed prior to offering sacrifice, particularly when one has been to a funeral, birthed a child, or had sexual intercourse (2.198). He then expounds on these rites of purification in moral terms, warning against adultery, abortion, and other sexual misdeeds, as well as seeking to explain anthropologically why lawful sex also required ablutions (2.199–203).[20] Interestingly, the rationale for corpses causing ritual impurity is explicitly moral, namely, "so that anyone who has committed murder might be far from seeming to be pure [καθαρός]" (2.205).[21] In other words, the observance of ritual purification after contact with corpses is piety toward God that makes one bound to judge the murder of a person as utterly morally defiling (cf., also, Philo, *Spec. Laws* 3.205–207). The observance of purity, then, is among the matters Josephus finds involved in his statement that all "must worship [God] by exercising virtue" (τοῦτον θεραπευτέον ἀσκοῦντας ἀρετήν, *Ag. Ap.* 2.192). Since that sentence leads directly into Josephus's discussion of the temple, sacrifice, and purity (2.193–205), one rightly infers that the Jewish laws regarding worship involve virtuous lives in the world.

Josephus's work on purity in *Ag. Ap.* 2.199–205 coheres with the way that he elsewhere morally evaluates human action with the terminology of (im)purity. Josephus predicates purity (καθαρός) of those whose lives are free from certain sins and vices, such as theft (κλοπή; *J.W.* 2.141), wickedness (πονηρία, κακία; *Ant.* 1.75; 4.114, 8.120), adultery (*Ant.* 2.50–2), and bloodshed (φόνος, αἶμα; *Ant.* 4.222; 6.303). And Josephus often speaks of sin's defilement (μιαίνω, μιαρός) in relation to bloodshed (cf., e.g., *J.W.* 3.391; *Ant.* 2.24, 31), as well as sexual misdeeds (*J.W.* 4.562), idolatry among Israelites (*Ant.* 8.245; 9.272–3), and theft from God (*Ant.* 5.42). But for Josephus no sin is so severe as bloodshed within holy precincts. Josephus claimed that the defilement of the temple through bloodshed by John of Gischala and the Sicarii is the reason that God caused the Romans to destroy the temple. Bloodshed in the temple was for Josephus a dangerous mixture of injustice and impiety (*J.W.* 6.99–110, cf., also,

---

[18] Géza Vermès, "A Summary of the Law by Flavius Josephus," *NovT* 24.4 (1982): 301.

[19] Vermès, "Summary of the Law," 293.

[20] It seems to me that Josephus's statement about purification (2.198) frames his discussion on sexual ethics and death (2.199–206), but others do not make the connection quite the same way. For example, Barclay, *Against Apion*, 282 fn.795, interprets these sentences as a new section of text dealing with household matters. But that disjunction obscures the reason why Josephus twice returns to matters of purity, first with respect to sex and childbearing (2.202–3) and then with respect to death (2.205). Even so, Barclay recognizes that for Josephus "purity is defined in moral terms. ... worship of God can be understood as a matter of both ritual and virtue" (281, fn. 788). See also Barclay's helpful interpretation of Josephus's obscure anthropological explanation for why lawful sex defiles, see (286–7, fns. 816–19).

[21] Barclay notes that the bracketing of the Greek text of 2.205 in the Loeb edition "is without textual warrant" (*Against Apion*, 288, fn. 829).

4.201; 4.323; 5.17–19; *Ant.* 11.297–301).[22] Josephus's evaluation of their actions using the rich, metaphoric language of purity grounds his theological claim about God's agency in the temple's destruction. Josephus later mentions that John of Gischala not only murdered people close to him, he also "abandoned the established rules of purity of our forefathers [πάτριον ἐξεδιῄτησεν ἁγνείαν]; so that it could no longer excite surprise, that one guilty of such mad impiety towards God failed to observe towards men the offices of gentleness and charity" (*J. W.* 7.264–65 [Thackeray]). It almost sounds as if Josephus is saying, "John murdered people, and, what is worse, he failed to observe the laws of purity." In truth, Josephus finds that piety toward God—especially in the observance of purity—and loving regard for human beings are inseparable (cf., also, *J. W.* 4.150). In other words, for Josephus ritual purity as piety toward God had to correspond to moral purity in one's relations to others.

In fact, for both Josephus and Philo, ritual purity was intended to correspond to moral purity. For Josephus, ritual purification after sexual relations was to be matched in a moral purity that precluded sexual misdeeds, and ritual purification after contact with a corpse was to correspond to moral purity from murder (*Ag. Ap.* 199–205). The correspondence between ritual and moral purity is so close for Josephus that the failure to observe ritual purity suggests to him a deficiency in moral life, as in the case of John of Gischala. In other words, for Josephus, if one shows piety toward God in the observance of ritual purification, one is likely to live in a manner pure from murderous sins against human beings. Philo is similar to Josephus in this respect, except that he associates ritual purity with the body and moral purity with the soul.[23] He also expands the scope of moral impurity to include all kinds of vices and passions. For Philo, the ritual purification of the body with water counts for nothing if it is not matched with the moral purification of the soul from vice and passion. Philo writes:

> For it is absurd that a man should be forbidden to enter the temples save after bathing and cleansing his body, and yet should attempt to pray and sacrifice with a heart still soiled and spotted. The temples are made of stones and timber, that is of soulless matter, and soulless too is the body in itself. And can it be that while it is forbidden to this soulless body to touch the soulless stones, except it have first been subjected to lustral and purificatory consecration, a man will not shrink from approaching with his soul impure the absolute purity of God and that too

---

[22] Mason finds that (im)purity and the cult form a cluster of themes integral to Josephus's *War*, which intertwine with Greek tragic elements and escalate throughout his account until the rebels' murder of their compatriots defiles the city with their blood, all while they claim as an ally the God whose dwelling they defiled ("Pollution and Purification in Josephus's Judean War," 181–207). Mason interprets these themes against Josephus's Roman context, even as he recognizes that Josephus's understanding of purity is not "simply Judean or simply Greek" (205). For a reading on the defilement of the temple by the sin of bloodshed that attends to its early Jewish context, see Klawans, *Josephus and the Theologies of Ancient Judaism*, 187–91.

[23] On the analogy in Philo between ritual and moral purity and its relation to his anthropology, see Klawans, *Impurity and Sin*, 64–6. However, whereas Klawans uses the term analogy is a relationship constructed between dissimilar things, I prefer the term correspondence, as it denotes a reciprocal relationship between similar things.

when there is no thought of repentance in his heart? (*Unchangeable* 8 [Colson and Whitaker])

For Philo, just as the body corresponds to the soul, so ritual purity ought to correspond to the moral purity needed for worship. Philo excoriates those who purify their bodies and not their souls as having an "impure purity" (ἀγνείαν ἄναγνον, *Cherubim* 94). Both Josephus and Philo, then, understood ritual purity as an analogue of moral purity. Attention to ritual purity could occasion evaluation of human action in terms of moral purity. Arguably, the correspondence drawn between ritual and moral purity in Josephus and Philo helps to explain how Jesus's washing of his disciples' feet relates to his judgment that they are pure.

Having considered how the language of purity figures into ethical discourse in Philo and Josephus, early Jewish testaments in which the language of (im)purity is employed for moral evaluation and instruction will now be analyzed, in particular, T. 12 Patr., the Testament of Qahat, and Abraham's speech in *Jub.* 20. The Fourth Gospel's Farewell Discourse for which the footwashing is a prelude resembles such early Jewish testaments, the defining feature of which is "that [a testament] is a discourse delivered in anticipation of imminent death" (Jn 13–17; cf., e.g., Gen. 49; Deut. 33:1–34:8; *Jub.* 20.1–23.7; T. 12 Patr.; T. Mos.).[24] As moral reflection and exhortation were common features of early Jewish testamentary literature, attention to the concept of moral purity in these texts may shed light on what Jesus predicates of his disciples in calling them pure.

Whatever else may be said about the ethics of the T. 12 Patr., its use of the language of (im)purity in ethical discourse is coherent with an early Jewish metaphoric network in which the language of purity encapsulates moral life in relation to the worship of Israel's God, with certain defiling sins demarcated as those by which relations between human beings and God are ruptured. The provenance and date of the T. 12 Patr. are highly contested. Whereas some scholars construe this as an early Jewish writing composed as early as the second century BCE and interpolated by early Christians, others argue it is an early Christian composition that incorporated early Jewish source material in the second century CE.[25] The matter will not be settled here, and is not

---

[24] John J. Collins, "Testaments," in *Jewish Writings of the Second Temple Period: Apocrypha, Pseudepigrapha, Qumran, Sectarian Writings, Philo, Josephus*, ed. Michael E. Stone (Assen: Van Gorcum; Philadelphia, PA: Fortress, 1984), 325. To be sure, the Farewell Discourse is not constricted to the literary form of the testament, since the Fourth Gospel is known to "bend genres," on which see Harold W. Attridge, "Genre Bending in the Fourth Gospel," *JBL* 121.1 (2002): 3–21. Furthermore, George L. Parsenios demonstrates that the Farewell Discourses is not confined to the testamentary genre by pointing out Greco-Roman generic figures such as the delayed exit in Jn 14:31 (*Departure and Consolation: The Johannine Farewell Discourses in Light of Greco-Roman Literature*, NovTSup 117 [Leiden: Brill, 2005], 1–76).

[25] See the summary of scholarship on the matter in Robert A. Kugler, *Testaments of the Twelve Patriarchs*, Guides to Apocrypha and Pseudepigrapha (Sheffield: Sheffield Academic, 2001), 31–8. On the early Jewish provenance of the T. 12 Patr., see, for example, Howard C. Kee, "Testaments of the Twelve Patriarchs," in *Old Testament Pseudepigrapha*, ed. James H. Charlesworth, vol. 1 (New York: Hendrickson, 1983), 776–8. The most vocal proponent of the Christian composition of the T. 12 Patr. is Marinus de Jonge. Of his many publications on the matter, see, for example, Marinus de Jonge, *Jewish Eschatology, Early Christian Christology and the Testaments of the Twelve Patriarchs: Collected Essays*, NovTSup 63 (Leiden: Brill, 1991), 233–43. Supporting de Jonge's

absolutely essential for the argument of this chapter. Suffice to say, if the former is the case, then the T. 12 Patr. provides corroborative evidence for how ancient Jews spoke about moral purity. If the latter, then these documents show one way in which the language of purity continued to be used within ethical discourse among early Christians. In either case, proponents of both early and late dates for T. 12 Patr. have found its ethics to be consistent with other early Jewish writings in Greek, such as 3–4 Maccabees and the Wisdom of Solomon.[26]

The T. 12 Patr. are framed as the legacy given by the sons of Jacob to their children (see, e.g., T. Benj. 10.2–4). Each testament is usually made up of three sections: the patriarch's reflections on his own life, the moral exhortations that he gives to his children, and an eschatological forecast, which often concerns the sin, exile and return of Israel from Babylon, but sometimes anticipates a savior who will come beyond that time.[27] It is no exaggeration to say that the purpose of the whole composition is ethical, as even the biographies are designed to be exemplary, with Joseph's life in particular being set forward as a pattern for the love of God and love of others (T. Benj. 3.1; cf. T. Jos. 17).[28]

The language of purity is used in the ethical discourse of T. 12 Patr. in ways largely consistent with what was seen in Philo and Josephus and can be summarized in three points. First, the language of impurity (ἀκαθαρσία, ἀκάθαρτος), defilement (μιαίνω), and abomination (βδέλυγμα) is used to describe certain defiling sins and the ruptured relation between the people and God caused by moral defilement. Counted among sins that defile are sexual misdeeds (T. Reu. 1.6; 4.6–8; 6.1; T. Levi 9.9; 14.6–15.1; T. Jos. 4.6), intentions to murder (T. Sim. 2.13), theft from God and from the poor (T. Levi 14.4–15.1; T. Ash. 2.5), and possibly idolatry (T. Reu. 4.6–8; T. Levi 17.8; T. Zeb. 9.5).[29] In T. Levi, the patriarch forecasts that on account of these defiling sins, "the sanctuary

---

contention from the perspective of material culture are the arguments of Kraft, who asserts that one should assume Christian provenance for manuscripts transmitted by Christians until persuasively argued otherwise; see Robert A. Kraft, *Exploring the Scripturesque: Jewish Texts and Their Christian Contexts*, JSJSup 137 (Leiden: Brill, 2009), 1–33; Robert A. Kraft, "Setting the Stage and Framing Some Central Questions," *JSJ* 32.4 (2001): 371–95. Building on Kraft's work, James Davila expounds on the complexity and ambiguity of the terms *Jewish* and *Christian* in discussion over the provenance of OT pseudepigrapha; see *The Provenance of the Pseudepigrapha: Jewish, Christian, or Other?*, JSJSup 105 (Boston: Brill, 2005), 2–73. My own view of the T. 12 Patr. aligns with that of Joel Marcus, who provides a modest corrective to de Jonge by arguing that it is a Jewish-Christian composition ("The Testaments of the Twelve Patriarchs and the Didascalia Apostolorum: A Common Jewish Christian Milieu?" *JTS* 61.2 [2010]: 596–626).

26. On the basis of correlation between the ethical language of Middle Stoicism and T. 12 Patriarchs, Howard C. Kee argues that the ethics of the latter may be located alongside other Hellenistic Jewish writings ("Ethical Dimensions of the Testaments of the XII as a Clue to Provenance," *NTS* 24.2 [1978]: 259–70). And, focusing on the way Joseph is an ethical exemplar, H. W. Hollander argues for the preeminence of ethics in the T. 12 Patr., and finds that its ethical vision discloses continuity between Hellenistic Jewish and early Christian ethics (*Joseph as an Ethical Model in the Testaments of the Twelve Patriarchs*, SVTP 6 [Leiden: Brill, 1981], 1–15).

27. This pattern in T. 12 Patr. is observed by Kugler, *Testaments*, 12–15.

28. So Kugler, who writes that "by most accounts ethics are the *Testaments*' central theme" (*Testaments*, 17).

29. Citations of the Greek text of T. 12 Patr. follow R. H. Charles, *The Greek Versions of the Testaments of the Twelve Patriarchs: Edited from Nine MSS Together with the Variants of the Armenian and Slavonic Versions and Some Hebrew Fragments* (Oxford: Clarendon Press, 1908).

which the Lord chose shall become desolate through your uncleanness (ἔρημος ἔσται ἐν ἀκαθαρσίᾳ), and you will be captives in all the nations" (15.1, [Kee]).[30] Second, the language of (moral) purity and purification (καθαρίζω, καθαρεύω, καθαρός) is used to denote the absence of sin in general and sexual misdeeds in particular (cf. T. Reu. 4.8; 6.1–2; T. Levi 14.2; T. Jos. 10.2) as well as the moral capacity to do God's will (cf. T. Ash. 4.4–5; T. Benj. 6.5–7; 8.1–3). The purity of one's life is related to the worship of God at a critical moment in Joseph's biography. When the Egyptian woman promises to convert to the worship of God if Joseph will have sexual intercourse with her, he tells her that

> the Lord did not want worshipers who come by means of uncleanness [ἐν ἀκαθαρσίᾳ], nor would he be pleased with adulterers [τοῖς μοιχεύουσιν], but with those who were pure in heart and undefiled in speech [ἀλλὰ τοῖς ἐν καθαρᾷ καρδίᾳ καὶ στόμασιν ἀμιάντοις αὐτῷ προσερχομένοις]. (T. Jos. 4.6)

Joseph's endurance in the face of temptation is presented as one of the exemplary aspects of his life, and is bound up with his speech about the moral purity needed for the Lord to be pleased with worship.

Finally, the language of (im)purity in T. 12 Patr. is employed to instruct readers about how to discern right conduct (T. Naph. 3.1; T. Ash. 2.1–4.5). In T. Naph., the purity of heart (καθαρότητι καρδίας) is necessary for understanding God's will, which is inscribed in creation's order. More interestingly, T. Ash. employs purity in the two-ways tradition of ethical discourse as a means of discernment in morally ambiguous situations, as in the case of a person who is economically exploitative, but charitable to the poor (T. Ash. 2.5).[31] Such action "defiles the soul" (τὴν ψυχὴν σπιλοῖ), and such people are compared to rabbits and wild pigs. They appear "half pure" (ἐξ ἡμισείας εἰσὶ καθαροί) but "in truth they are impure" (ἀληθὲς ἀκάθαρτοί εἰσιν, 2.9). By contrast, those whose zeal for good involves the destruction of evil are likened to gazelles and deer, because they seem impure (δοκοῦσιν ἀκάθαρτοι), but, in fact, are wholly pure (πᾶν καθαροί εἰσιν, 4.5). Thus, by analogy to the dietary laws, the language of purity is used to evaluate moral character and action.

The concept of moral purity is also employed in the ethical discourse of the fragmentary Testament of Qahat and the farewell discourse of Abraham in *Jubilees*. In the Testament of Qahat, to align oneself with Jacob's legacy is first and foremost to be "holy and pure from all [uncleannesses] … complying with the truth and walking in uprightness and not with a double heart, but with a pure heart and with a truthful and good spirit" (4Q542 1.10b–13). In this moral exhortation, righteous conduct requires a pure heart and good spirit, which is perhaps an echo of the psalmist's prayer for God to restore a pure heart and right spirit to the penitent (Ps. 51:10).

The most remarkable moral use of the language of purity in view of the Fourth Gospel is in one of Abraham's final speeches in *Jubilees*. In Abraham's testamentary speech, moral impurity is defined in opposition to the love and worship of God.

---

[30] Unless otherwise noted, translations of T. 12 Patr. follow Howard C. Kee, *OTP* 1:782–828.
[31] On the use of the tradition of the two ways in T. Ash., see Collins, "Testaments," 336–7; Kee, "Ethical Dimensions," 266.

Abraham exhorts those gathered around him to "guard yourself from all fornication and impurity, and from all corruption of sin," for which the alternative is to "love the God of heaven and be joined to all of his commandments" (*Jub.* 20.6–7). This is followed by a warning not to "go after their idols and after their defilement," but, instead, to "worship the Most High God" (20.7, 9). So moral impurity is produced by certain defiling sins— sexual misdeeds and idolatry in particular—and the form of action commended as an alternative is the love of God, the keeping of God's commandments, and the worship of God. In such things, moral purity consists. This contrast is particularly interesting for John's Gospel, since the disciples whom Jesus calls pure are closely thereafter commanded to love one another as Jesus had loved them (13:34–35; 15:12–17), and the disciple whom Jesus did not call pure is characterized as one defiled by sin—a thief (Jn 12:6) and one complicit in the death of Jesus (see, e.g., 12:4; 13:21–30).

The moral use of the language of purity in these writings may be summarized in terms of ethics, theology, and relationship to ritual purity. First, the language of (im)purity in these early Jewish writings is used with consistency in ethical contexts, being associated primarily with bloodshed, sexual misdeeds, idolatry, and theft from the poor. Those who do such things could not be more morally impure, and those who are unsullied by defiling sins and devoted to the love of God are pure. Philo is exceptional insofar as he expands moral impurity to include passions and vice, but traditional insofar as he conceives of passions and vice as subsets of the defiling sin of idolatry. Second, while the language of purity is used in ethical contexts to evaluate human action or commend certain patterns of human conduct, the language is nevertheless theologically charged. In contrast to more ordinary sins, the practice of defiling sin definitively ruptures the relationship between the people and God. In such contexts, the language of purity is at once ethical and theological. So, for instance, Josephus's claim that God caused the Romans to destroy the temple is warranted by bloodshed in its precincts. Similarly, Philo's connection between moral life and worship is established by linking the moral purity of worshippers to the preciousness of their sacrifices in God's sight. Third, moral (im)purity does not replace ritual (im)purity in these early Jewish writings, and ritual and moral purity are not thought to contradict one another.[32] Instead, Philo and Josephus construct a relationship of correspondence between ritual and moral purity. For Josephus, the observance of ritual purity mirrors the moral purity characterized by regard for human and animal life. And Philo appeals to the necessity of one's bodily ritual purity in order to emphasize the indispensability of the moral purity of one's soul. For this reason, rites of ritual purification could occasion reflection on moral character and action in terms of moral purity.

Turning toward the analysis of the disciples' purity and impurity in the Fourth Gospel, there are three primary points of affinity with the preceding exploration of moral purity. First, the reason given for Judas not being counted among the pure is

---

[32] It has been noted that the T. 12 Patr. neglect significant attention to the laws of ritual purity, which is true. Even so, T. Levi references priestly washings (8.5; 9.11), and the ethical use of the levitical dietary laws depends on the legitimacy of the classification of some animals as pure and others as impure (T. Ash. 4.1–5). On this matter see Dixon Slingerland, "The Nature of Nomos (Law) within the Testaments of the Twelve Patriarchs," *JBL* 105.1 (1986): 45–6.

his betrayal of Jesus to the death. Judas is defiled by his intention to shed innocent blood and (eventually) by his complicity in the death of Jesus (13:2, 10–11). The Fourth Gospel's unique portrayal of Judas as one who stole from the poor also underscores the defilement of Judas by sin (12:6). In other words, Judas's impurity on account of bloodshed is explicable in terms of an early Jewish concept of moral impurity. No murderer could be morally pure, and even the intention to murder was sometimes thought to be defiling sin (see, e.g., T. Sim. 2.13–14; Philo, *Spec. Laws* 3.208–209). Second, similar to the way that moral purity is understood as indispensable to honoring God in Philo, Josephus, T. 12 Patr., and *Jub.*, in the Fourth Gospel the disciples' purity is spoken of in close connection to their keeping of the commandment that Jesus gave them, namely, that they love one another (13:34–35; 15:12). Third, Jesus evaluates the moral purity of his disciples just before a Passover for which they had likely already been ritually purified (11:55). Not unlike other early Jewish writings, the Fourth Gospel maintains a difference *and* correspondence between ritual and moral purity. All these points of affinity will be treated at more length presently.

4.2 The Purity of Jesus's Disciples

Only in the Fourth Gospel does Jesus call his disciples pure. He says to his disciples, "you are pure" as he is washing their feet, and again afterward when he speaks to them with the image of vine and branches. In both instances, Jesus's words about his disciples' purity are placed just before the Passover. The association between Passover and purity is well attested. Josephus, for example, remarks that almost three million people would travel to Jerusalem to celebrate the Passover, "all being pure and holy" (καθαρῶν ἁπάντων καὶ ἁγίων, *J.W.* 6.425), and Philo interprets Passover allegorically in terms of the "purification of the soul" (ψυχῆς κάθαρσιν, *Spec. Laws* 2.147–8). As was mentioned, this is the third Passover that is narrated in the Fourth Gospel, but the only one in which ritual purity is foregrounded.[33] In fact, the arrival of this Passover is first announced along with the practice of ritual purification, as "many went up from the country to Jerusalem before the Passover to purify themselves" (ἀνέβησαν ... πρὸ τοῦ πάσχα ἵνα ἁγνίσωσιν ἑαυτούς, 11:55). Although the ritual purification of the disciples is not narrated, it is difficult to imagine that Jesus and his disciples were not also already in a state of ritual purity in preparation for the Passover. This setting during the Passover brings the moral purity of the disciples into focus through attention to their ritual purity. As in Philo and Josephus, where ritual purity is thought to correspond to moral purity, so in the footwashing does Peter's focus on washing for ritual purification make room for reflection on the disciples' moral purity. I will first argue that the footwashing is not the *cause* of the disciples' ritual or moral purity, but

---

[33] Busse argues that purity in the Fourth Gospel is connected to Jesus's renewal of the temple, with the disciples' purity making possible worship even after the Jerusalem temple was destroyed ("Reinigung und Heiligung," 147, 157–8). This does seem to be implicit in the Fourth Gospel. In my analysis, however, I try to follow the Fourth Gospel's emphases on purity, which, interestingly, are not explicitly connected to the temple's renewal, but instead to the disciples of Jesus.

is the *setting* that occasions Jesus's judgment that his disciples are (already) morally pure, with the exception of Judas. I will deal with ritual purity in this section because it is suggested by the language of bathing and washing, but the function of ritual purity in the footwashing is to bring forth Jesus's judgment about his disciples' moral purity. I will then show that Judas is disqualified from among the morally pure on account of his complicity in a sin that ancient Jews widely regarded as defiling, namely, bloodshed. By contrast, the disciples whom Jesus calls pure are to have lives that are morally pure, characterized by the kind of lowly love Jesus demonstrated for them in the footwashing, and, subsequently, in laying down his life on the cross.

4.2.1 One Who Has Bathed Is Entirely (Ritually) Pure

The footwashing did not cause the disciples to become ritually or morally pure. The time of Passover suggests they were ritually pure already. Furthermore, the disciples (Judas excepted) were morally pure already on account of Jesus's ministry of restoration, as was argued in Chapter 3. There are simply no warrants in early Jewish practice or thought to conceptualize footwashing as an act that makes pure from sin, even if some evidence suggests early Christians came to regard footwashing in such a way.[34] Instead, what may be said about footwashing and purity in light of early Jewish evidence is that footwashing was at most an incomplete act of ritual purification when practiced on its own.[35] Nearly every ancient Jewish text that mentions the washing of feet for ritual purification also mentions the washing of hands. What is more, the washing of feet and hands pertains only to priests as they prepare for their liturgical duties in the temple (Exod. 30:17–21; 40:30–32; *Jub.* 21.15–17; Philo, *Moses,* 2.138; Josephus, *Ant.* 3.114; 8:85–87; m. Yoma 3:2–3).[36] One notable exception is Philo's reference to a saying about how those with unwashed feet defiled the places where they walked (*Spec. Laws* 2.6). This suggests that the feet were sometimes washed to maintain an otherwise complete ritual purity. Moreover, Deines has catalogued the discovery in Jerusalem of several footbaths placed next to the entrance of pools built for ritual immersion, which he takes as an indication that footwashing accompanied the bathing of the whole body.[37] So footwashing was at most a marginal, ritual purification. It may be thought

---

[34] Thomas argues that the footwashing signified the removal of post-baptismal sin for the Johannine community and for some early Christians (*Footwashing in John,* 150–77). But see the critique of Thomas's reading of the patristic evidence in Bauckham, *The Testimony of the Beloved Disciple,* 205–6, who interprets the footwashing as a radical reversal of social hierarchy.

[35] Footwashing on its own is often practiced as a form of hospitality, as Arland J. Hultgren pointed out based on texts such as Gen. 18:4, 1 Sam. 25:41, and Lk. 7:44 ("The Johannine Footwashing [Jn 13:1–11] as Symbol of Eschatological Hospitality," *NTS* 28.4 [1982]: 539–46). Based on Hultgren and her own earlier work, Mary L. Coloe develops a reading of the footwashing as one aspect of Jesus's welcome of his disciples into the household of God ("Welcome into the Household of God: The Foot Washing in John 13," *CBQ* 66.3 [2004]: 400–15).

[36] For these primary source references on the washing of feet in cultic contexts, I am indebted to Bincy Mathew, *The Johannine Footwashing as the Sign of Perfect Love: An Exegetical Study of John 13:1–20,* WUNT 2/464 (Tübingen: Mohr Siebeck, 2018), 82–6, 52–4. The two exceptions I found to my claim are P. Oxy 840 and Philo's *QE* 1.2, which mention only the washing of feet. Even so, in every case, priests would wash their own feet, rather than having their feet washed by another.

[37] Deines, *Jüdische Steingefässe,* 92–3.

of as nothing more than a way to maintain an otherwise complete condition of ritual purity.[38]

The insufficiency of footwashing for ritual purification is perhaps why Peter inexplicably shifts from resisting the washing of his feet ("You will never wash my feet," 13:8) to requesting additional washing by Jesus: "Lord, not my feet only [μὴ τοὺς πόδας μου μόνον] but also my hands and my head!" (13:9). Peter's request for these washings appears to be a request for a more complete ritual purification.[39] To be sure, there is no extant historical precedent for the ritual purification of hands, feet, and head together. It seems, rather, that these three parts of the body may have sometimes stood for the whole person, as in the anointing of priests on ear, thumb, and toe with blood and oil (Lev. 14:14, 17).[40] Since there was not likely to have been a pool built for ritual immersion at hand, the washing of head, hands, and feet might have been the closest Peter thought he could get to being wholly ritually purified by Jesus. But the rationale for Peter's request for additional washing is opaque, particularly because he was likely already in a state of ritual purity and because he had only moments before he resisted the washing of his feet at all. Perhaps Peter thought he needed all the washing he could get after Jesus's foreboding words that "unless I wash you, you have no share with me" (13:8). Peter's self-consciousness about his condition of ritual purity is not unfounded. Ancient Jews were expected to be able to discern whether they were ritually pure, particularly during holy times and at holy places. The levitical injunction that the people were to learn to distinguish between the ritually impure and pure had taken root in early Jewish imagination (Lev. 10:10–11; cf. Ezek. 22:26). Philo remarks that the failure to make such distinctions is "the way of lawlessness" (*Drunkenness* 143), and Josephus expects that people will know their condition of ritual impurity and avoid crossing certain boundaries of holiness in Jerusalem (*J. W.* 5.193–199; 227–229; 236).[41] Since the disciples were in Jerusalem just before the Passover and ritual purification for the feast involved multiple ablutions and washings (cf. *Spec. Laws* 1.261), Peter's concern about whether he was actually ritually pure is understandable, even if he turned out to have discerned wrongly that he was not already ritually pure.

---

[38] On the footwashing as "supplementing" an otherwise complete purification see Thomas, *Footwashing in John*, 114, 192. Also Thompson, who based on the footwashing's relation to Jesus's death, speaks of his death as "completing" the disciples' purification, which would mean that at the time of the footwashing their (moral) purification would already have been nearly complete (*John: A Commentary*, 282).

[39] Similarly, Brown, *The Gospel according to John*, 2:566.

[40] Philo interprets the anointing of the right ear, hand, and foot of priests as a symbol of the whole person's purification, writing, "in this figure, he indicated that the fully-consecrated must be pure in words and actions and in his whole life (δεῖ τὸν τέλειον καὶ λόγῳ καὶ ἔργῳ καὶ βίῳ παντὶ καθαρεύειν); for words are judged by the hearing, the hand is a symbol of action, and the foot of the pilgrimage of life" (*Moses* 2.150 [Colson]).

[41] Similarly, both m. Kelim 1:6–9 and the Temple Scroll give instructions regarding who may go where depending on their condition of ritual impurity, on which see Orian, "Josephus's Seven Purities and the Mishnah's Ten Holinesses," 183–211. Balberg, furthermore, argues that the mishnaic expansion of the observance of purity, which caused persons to attend carefully and continually to their state of ritual purity, worked to construct a particular kind of self in relation to the Torah (*Purity, Body, and Self*, 3).

A more plausible interpretation, though, for why Peter suddenly moves from resisting to requesting washing is that Peter did not want to receive the footwashing as an act of lowly service, so he wrongly reinterpreted it as just one step in a special purifying rite administered by one who was above him. Interestingly, prior to Peter's request for the washing of his hands and head, purity did not figure into the account of the footwashing. The dialogue was wholly absorbed with attention to the social scandal of Jesus's washing of his disciples' feet. Peter initiates the dialogue:

> He came to Simon Peter, who said to him, "Lord, are you going to wash [νίπτω] my feet?"
> Jesus answered, "You do not know now what I am doing, but later you will understand."
> Peter said to him, "You will never wash [νίπτω] my feet."
> Jesus answered, "Unless I wash you [νίπτω], you have no share with me."
> (Jn 13:6–8)

As both Bincy Mathew and John Christopher Thomas have demonstrated, in ancient Jewish and Greco-Roman contexts, footwashing was a lowly act of service that was always administered by those of inferior social status, unless one was to wash one's own feet. Jesus's act is simply unprecedented in the ancient world, and radical insofar as Jesus practices lowly service for those who called him Lord (cf. 13:12–17).[42] The social scandal of Jesus washing feet is not lost on Peter, apparent in his two-fold address of Jesus as Lord (κύριος, 13:6, 9), the emphatic use and position of pronouns as he resists Jesus's act of lowly service (σύ μου νίπτεις τοὺς πόδας, 13:6), and his resistance to Jesus washing his feet at all (13:8).[43] In light of this resistance to Jesus's lowly service, Peter's request for the washing of head and hands in addition to his feet is surprising. It makes sense, however, if one finds in Peter's request a relocation of footwashing from a conceptual schema of service (in which Jesus is a lowly servant) to purification (in which Jesus is a special agent, not unlike John the Baptist was before him). That is, Peter can resolve his cognitive dissonance by reimagining foowashing as purification rather than service.

Jesus's refusal to wash Peter's hands and head is predicated on the fact that Peter and the other disciples were already ritually pure on account of having already bathed. Jesus answers Peter in such a way that denies his request for the washing of his head and hands while insisting on the washing of his feet:

---

[42] Both Mathew and Thomas review almost all of the same ancient texts related to footwashing, both finding that footwashing was practiced for the sake of cultic practice, hygiene, and hospitality. Mathew also finds that footwashing is sometimes an expression of love. Mathew does more analytical work than Thomas to show how she interprets footwashing in those ancient texts, and she critically assesses how the Fourth Gospel's representation of the footwashing relates to its ancient context. Among the conclusions they share is the utter uniqueness of the Fourth Gospel's account of a person of superior social status washing the feet of an inferior. See Mathew, *The Johannine Footwashing*, 69–127; Thomas, *Footwashing in John*, 17–54.

[43] I owe these observations to Marianne Meye Thompson, "'His Own Received Him Not': Jesus Washes the Feet of His Disciples," in *The Art of Reading Scripture*, ed. Ellen F. Davis and Richard B. Hays (Grand Rapids, MI: Eerdmans, 2003), 265–6.

Jesus said to him, "One who has bathed [ὁ λελουμένος] does not need to wash [νίπτω], except for the feet [εἰ μὴ τοὺς πόδας], but is entirely pure [ἔστιν καθαρὸς ὅλος]. (13:10a)

Until this point in the dialogue, Jesus has addressed Peter in the second-person singular, which gives this third-person statement about one who bathes a proverbial quality. In that respect, it is not unlike other sayings in the Fourth Gospel where Jesus appeals to received wisdom—such as the way the wind blows (3:8), the disparity between sowers and reapers (4:37–38), and the need to work while it is day (9:4)—in order to disclose some kind of truth to his hearers.[44] In other words, Jesus's statement is not referential in the sense of pointing to one particular moment when Peter was bathed, but proverbial in the sense that Jesus is reminding Peter of the way the world works.[45] Jesus communicates to Peter a common levitical principle: "one who has bathed … is entirely pure" (ὁ λελουμένος … ἔστιν καθαρὸς ὅλος; 13:10).[46] In Israel's priestly tradition, a man ritually defiled by a discharge of semen (Lev. 15:8, 13 LXX) or persons made ritually impure by skin disease or contact with a corpse (Lev. 14:9; Num. 19:19 LXX), were (among other things) to bathe with water (λούω) and thus find themselves ritually pure (καθαρός; cf., e.g., Philo, *Dreams*, 1.81; Josephus, *J.W.* 2.129). Jesus appeals to the basic causal relation between washing with water and the ritual purification of the body to remind Peter of his own ritual purity.[47] If the body is bathed with water then it is ritually pure. So, on account of his complete ritual purity—except for the feet—Jesus rebuts Peter's request that he wash his hands and head, but prevails on him about his feet being washed. Like the other *Ioudaioi* who had traveled

[44] On wind as a figure of incomprehensibility and the proverbial saying about sowers and reapers, see, for example, Bultmann, *The Gospel of John*, 142, fn. 3; 198; on the need to work while it is day as proverbial wisdom, see Dodd, *Historical Tradition*, 186.

[45] Jn 13:10a has proved immensely challenging for interpreters, whose search for the referent(s) of λούω and νίπτω is frustrated by the fact that the Fourth Gospel nowhere narrates the purification of these disciples, either by bathing or washing. Mathew chronicles seven different scholarly proposals for the referent of λούω—including different kinds of baptisms or ablutions, or else the word of Jesus, discipleship, or Jesus's death—and eleven different interpretations of the meaning of νίπτω—including variations on the Eucharist, the removal of sin, and Jesus's death (*The Johannine Footwashing*, 58–9).

[46] Syntactically, it is clear that ὁ λελουμένος is the implied subject in the clause ἀλλ' ἔστιν καθαρὸς ὅλος. Brower also finds in the first part of Jesus's response to Peter an appeal to levitical teaching on ritual purity ("Purity in the Gospel of John," 124). Although Jean Owanga-Welo also reads 13:10a as a proverbial statement, he focuses on the relationship between bathing and washing by appeal to Roman bathing practices, whereas I focus on the relationship between bathing and purity by appeal to the early Jewish association between immersion in water and purification ("The Function and Meaning of the Footwashing in the Johannine Passion Narrative: A Structural Approach" [PhD diss., Emory University, 1980], 239–41).

[47] Not unlike the supersessionistic interpretation of purity at Cana still repeated today, studies of the footwashing in the early twentieth century tended to interpret Jn 13:10 as a polemic against ritual purifications of various kinds, claiming that Jesus's purifying death rendered these purifications superfluous (on which, see Georg Richter, "Die Fußwaschung Joh 13, 1–20," *MTZ* 16.1–2 [1965]: 15–16). Against these interpretations, one may observe here Jesus's reception and validation of the practice and effectiveness of ritual purification with water, while, at the same time, using this focus on ritual purity to reflect on the disciples' moral purity.

to Jerusalem for the feast to purify themselves, Peter and the disciples were already entirely ritually pure, except for their feet (11:55; 18:28).

When the focus falls on the rest of Jesus's proverbial statement—that the parts of a pure body need no washing, except for the feet—two critical issues come to the forefront. The first is a matter of textual criticism, namely, whether the phrase εἰ μὴ τοὺς πόδας belongs to the initial text (Jn 13:10). The second is whether the terms λούω and νίπτω are synonyms. The two matters are interconnected. Codex Siniaticus is the most significant witness to the shorter reading: ὁ λελουμένος οὐκ ἔχει χρείαν νίψασθαι, ἀλλ᾽ ἔστιν καθαρὸς ὅλος, which may be translated as "the one who is bathed does not have need to wash, but is completely pure." The shorter reading suggests that bathing (λούω) makes pure, to the effect that any kind of washing (νίπτω) is superfluous, thereby making the two verbs more or less synonymous.[48] However, the longer reading is much to be preferred on the basis of the external evidence, with variations of this reading preserved in B, 𝔓[66], and 𝔓[75].[49] Moreover, in his careful study of six papyri, including 𝔓[66] and 𝔓[75], James Royse concludes that scribes were more likely to omit text than to add to it, which suggests that the longer reading is more likely to belong with the earliest attainable text.[50] When one interprets Jesus's statement with the inclusion of the phrase εἰ μὴ τοὺς πόδας, it disposes one to distinguish between the terms λούω and νίπτω, with the former denoting full immersion and the latter the washing of only part of the body, a distinction maintained in a number of early Jewish writings in Greek.[51] In light of this, we might freely paraphrase Jesus's proverbial response to Peter's request that his head and hands also be washed (13:10a): "Peter, as is well known, one who has ritually bathed in water is already ritually pure, the only exception being the feet, which are washed to maintain an otherwise complete ritual purity."

Given that the narrator frames the footwashing as an act of love that Jesus undertakes in anticipation of his death (13:1–5) and has Jesus go on to explain the footwashing in terms of lowly service (13:12–20), it would seem that Peter's interpretation of the footwashing as an act of purification is somewhat beside the point. The footwashing does not primarily function as an act of purification, but rather, an act of lowly service

---

[48] For example, Bultmann interprets λούω allegorically as the disciples' faith or the word of Jesus, such that even Christian baptism is displaced (*The Gospel of John*, 470–3). Brown understands λούω as the footwashing and on that basis interprets the death of Jesus as a purification from sin, to the exclusion of any other washing besides Christian baptism (*The Gospel according to John*, 2:566–8).

[49] For a table of variant readings in textual witnesses see Mathew, *The Johannine Footwashing*, 41–3. Mathew compellingly argues for the longer reading, marshaling evidence from manuscript traditions and archeology as well as appealing to grammatical and lexicographical considerations (41–68).

[50] James R. Royse, *Scribal Habits in Early Greek New Testament Papyri, Scribal Habits in Early Greek New Testament Papyri*, NTTSD 36 (Brill, 2007), 710–36. Royse goes so far as to say that "the longer reading is to be preferred, except where: 1) the longer reading appears, on external grounds, to be late; or 2) the longer reading may have arisen from harmonization to the immediate context, to parallels, or to general usage; or 3) the longer reading may have arisen from an attempt at grammatical improvement" (735). None of these exceptions apply to the longer reading in Jn 13:10.

[51] See the citation and analysis of the distinction between these two terms in Lev. 15:11 LXX, Tobit 7:9, Philo, *Dreams* 1.148, T. Levi 9:11-12, and P. Oxy. 840 in Mathew, *The Johannine Footwashing*, 48–55, who concludes that in every instance (with the possible exception of P. Oxy 840) a distinction between them is maintained in terms of the scope of the action.

in love. The footwashing demonstrates that there is no depth to which the love of God will not descend to bring life to the world.[52] That is, as van der Watt argues, the love of Jesus (13:1) and the love of the disciples for one another (13:34–35) indicate that the footwashing is about the intensity of Jesus's love expressed in lowly service.[53] Love's presence in the debasement of washing feet signals how the love of God can be given in Jesus's laying down of his life on the cross. What Peter cannot understand until after Jesus is glorified in the cross and resurrection is that love's form in the world is a life-giving death (see, e.g., 3:16; 13:1, 7; 15:13).[54] Peter's reception of Jesus's lowly act of washing feet would signify his willingness to receive the death of Jesus as an act of God's love, and thus secure his place with Jesus in the future. For these reasons, Culpepper suggests that the footwashing "functions metaphorically and proleptically in relation to Jesus' death."[55] After that death, Peter will understand that the share he was to have with Jesus would be to lay down his own life for God's glory, having loved Jesus and tended to his sheep (13:8; cf. 13:34–38; 20:15–19).[56] Everything a reader needs in order to associate the footwashing with the death of Jesus has been given prior to the introduction of purity into the dialogue: how Jesus's knowledge of his death precipitates the footwashing (13:1–5), how the footwashing anticipates things to come (13:7), and how Peter's heritage with Jesus is conditioned on receiving his lowly act of love in washing his disciples' feet (13:8). Jesus's responses to Peter's resistance defer the meaning of the footwashing until a later time, namely, when his death reveals God's work of love for the world. Jesus's act of lowly love is the pattern of life to which his morally pure disciples are to conform.[57] In other words, the footwashing does not cause the disciples' moral purity, but it does show in what that moral purity consists.

---

[52] M. E. Boismard influentially argued that the footwashing is portrayed in 13:6–10 as a prefiguration of the sacrament of baptism, which was a later addition to the ethical teaching in 13:12–20 ("Le lavement des pieds [Jn 13:1–17]," *RB* 71.1 [1964]: 5–24). In her survey of recent scholarship on the footwashing, Bincy Mathew finds that scholars tend to interpret the action of footwashing either soteriologically or sacramentally (*The Johannine Footwashing*, 12–38). The sacramental interpretation of Jn 13:6–11 seems doubtful to me both because of the deliberate connection between the footwashing and Jesus's death (13:1–5) and the intelligibility of the language of washing and bathing in terms of early Jewish concepts of purity, quite apart from reference to Christian baptism.

[53] Jan G. van der Watt, "The Meaning of Jesus Washing the Feet of His Disciples (John 13)," *Neot* 51.1 (2017): 25–39.

[54] I owe the reading of this dialogue in terms of God's love in Jesus and Peter's resistance primarily to Thompson, "His Own Received Him Not," 265; and van der Watt, "The Meaning of Jesus Washing the Feet of His Disciples," 25–39.

[55] R. Alan Culpepper, "The Johannine *Hypodeigma*: A Reading of John 13," *Semeia* 53 (1991): 139.

[56] Drawing attention to the oft-neglected temporal dimension of Johannine ethics, Olivia Rahmsdorf examines how the Fourth Gospel characterizes Peter as one "out of time," arguing that Peter surmised the washing of his feet was a sign of a death that he was not yet ready to undergo (" 'You Shall Not Wash My Feet εἰς τὸν αἰῶνα' [John 13.8]: Time and Ethics in Peter's Interactions with Jesus in the Johannine Narrative," *JSNT* 41.4 [2019]: 458–77, 470).

[57] Fernando F. Segovia advances a forceful argument for the incommensurability of 13:6–10 and 13:12–20, arguing that "harmonizing approaches" have not adequately dealt with eight problematic features for the text's unity, the most significant of which to my mind is that the former makes footwashing indicative of a singular, saving event and the latter makes it a repetitive, communal practice ("Jn 13:1–20: The Footwashing in the Johannine Tradition," *ZNW* 73.1–2 [1982]: 31–7). But the interpretive tendency in which soteriological and ethical aspects of the text are bifurcated is best answered with recognition of what Thompson refers to as "the intrinsic connection between

4.2.2 You Are (Morally) Pure—But Not All of You

To this point, I have sought to show that the footwashing does not *cause* the disciples' moral or ritual purity, but it does occasion reflection on ritual purity. That reflection on ritual purity, as will be presently argued, leads by analogy into Jesus's evaluation of the disciples' moral purity:

> Jesus said to him, "One who has bathed [ὁ λελουμένος] does not need to wash [νίπτω], except for the feet [εἰ μὴ τοὺς πόδας], but is entirely pure [ἔστιν καθαρὸς ὅλος]. And you are pure, though not all of you" [καὶ ὑμεῖς καθαροί ἐστε, ἀλλ᾽ οὐχὶ πάντες]. For he knew who was to betray him; for this reason he said, "Not all of you are pure" [οὐχὶ πάντες καθαροί ἐστε]. (13:10–11 NRSV, trans. mod.)

As was seen, Jesus explains to Peter that he does not need a complete bathing because one who has bathed with water is already ritually pure, except for the feet (13:10a). But then Jesus immediately follows with a statement about the disciples' purity that excludes Judas for reasons unrelated to ritual purity (13:10b–11). That is, Jesus transitions from a third-person statement about the causal relation between washing with water and ritual purity to a second-person plural statement evaluating the disciples' moral purity, with Judas's complicity in Jesus's death given as the reason he is not included among the pure. The twelve disciples had all been bathed, apparently, and Jesus washed the feet of all of them. And yet, only eleven of them are called pure by Jesus. As with Philo, Josephus, and the T. 12 Patr., reflection on ritual purity gives way to consideration of moral purity. There is correspondence between the ritual and moral purity of the disciples, except in the case of Judas, where there is a disjunction. Judas is in the contradictory condition of "impure purity" (cf. *Cherubim* 94).[58] All this is to be explored in more depth presently.

Jesus's statement to the disciples, "you are pure, though not all of you," is the first time that the dialogue between Peter and Jesus opens up to the rest of the disciples, as indicated by the second-person plural address as well as Jesus's qualification that not *all* of his disciples are pure. Some interpreters have sensed a contrast between the purity God gives to the disciples through Jesus and the ritual purification effected by washing with water, so that the former represents God's free gift of salvation, while the latter reflects human attempts to make oneself righteous before God.[59] This reading of purity cannot be warranted by the language of purity in its early Jewish context. As was seen in the earlier selection of early Jewish writings, moral purity is inseparable

God's action in Christ, which constitutes the community of his followers, and the life of that community" (cf. 14:12–21; 15:1–8); see "His Own Received Him Not," 259.

58　It seems likely that the *Ioudaioi* who maintained ritual purity for the Passover even as they were complicit in Jesus's death with Judas were also in a state of impure purity, that is, they are represented as ritually pure and morally impure (Jn 18:28).

59　One recent example of this reading is from Stare, who I think is incorrect in her assumption that ritual purification was an attempt to "sich … den Zugang zu Gott selbst verschaffen," but right in her assertion that the purity of Jesus's disciples is the result of God's work in Jesus ("Die Reinheitsthematik," 89, 92). Brown, with tacit approval, refers to past interpreters who understood 13:10 as a polemic against washings of various kinds (*The Gospel according to John*, 2:566).

from Israel's life before God. And, as will be seen, the language of moral (im)purity was sometimes used to articulate the need for unilateral divine action for anthropological transformation, that is, a change in humanity that would make human beings capable of reflecting God's holiness without any blemish or adulteration. So Jesus is not replacing an early Jewish discourse of purity with something new and unprecedented, but indicating to Peter and the rest of the disciples that the moral purity that was to come with Israel's restoration is theirs already—or not. One may discern a movement of correspondence between the two sentences. Just as all the disciples are completely, ritually pure (except for the feet), so are all the disciples morally pure (except for Judas). The move between ritual and moral purity is similar to Isaiah's call to "wash yourselves; become pure" (λούσασθε, καθαροὶ γένεσθε; Isa. 1:16 LXX; cf. Jer. 4:14), or the Psalmist's plea for God to "wash me thoroughly from my lawlessness and from my sin purify me" (ἐπὶ πλεῖον πλῦνόν με ἀπὸ τῆς ἀνομίας μου καὶ ἀπὸ τῆς ἁμαρτίας μου καθάρισόν με, Ps. 50:4 NETS, trans. mod.). But whereas those texts employ the language of ritual purity metaphorically to speak of purification from sin, Jesus moves from speaking of ritual purification as such to predicating moral purity of his disciples. One could say that the footwashing is the setting of Jesus's words about the disciples' moral purity, but not the cause of that purity. That is, they are morally pure already before the footwashing, and Jesus only discloses this to them at the footwashing.

Before attending to the moral purity predicated of the disciples, it will be beneficial to understand the grounds given for Judas's impurity, so that by contrast we can deduce the character of the disciples' purity. The narrator explains that Jesus qualified his statement about the purity of the disciples on account of his knowledge of Judas's imminent betrayal: "for (γὰρ) he knew who was to betray him; for this reason (διὰ τοῦτο) he said, 'Not all of you are pure'" (οὐχὶ πάντες καθαροί ἐστε, 13:11 NRSV, trans. mod.). What sort of impurity is implicit in such an act as handing Jesus over to the death?[60] Ritual impurity, ordinarily caused by semen or menstrual blood, skin disease, or contact with corpses, is excluded. Judas's impurity must be the defilement caused by sin.[61] Judas was complicit with devil in the death of Jesus (13:2, 27), so that his hands are stained with blood. Although he had not yet handed over Jesus to the death, the intention to murder was enough to defile him (Jn 13:2; cf. T. Sim. 2.13–14; Philo, *Spec. Laws* 3.208–209). Bloodshed, as was seen earlier, was chief among those sins conceptualized as defiling. And Judas is portrayed in the Fourth Gospel as chief among those who handed over Jesus to death (6:64, 70–71; 12:4; 13:2, 21; 18:2), thus making him complicit in bloodshed. He is also exposed by the narrator to be a thief who stole from gifts to the poor (Jn 12:6), and theft was sometimes also considered a

---

[60] On the translation of the term παραδίδωμι as *handing over* in the Fourth Gospel, such that it denotes Judas's complicity in the death of Jesus with some implication of betrayal, see the discussion in Thompson, *John: A Commentary*, 161.

[61] Stare rightly notes that the disciples' purity is a result of God's work in Jesus ("Die Reinheitsthematik," 88–90). This makes Judas's impurity and complicity in Jesus's death a theological problem for the Fourth Gospel. Perhaps it is enough to point out that the Fourth Gospel treats it as a problem, invoking a number of different agencies in its representation of Judas's act, including the devil (13:2, 27), Scripture (13:18), and soldiers, chief priests, and Pharisees (18:1-11).

defiling sin (cf. Jer. 7:9–10; *Ant.* 5.42; T. Levi 14.4–15.1; T. Ash. 2.5). Because of these moral deficiencies, Judas cannot possibly be considered morally pure.

Interestingly, although Judas is complicit in the death of Jesus, he is not blamed for it. Jesus has already told his disciples that "no one takes [my life] from me, but I lay it down of my own accord. I have power to lay it down [τίθημι], and I have power to take it up again [λαμβάνω]" (10:18). This saying is echoed in Jesus's laying aside of his robes before the footwashing (τίθημι, 13:5), and taking them up again afterward (λαμβάνω, 13:12).[62] Judas cannot take away the life of Jesus, but his complicity in the death of Jesus will be for him a practically incurable impurity. That is, Judas is judged by Jesus not to be among the pure on moral grounds.

Unlike each disciple that Jesus called pure, Judas will not do as Jesus had modeled in the footwashing and enter blessedness alongside the other disciples. Just as Jesus qualifies his statement that his disciples are pure by pointing to the one exception (13:10–11), so Jesus qualifies his promise of blessing to his obedient disciples:

> "I am not speaking (λέγω) of all of you; I know (οἶδα) whom I have chosen. But it is to fulfill the scripture, 'The one who ate my bread has lifted his heel against me.'" (13:18).

Jesus's knowledge of whom he had chosen may be interpreted as a statement that Judas was *not* among the chosen.[63] But this contradicts Jesus's earlier words, which hold together Jesus's choice of Judas with his knowledge that Judas was to betray him (6:70–71). Thus, Jesus's knowledge of those whom he had chosen is the knowledge that one of them would "lift his heel" against him and hand him over to the death.[64] That same knowledge of Judas's complicity in his death is also the reason given for Jesus not considering Judas among the pure (13:11). Judas's imminent betrayal of Jesus to the death is a sin that defiles him, and thus disqualifies him from among the pure. The footwashing shows that love's height is to lay down one's life for one's friends, but Judas does exactly the opposite of what Jesus commands his disciples to do. He will not lay down his life, but he will take the life of another. The moral impurity of Judas suggests that those sins that were conceptualized as defiling—bloodshed, sexual misdeeds, idolatry, and theft among them—are absolutely incompatible with the commandments that Jesus gives to his disciples. One cannot steal from the poor or be complicit in murder and, at the same time, do what Jesus had done in the footwashing (13:15) or love as Jesus had loved his disciples (13:34–35). In speaking of the impurity of Judas based on the knowledge of his character, Jesus "judges with right judgment" (7:24), articulating his right moral judgment with the language of purity.

In contrast to Judas, it can be said that the purity predicated of the disciples is indicative of their moral purity. In the Fourth Gospel, as was discussed in the last

---

[62] As observed by Culpepper, "The Johannine *Hypodeigma*," 137.

[63] Barrett weighs the possibility that Judas was not among the chosen, but favors the view that the sentence refers to Jesus's knowledge of his betrayer (*The Gospel according to St. John*, 444).

[64] For this reading of Jesus's knowledge and Judas's election I am indebted to Mathew, *The Johannine Footwashing*, 294–5, who finds that Jesus practices love and graciousness even toward Judas in Jn 13.

chapter of this book, moral purification is a divine, eschatological work of God carried out in Jesus, which was to enable Israel to see and enter the life of God. It is difficult to imagine that the Fourth Gospel does not call forth a moral vision for how one is to live when one's life has become bound to the life of God, mediated by God's Son.[65] And here the Fourth Gospel's disclosure of its rhetorical programme may come to be regarded as ethically oriented: "these are written … that through believing you may have life in his name" (ἵνα πιστεύοντες ζωὴν ἔχητε ἐν τῷ ὀνόματι αὐτοῦ, 20:31). The life that one has through faith in the Son of God is eternal life in the sense that its origin and end is with the living God.[66] But to *have* such life is not to possess in such a way that it is at one's disposal to do with it whatever one wills. Rather, to have eternal life is to be disposed toward the life of God, such that God's judgment reveals that one's works have been carried out in God (3:21).[67] The quality of such life has as its standard Jesus, resulting in an "ethics of life" for Jesus's disciples constituted by the "abundance and abandonment" of life in company with others.[68] Another name given to such abundant, abandoned life is love, for love's height is to lay down one's bodied life (ψυχή) for those one regards

---

[65]   For some time there was a consensus that the Fourth Gospel set forth no moral vision. Wayne A. Meeks, for example, cannot speak of ethics in the Fourth Gospel except as an oxymoron, since in it he finds no practicable ethical directives, no universalizable moral principles, no exemplary characters to imitate, no rationale with which moral decisions can be made, and no appeals to humans as responsible moral agents ("The Ethics of the Fourth Evangelist," in *Exploring the Gospel of John: In Honor of D. Moody Smith*, ed. R. Alan Culpepper and C. Clifton Black [Louisville, KY: Westminster John Knox, 1996], 318–20). The basic methodological premise of recent studies of the Fourth Gospel's ethics is that one ought not to make judgments about what kind of ethics are present in the Fourth Gospel based on what kind of ethics are absent from it. While the Gospel of John lacks discursive reflection on ethical situations, it may be understood to have what Ruben Zimmermann calls an "implicit ethics," insofar as it is a text that generates ethical reflection, on which see "The 'Implicit Ethics' of New Testament Writings: A Draft on a New Methodology for Analyzing New Testament Ethics," *Neot* 43.2 (2009): 399–423. For surveys of recent scholarship on ethics in the Fourth Gospel, see especially Shin, *Ethics in the Gospel of John*, 3–25; Jan G. van der Watt, "Ethics in Community in the Gospel and Letters of John," in *The Oxford Handbook of Johannine Studies*, ed. Judith Lieu and Martinus C. de Boer, Oxford Handbooks (Oxford: Oxford University Press, 2018), 363–80. Overlooked so far in these approaches to ethics in the Fourth Gospel is the way that the language of purity is employed to signal the moral qualities and moral capacity given to the disciples, which enables them to love as Jesus commanded.

[66]   For a reading of eternal life in John's Gospel in its relation to God, Jesus, soteriology, and love see Marianne Meye Thompson, "Eternal Life in the Gospel of John," *ExAud* 5 (1989): 35–55.

[67]   Karl Weyer-Menkhoff takes a cognitive-linguistic approach to the language of action in the Fourth Gospel (ἔργον, ἐργάζομαι, ποιέω), and makes note of the essentially responsive nature of human ethical work in relation to God (*Die Ethik des Johannesevangeliums im sprachlichen Feld des Handelns*, WUNT 2/359 [Tübingen: Mohr Siebeck, 2014], 253–60; "The Response of Jesus: Ethics in John by Considering Scripture as Work of God," in *Rethinking the Ethics of John: "Implicit Ethics" in the Johannine Writings*, ed. Jan G. van der Watt and Ruben Zimmermann, WUNT 291 (Tübingen: Mohr Siebeck, 2012), 159–74.

[68]   Ruben Zimmermann observes that ancient Greco-Roman ethics tended to focus on how to live a good life and not on what decisions to make in certain situations, which leads him to speak of the Fourth Gospel's "ethics of life" in connection with its language of life ("Abundant and Abandoning Life: Towards an 'Ethic of Life' in the Gospel of John," *ABR* 64 [2016]: 31–53). I am dependent on Zimmermann for the phrase "abundant and abandoned life." See also Mira Stare's treatment of the ethics of life in the Fourth Gospel, which begins with a close analysis of ζωή in Jesus's discourse on the bread of life (Jn 6:25–71) and expands to several passages in the Farewell Discourse (Mira Stare, "Ethics of Life in the Gospel of John," in *Rethinking the Ethics of John: "Implicit Ethics" in the Johannine Writings*, ed. Jan G. van der Watt and Ruben Zimmermann, WUNT 291 [Tübingen: Mohr Siebeck, 2012], 213–28).

as one's friends (15:13; cf. 3:16).[69] That the Fourth Gospel was written for its readers to "have life in his name" can therefore be considered programmatic not only with respect to its soteriology, but also to its ethics.[70] In the Fourth Gospel's language of life (ζωή), soteriology and ethics become nearly indistinguishable.[71] In washing the feet of his disciples and laying down his life for them, Jesus exemplifies the pattern of God's life in the world (ὑπόδειγμα, 13:15). And in conferring the life of God to his disciples, they become conformed to that pattern of life. The Fourth Gospel is written down so that such life might be found in Jesus's disciples (20:30–31).

Taking this into account alongside the way that the language of purity is used to denote particular moral qualities in early Jewish writings, the disciples' moral purity seems to be the moral quality of their lives that will enable them to live as those who have seen and entered the life of God. This entails both an absence and a presence. The Fourth Gospel gives us no reason to think that any of the Twelve, besides Judas, were ever captive to defiling sins such as bloodshed, idolatry, sexual misdeeds, or theft. Even so, the use of this language in its early Jewish context must at least predicate of these disciples an absence of those defiling sins, since those particular sins constitute a break between God and God's people. It is for sins like these, after all, that Judas is not counted among the pure. However, the Fourth Gospel seems to define the disciples' moral purity positively, with reference to life in the pattern of Jesus's love. Jesus commands his disciples to "do as I have done to you" (καθὼς ἐγὼ ἐποίησα ὑμῖν καὶ ὑμεῖς ποιῆτε, 13:15), and promises that "if you know these things, you are blessed if you do them" (μακάριοί ἐστε ἐὰν ποιῆτε αὐτά, 13:17). The paradigm that Jesus gives to his disciples parallels the new commandment he gives to his disciples shortly thereafter, namely, "that you love one another. Just as I have loved you, you also should love one another" (13:34).[72] In each case Jesus's life is the pattern and paradigm for the lives of the disciples. As was seen earlier, Abraham's testamentary speech in *Jubilees* warns those gathered with him against defiling sins such as sexual misdeeds and idolatry, and commends the love and worship of God as a way of life for them (*Jub.* 20.6–9). One finds something similar in the footwashing. The disciples' purity anticipates that defiling sin will be absent from their lives, and the animating presence of the love of God will be realized in their love for one another.[73] In the Fourth Gospel, the moral

---

[69] Thompson helpfully distinguishes between the life that cannot be lost (ζωή) and mortal life (ψυχή) in the Fourth Gospel, and later speaks of the "inescapable social dimension" of ζωή, which is love ("Eternal Life," 38–9, 47).

[70] Surprisingly, neither Zimmermann nor Stare clearly connect the programmatic statement in Jn 20:30–31 to the ethics of life about which they speak.

[71] In her analysis of ζωή in Jn 6, Stare finds "a complex link between the christological, theological, pneumatological and soteriological dimensions of the reality of life" ("Ethics of Life," 220).

[72] Coloe notes the parallel between Jesus's ὑπόδειγμα (13:15) and the new commandment (13:34) in that both are given by Jesus (δίδωμι), and Jesus is the model of his disciples' action in both ("Welcome into the Household of God," 410).

[73] For those who find helpful the analytical distinction between ethics (reflection on action in the form of commandment) and ethos (assumed, habitual behavior and values), one might say that the moral purity of the disciples is embedded within an early Jewish ethos where bloodshed, idolatry, and sexual misdeeds were assumed to be morally defiling. For a helpful discussion of this distinction with respect to the "household ethics" of the Fourth Gospel, see Jan G. van der Watt, "Ethics and Ethos in the Gospel According to John," *ZNW* 97 (2006): 152–75.

purity of the disciples will be actualized in their love for one another in the pattern of Jesus's love, having been located within God's own life by their companionship with Jesus.

Given the moral orientation of the disciples' purity, it is somewhat peculiar that Jesus does not warn his disciples of impurity or command them to be pure. He simply calls his disciples pure. The disciples' purity is not to be regarded as the result of their works of love, but as the necessary condition for love's actualization among them. The disciples that Jesus called pure will be capable of doing what he commands. Volker Rabens is one of the few scholars who have written on moral capacity in the Fourth Gospel.[74] Rabens attends to how "Jesus' love for [the disciples] is not only the model but also the enabling force of their love," arguing that the term καθώς in the love command is not only comparative, but also causative (13:34).[75] In other words, without the love of God revealed in Jesus's works, the disciples would not be able to love each other as Jesus loved them. Thus, the disciples' practice in love is nothing if not responsive to the love that Jesus had for them, and, in that sense, reflects the Fourth Gospel's irreducibly relational, responsive approach to ethics.[76] So, Jesus commands his disciples to love one another in the pattern of his own love, and that love for his disciples enables them to love one another. Rabens, however, overlooks how the language of purity advances this vision of enablement. For such love to be actualized among the disciples, the disciples must be able to love. The disciples' purity, given to them by God's work in Jesus, enables them to love. It almost goes without saying that not everyone who is loved returns love. Jesus's love for Judas is unrequited, for example. The loving paradigm for life given by Jesus to his disciples would not be actualized in the life of Judas (13:18).[77] Judas, far from practicing love that abandons life, abandons Jesus to death. And this is precisely what his impurity entails—not only bloodshed, but what appears to be the inability to do otherwise. By contrast, Jesus pronounces blessing on every disciple whom he called pure, who would do as he had done for them in the footwashing (13:17–18; cf. 14:12–14).

This association between purity and moral enablement is to be explored in the next section. That is, now morally pure, the disciples are enabled to live in the pattern of Jesus's love, and will do it. As will be seen, the language of purity or impurity was sometimes employed in early Jewish writings to speak of the anthropological (im)possibility of reflecting God's holiness and keeping God's commandments. While

---

[74] Volker Rabens notes that Bultmann, Caragounis, and Buch-Hansen are among the few who have written on this subject ("Johannine Perspectives on Ethical Enabling in the Context of Stoic and Philonic Ethics," in *Rethinking the Ethics of John: "Implicit Ethics" in the Johannine Writings*, ed. Jan G. van der Watt and Ruben Zimmermann, WUNT 291 [Tübingen: Mohr Siebeck, 2012], 114–20). What I refer to as ethical capacity, Rabens variously refers to as "ethical enabling," "ethical empowerment," and "relational empowering." See also the work of Charles H. Talbert, who interprets mutual indwelling (cf. Jn 15:4–5) in terms of divine enablement for discipleship ("The Fourth Gospel's Soteriology between New Birth and Resurrection," *PRSt* 37.2 [2010]: 133–45).

[75] Rabens, "Johannine Perspectives on Ethical Enabling," 120.

[76] Rabens, "Johannine Perspectives on Ethical Enabling," 122–30. Rabens appeals to Philo of Alexandria's work on ethical enabling and life with God in order to help warrant his claims about ethical enabling in John's Gospel (134–9). On the Fourth Gospel's relational, responsive approach to ethics, see Weyer-Menkhoff, *Die Ethik*, 253–60; Zimmermann, "Is There Ethics," 80.

[77] So Mathew, *The Johannine Footwashing*, 294.

there is a hint of purity's relation to moral capacity in the footwashing, it is explicit when Jesus calls his disciples pure in the discourse on the vine. As ought to be clear from the preceding discussion, though, this moral capacity is connected to a quality of life conducive to the kind of love embodied in Jesus and repellent to the sins that defile—bloodshed, sexual misdeeds, idolatry, and theft from the poor. The life of God brought through Jesus is to be replicated among the disciples.

4.3 Pure from "the Impurity of the Human Being"?
Moral Purity and Moral Capacity

Moral purification was sometimes conceptualized in ancient Jewish writings as a divine transformation of humanity, which was to make possible the keeping of God's commandments. That is, the language of purity could denote not only the moral quality of one's life but also the capacity to conform to what God required of humanity. Likewise, the language of impurity sometimes captured the human incapacity for keeping the commandments of God. In other words, "the impurity of the human being" (to borrow a phrase from 1QS 11.14) made it impossible to keep the Law given by God.

The early Jewish perception that human beings lacked the capacity to keep the Law that was given to them may briefly be illustrated by a passage in 4 Ezra:

> And your glory passed through the four gates of fire and earthquake and wind and ice, to give the Law to the descendants of Jacob, and your commandment to the posterity of Israel. *Yet you did not take away from them their evil heart, so that your Law might bring forth fruit in them.* (4 Ezra 4.19–20, emphasis mine; cf. 7.48)[78]

Karina Martin Hogan argues that the dialogue between Ezra and Uriel, of which Ezra's complaint is a part, reflects a contentious debate among ancient Jews about moral responsibility in the keeping of the Law (cf. Sir. 15:11–15). Hogan suggests that those like Ezra have drawn a notion similar to the rabbinic concept of the "evil inclination" (יצר הרע) from Gen 3 in order to place some responsibility on God for human failure to keep the Law, whereas those such as Uriel emphasize human capacity to choose to act in accordance with the Law.[79] That is, for Uriel, the problem is a matter of *will*, but for Ezra, the problem is a matter of *ability*. Ezra agonizes over why God did not take away the "evil heart" from the people, which made it impossible for the Law to produce good fruit in them (4 Ezra 4.22). Human beings could not choose to keep the Law. To Uriel's unflinching demand for human beings to conform exactingly to God's Law, Ezra might say, "We would if we could, but we cannot!" What was needed was a fundamental change in humanity's inner being, that is, the removal of the "evil heart," which would make possible the Law's fruit in humanity.[80] That is, God needed to transform humanity

---

[78] Bruce Metzger, *OTP* 1:529.
[79] Karina Martin Hogan, *Theologies in Conflict in 4 Ezra: Wisdom, Debate, and Apocalyptic Solution,* JSJSup 130 (Leiden: Brill, 2008), 112–20.
[80] Hogan, *Theologies in Conflict in 4 Ezra,* 120.

so that humanity would be able to keep God's commandments. In Ezra's view, once humanity had the capacity for obeying God's commandments, then the fruit of the Law would be actualized in Israel. Although 4 Ezra does not frame the problem of the evil heart and the inability to keep the Law in terms of moral (im)purity, other early Jewish writings do conceive of the problem in such terms. In other words, once God purified humanity from sin and made them able to observe righteousness, then the intention to conform to God's commandments would be actualized.

Purity's association with moral capacity has its root in the oracle of Ezekiel that anticipates God's moral purification of Israel in its restoration and regathering (Ezek. 36:25–27). This oracle of purification can be understood as the positive counterpart to Ezekiel's earlier portrayal of the wilderness generation. Ezekiel represents God as having given them "ordinances that were not good and statutes whereby they shall not live" (δικαιώματα ἐν οἷς οὐ ζήσονται ἐν αὐτοῖς, Ezek. 20:25 LXX). In so doing, God defiled them (μιαίνω, Ezek. 20:26). By contrast, Ezekiel supposes that when God purifies Israel, Israel will be conformed to God's commandments:

And I will sprinkle pure water upon you, and you shall be purified from all your impure acts and from all your idols, and I will purify you. And I will give you a new heart, and a new spirit I will give in you, and I will remove the stone heart from your flesh and give you a heart of flesh. And I will give my spirit in you and will act so that you walk in my statutes and keep my judgments and perform them [ἐν τοῖς δικαιώμασίν μου πορεύησθε καὶ τὰ κρίματά μου φυλάξησθε καὶ ποιήσητε]. (Ezek. 36:25–27 NETS, trans. mod.)

God's purification is the reconstitution of Israel's humanity: a new spirit is to be found in Israel, and stone hearts are to become hearts of flesh. The result of this divine purification of humanity is anthropological transformation, a change in the inner being that would make Israel able to observe and enact God's commandments, which they would no longer fail to do. As Christine Hayes observes about the representation of divine law in Ezekiel, "it is not the law that will change in the messianic future. The same laws and rules will continue to function as residency requirements for those who would live in Yahweh's land. What will change is *human nature*."[81] God's act of purification was to make Israel able to keep God's commandments, and the Prophet expects that, once purified from idolatry and given a new heart, Israel would in actuality walk in God's ways. To put it in Augustinian terms, Ezekiel's understanding of Israel's purification by God entailed its transformation from not being able not to sin (*non posse non peccare*) to not being able to sin (*non posse peccare*). This oracle of Ezekiel was profoundly generative in early Jewish thought about purification in relation to moral capacity.

The Community Rule draws from this text in Ezekiel in order to portray the condition of humanity as what Gudrun Holtz terms *constitutional impurity*.[82] For

[81] Christine E. Hayes, *What's Divine about Divine Law?: Early Perspectives* (Princeton, NJ: Princeton University Press, 2015), 48.
[82] Holtz, "Purity Conceptions in the Dead Sea Scrolls," 522–9. On the connection between Ezek. 36, Ps. 51, and 1QS 1–3, see p. 529.

Holtz, constitutional impurity denotes human incapacity for true holiness, for as
bodily life involves the ritual impurities that emerge from the body, so moral life entails
a predilection toward wrongfulness.[83] It is an understanding of impurity that both
overlaps and exceeds the ritual and moral aspects of impurity, because purity in either
aspect cannot be chosen or achieved by human action. Holtz finds this constitutional
impurity connected both to anthropological humiliation before the holiness of God
(1QS 11.9–15) and to the duality between the spirits of truth and deceit, and between
the members of the community and those who were not so predestined (1 QS 3.13–
4.26).[84] To take two excerpts from the former text:

> I belong to evil humankind
> to the assembly of wicked flesh;
> my failings, my transgressions, my sins, ...
> with the depravities of my heart,
> belong to the assembly of worms
> and of those who walk in darkness. (1 QS 11.9–10)
> in his justice he will cleanse me
> from the uncleanness of the human being [מנדת אנוש]
> and from the sin of the sons of man,
> so that I can extol God for his justice
> and The Highest for his majesty. (1QS 11.14–15)

The extraordinary phrase, "the impurity of the human being" (מנדת אנוש) captures the
depth of impurity in human constitution that Holtz is describing. Such impurity only
God can remove, which was imagined to be a divine eschatological act earlier in the
Community Rule (1 QS 4.20–22). On this, Holtz writes, "As humans in this time
cannot but perform both good and evil works, according to their portion of the two
spirits, so eschatologically purified humans cannot but act according to the will of
God."[85] Here, then, the language of impurity denotes a fundamental human incapacity
for unadulterated holiness in life and conduct. By contrast, the eschatological
purification brought on by God makes possible the full actualization of God's praise
and humanity's praiseworthy conduct. To put it differently, whereas the impure human
being was not able to will obedience to God's commandments, the human being that
God purified would be able to do nothing other than be completely holy.

A similar concept of constitutional impurity is found in Philo, but it is developed
with reference to Job rather than Ezekiel. Philo describes human incapacity for
complete virtue in terms of moral impurity. The passage in question appears within

---

[83] Or, in Holtz's own words, "In 1QH 9 and 1QS 3, ... humans do not have the capability to act
    morally. They are subject to circumstances that only allow them to sin. As little as they are able to
    influence the state of their bodily purity, so are they unable to affect their actions. The related type
    of impurity here is described as 'constitutional' impurity" ("Purity Conceptions in the Dead Sea
    Scrolls," 524).

[84] Holtz, "Purity Conceptions in the Dead Sea Scrolls," 524–7.

[85] Holtz, "Purity Conceptions in the Dead Sea Scrolls," 527. Holtz, it ought to be noted, also finds that
    the Hodayot present human beings as constitutionally impure.

Philo's comment on God's appearance to Abraham, in which God says, "I am your God; be well pleasing (εὐαρεστέω) before me, and become blameless (ἄμεμπτος)" (Gen. 17:1 LXX). Philo interprets the first phrase ("be well pleasing") as essentially out of human reach and the second phrase ("become blameless") as a divine concession to humanity's moral incapacity. Philo employs the language of impurity to discuss the human impossibility (ἀδύνατος) of acquiring all virtues:

> For who, as Job says, is pure from defilement [καθαρὸς ἀπὸ ῥύπου], even if his life be but for one day? Infinite indeed are the defilements that soil the soul [τὰ καταρρυπαίνοντα τὴν ψυχήν], which it is impossible to wash and scour away altogether [ἐκνίψασθαι καὶ ἀπολούσασθαι παντελῶς οὐκ ἔνεστιν]. For there still remain evils which are bound up with the life of every mortal, which may well be abated but cannot be wholly destroyed [ἀναιρεθῆναι δ᾽ εἰσάπαν ἀδύνατον]. Should we then seek to find in the medley of life one who is perfectly just or wise or temperate or good in general? Be satisfied, if you do but find one who is not unjust, is not foolish, is not licentious, is not cowardly, is not altogether evil. We may be content with the overthrow of vices, and the complete acquisition of virtues is impossible for man, as we know him [ἡ ἐντελὴς κτῆσις ἀδύνατος ἀνθρώπῳ τῷ καθ᾽ ἡμᾶς]. (*Names* 49–50 [Colson and Whitaker])

We may notice three things about moral purity and moral capacity in this passage. First, Philo appeals to the language of purity in order to explain scriptural terms that he understands to be ethical (i.e., εὐαρεστέω and ἄμεμπτος), even though no mention is made of purity in Gen. 17. Again, this suggests that Philo employed the language of purity in order to reflect on human moral life. Second, Philo puts the language of impurity to work in relation to moral incapacity. He says that the soul's defilements *are not possible* to wash away (οὐκ ἔνεστιν). He proceeds to speak of the impossibility (ἀδύνατος) of removing all evil from one's life, as well as the impossibility (ἀδύνατος) of acquiring complete virtue. The rationale for this impossibility is grounded in the judgment that no one can be wholly pure from defilement (Job 14:4–5 LXX). Third, Philo qualifies his claims about moral incapacity with language for completeness (e.g., παντελῶς, εἰσάπαν, ἐντελής). That is, what is impossible is complete purity. For Philo, human beings can at least approximate moral purity, especially when what is lacking in the purity of their lives is matched with repentance from sin and resolve to do no more wrong (cf., e.g., *Unchangeable* 7–9). Nonetheless, Philo's moral vision is essentially tragic—humanity is so stained with moral impurity that it is impossible to remove. Even if one wants to please God, no one is able to live in such a way that is well-pleasing to God. Unlike the Community Rule, nowhere in his extant corpus does Philo allude to Ezekiel's promise that God would eventually remove moral impurity so that human beings would be able to keep God's commandments and do so.

As the language of impurity sometimes signified human incapacity for complete holiness, so the language of purity sometimes signified human moral capacity. Josephus, for example, adds to the prayer Solomon offers after the dedication of the temple that God would incline the heart of Israel to walk in the ways of God and to keep God's commandments (1 Kgs 8:54–61). To this petition, Josephus adds the language of purity in connection with keeping God's commandments. Solomon's prayer comes to be that:

> their minds might be kept pure from all evil [τὴν διάνοιαν αὐτοῖς καθαρὰν ἀπὸ πάσης ... κακίας] as they continued in righteousness and worship [ἐν δικαιοσύνῃ καὶ θρησκείᾳ] and in the observance of the commandments [τὰς ἐντολὰς τηρεῖν] God had given them through Moses; for thus would the Hebrew nation be happy and the most blessed [μακαριώτερον] of all races of men. (*Ant.* 8.120 [Marcus])

Interestingly, Josephus makes the people's worship and observance of the law contingent on God's act of preserving their minds in moral purity. That is, the divine preservation of the people in purity of mind would make possible their obedience and worship in the temple.

Finally, there is a striking reflection on the pure mind and moral capacity in the final testament in the T. 12 Patr., which belongs to Benjamin. The Testament of Benjamin may be understood as a summary of all the testaments in T. 12 Patr. because of the way it recapitulates the virtues of the other patriarchs, all the while presenting Joseph as the paradigmatic "good man" (ὁ ἀγαθὸς ἀνήρ, T. Benj. 4.1).[86] The paraenetic section begins with summons to love the Lord God (3.1) and one's neighbor (3.3) and ends with the command to avoid the "hatred of brothers" and to "cling to goodness and love" (8.1). Thus, practice at love for neighbor and brother forms an *inclusio* around the ethical section of T. Benj. This literary structure signals T. Benj.'s primary ethical aim: to inculcate that love in its readers that was seen first in Joseph (3.1–8). The final commandment to cling to goodness and love is explained further with reference to a pure mind in love (διάνοιαν καθαρὰν ἐν ἀγάπῃ, 8.2). It reads:

> For the person with a mind that is pure with love [διάνοιαν καθαρὰν ἐν ἀγάπῃ] does not look on a woman for the purpose of a sexual misdeed [εἰς πορνείαν]. He has no pollution in his heart [μιασμὸν ἐν καρδίᾳ], because upon him is resting the Spirit of God. For just as the sun is unpolluted [οὐ μιαίνεται], though it touches dung and slime, but dries up both and drives off the bad odor, so also the pure mind, though involved with the pollutions of earth [ὁ καθαρὸς νοῦς ἐν τοῖς μιασμοῖς τῆς γῆς], edifies instead and is not itself polluted [οὐ μιαίνεται]. (T. Benj. 8.2–3, [Kee, trans. mod.])[87]

That one with a pure mind will not be looking for sexual misdeeds has its model in Joseph's self-control (σωφροσύνην) and purity (ἁγνεία, T. Jos. 10.2). But what follows is an arresting analogy, broader in its focus, between the sun and the pure mind in the midst of the earth's moral defilements. The pragmatic force of the analogy is to

---

[86] On the way that T. Benj. summarizes the ethics of the rest of T. 12 Patr., see Kugler, *Testaments*, 85–6.

[87] I saw fit to modify Kee's translation in two ways. First, πορνεία is elsewhere called the "mother of all evils" (T. Sim. 5.3), so Kee's rendering of the term here as "sexual relations" is too sanguine. I have rendered it "a sexual misdeed." Second, I made Kee's translation of μιασμός and μιαίνω as "corruption" in 8.3 consistent with its translation in 8.2, where he rightly translated the term with the language of impurity and defilement.

communicate the possibility of moral life when one has a mind pure in love, despite the possibility of moral defilement all around. One with a pure mind will not be polluted, and may even build up another person in love. This hopeful analogy about the possibility of goodness and love for one with a pure mind contrasts with the dire eschatological forecasts that warn of sin and impurity eventually leading people into exile, and that wickedness would resume even after restoration (e.g., T. Levi 14–17; T. Benj. 10). In the end, the Testaments hold out the possibility for moral life, but only for those whose minds have become pure in love.[88]

That purity was a way to speak about moral capacity in Philo, Josephus, T. 12 Patr., and the DSS suggests that it was another facet of a far-reaching discourse about moral purification. As will be seen, the Fourth Gospel draws from this discourse on moral purification in order to predicate of the disciples of Jesus the moral capacity to keep his law, having been purified by the Father through the word of Jesus. As is especially clear in the discourse in the vine, this moral purity is not a result of the disciples' work, but is the unilateral work of God in Jesus, which locates the disciples within the restoration of Israel that God brings forth through the vine and its branches. Although the concept of purification through a word is unique to the Fourth Gospel, the concept of a moral purification by God by which moral capacity is restored is drawn from Israel's Prophets (especially Ezekiel) and informed by early Jewish ethical discourse.

4.4 Already You Are Pure: The Disciples' Purity and the Fruit of Love

Jesus's second statement about his disciples' purity, still located in the Farewell Discourse before the Passover, is embedded in the image of the vinedresser, vine, and branches. Although the imagery breaks for a moment as Jesus directly addresses his disciples as pure, Jesus's statement to his disciples that "you are pure already" is the culmination of an elaborate wordplay on αἴρω, καθαίρω, and καθαρός that closely associates the disciples' purity with the image of the vine:[89]

> I am the true vine, and my Father is the vinegrower. He removes (αἴρω) every branch in me that bears no fruit. Every branch that bears fruit he cleans up (καθαίρω) to make it bear more fruit. You are pure already (καθαρός) because

---

[88] Again, even if T. 12 Patr. contains early Jewish tradition, it is likely (but indeterminable) that the T. 12 Patr. reflects a Jewish Christian provenance that postdates the Fourth Gospel; see Marcus, "The Testaments of the Twelve Patriarchs and the Didascalia Apostolorum," 596–626). My argument is not that the T. 12 Patr. influenced the Fourth Gospel, but that, along with texts from an early Jewish provenance, the way it connects moral purity and capacity for moral life illuminates something about how the Fourth Gospel conceptualizes moral purity in relation to moral capacity.

[89] Busse notices the abrupt shift from the image of the vine to the direct statement about the disciples' purity ("Reinigung und Heiligung," 154). Among the numerous commentators who speak about this wordplay, one may consult Brown, *The Gospel according to John*, 2:660.

of the word that I have spoken to you. (ἤδη ὑμεῖς καθαροί ἐστε διὰ τὸν λόγον ὃν λελάληκα ὑμῖν, 15:1–3 NRSV, trans. mod.)[90]

Jesus's second pronouncement that his disciples are pure is a direct restatement of the first—ὑμεῖς καθαροί ἐστε—with two additions: the disciples are said to be pure *already* (ἤδη) and the cause of their purification is divulged, namely, the word that Jesus spoke to them (διὰ τὸν λόγον ὃν λελάληκα ὑμῖν, 15:3; cf. 13:10). These additions do not contradict what was said of the disciples' purity as spoken of in the footwashing, but make explicit what was then only implied.

Three questions about features of this text will help illuminate the language of purity in the vine discourse. First, the image of the vine is a figure of Israel or Israel's king in Israel's Scripture (cf., e.g., Jer. 2:21; 12:10–11; Isa. 5:1–7; 27:6; Ezek. 15:1–8; 17:1–21; 19:10–14; Ps. 80; Hos. 10:1–2; Joel 1:5–7).[91] How does the dizzying array of intertexts evoked by Jesus's words bear on the interpretation of this passage? Second, Jesus says that the Father "cleans up" (καθαίρω) the branches in order that they bear fruit, which brings the disciples' purity into close relation with their works, but what exactly is the relation? Third, Jesus identifies the word that he has spoken to the disciples as the cause of their purity. Although one may find in Israel's Scripture the word of God being instrumental in creation (e.g., Ps. 33:6) or deliverance (Ps. 107:20), for example, one struggles to find any precedent in Israel's Scripture for a word that purifies.[92] In what sense does Jesus's word purify the disciples? To these matters we now turn.

4.4.1 Cleaned Up by the Father: Pure Branches Bear Much Fruit

The image of the vine and the branches locates the disciples with Jesus in the restoration of Israel through an appeal to a particularly complex scriptural metaphor—that Israel (or Israel's king) is a vine—which is then employed metaphorically again when Jesus says, "I am the vine, you are the branches" (Jn 15:5, cf. 15:1). Gary Manning is among the many interpreters who have discerned in Jn 15:1–8 allusions to Jeremiah (in which God plants Israel as a 'true vine' [ἄμπελον … ἀληθινήν], but Israel becomes a 'foreign' vine by going after the nations' gods; Jer. 2:21), Isaiah (in which Israel is figured as a vineyard that produced thorns instead of grapes; Isa. 5:1–7), Ezekiel (where the vine is both Jerusalem that "is given to the fire for fuel" [Ezek. 15:6], and the house of King Zedekiah that will be judged in Babylon on account of breaking covenant with God [Ezek. 17:1–21; 19:10–14]), and a Psalm (in which Israel, or its king, is figured as a vine that the psalmist asks God to regard, Ps. 80:8–18).[93] The Fourth Gospel's image of the

---

[90] The NRSV translates διὰ τὸν λόγον instrumentally, but it is better to interpret it causally (so Brown, *The Gospel according to John*, 2:660). I tried to render the double meaning of καθαίρω played on in this text as "cleans up," which in English refers either to personal hygiene or tidying up any number of things, including plants. In agricultural contexts the term καθαίρω denotes pruning, whereas in other contexts it denotes purifying (BDAG, s.v. "καθαίρω").

[91] I am indebted to Thompson, *John: A Commentary*, 323 for a number of these primary-source references.

[92] Stare refers to purification by the word as "eine radikale Neuheit" ("Die Reinheitsthematik," 91).

[93] I am indebted to Manning for his concise analysis of these texts in relation to John 15 (*Echoes of a Prophet*, 135–40). Manning has a helpful chart that lays out the verbal parallels between these texts

vine appeals most directly to Ezekiel, as evidenced by the density of verbal parallels shared only between the two texts.[94]

The acute judgment of the vine in Ezekiel and other prophets (e.g., Isa. 5:1–7, Jer. 12:10–11; Hos. 10:1–2; Joel 1:5–7) has suggested to interpreters that there is a contrast implicit in Jesus's identification with the vine. That is, whereas Israel became a wild vine, Jesus is the true vine, so that the disciples must now be a part of Jesus instead of Israel.[95] Such interpretations of the vine image, however, are vulnerable to critique. As Thompson points out, the judgment of the vine "is not the whole story" in Israel's Scripture, for Isaiah anticipates the time when "Israel shall bud and blossom, and the world will be filled with his fruit" (Isa. 27:6b LXX) and the psalmist longs for God to "have regard for this vine" (Ps. 80:14–17 NRSV).[96] Moreover, based on Ezekiel's identification of the vine as King Zedekiah (Ezek. 17) and the royal, messianic hopes associated with the vine image in Psalm 80:14–16 among ancient Jews, Blumhofer argues that the Fourth Gospel's reception of the vine image represents Jesus the Messiah "as a vine with a singularly important role in bringing about the future restoration of Israel."[97] In other words, the vine image in John's Gospel identifies *not* the whole people of Israel, but that individual on whom Israel's future depends. That Jesus is the true vine helps his disciples to "know that *his* eschatological significance ensures their own place in Israel's eschatological future."[98] Thus the image of the vine and branches locates the disciples with Jesus in the restoration of Israel.

This brings us to the disciples' purity in relation to their moral capacity for the bearing of fruit. In the vine image, the disciples' place in the future of Israel is to be branches that bear fruit, which they will be able to do because the Father has pruned and purified them (15:2–3, 5). The difference between the disciples' purity in Jesus's vine discourse and the purification of the vine in Israel's Scripture is astonishing. Only two texts in the Septuagint (and, notably, not in the MT) directly connect the image of the vine to purification, and both cases involve dire judgment. For Ezekiel, the pruning of the vine shows only that it is useless for anything other than a fire's fuel.

---

and John 15 (p. 140), except that it omits Ps. 79 LXX, which refers to Israel as a vine (ἄμπελος, 79:9, 15 LXX) with branches that stretch out (κλῆμα, 79:12 LXX), which had once been burned with fire (πῦρ, 79:17 LXX).

[94] Manning notes that "Ezekiel's vine parables have 8 words (ἄμπελος, κλῆμα, φέρω, καρπός, καθαίρω/καθαρός/κάθαρσις, ξηραίνω, πῦρ, καίω/κατεσθίω) and two phrases (φέρειν καρπόν, τὸ κλῆμα … ἐξηράνθη/ἐξηράνθη ἡ ῥάβδος) in common with Jn 15. … Ezek. 15 and Jn 15 are the only two passages in either testament to use cognates of καθαίρω to refer to pruning. Ezekiel is the only book in the LXX that regularly uses κλῆμα for 'branch'; Jn 15 is the only passage in the NT to use the word at all" (*Echoes of a Prophet*, 140–1).

[95] So, for example, Manning, *Echoes of a Prophet*, 138; Brown, *The Gospel according to John*, 2:674–75 (who also connects the image of the vine to the viticultural ornamentation in the Jerusalem temple and the image on coins coined during the first Jewish revolt); Köstenberger, *A Theology of John's Gospel*, 502–4. Against such readings, see Blumhofer's critical evaluation of supersessionistic interpretations of the vine (*The Gospel of John and the Future of Israel*, 188–9).

[96] Thompson, *John: A Commentary*, 324.

[97] Blumhofer, *The Gospel of John and the Future of Israel*, 187–94; here, 192. Particularly important for Blumhofer's argument is the work of Thompson, *John: A Commentary*, 322–6 and Andrew Streett, *The Vine and the Son of Man: Eschatological Interpretation of Psalm 80 in Early Judaism*, Emerging Scholars (Minneapolis, MN: Fortress, 2014).

[98] Blumhofer, *The Gospel of John and the Future of Israel*, 188.

Of the vine, Ezekiel writes: "the fire consumes the yearly cleansing (κάθαρσις) of it, and it fails completely; shall it actually be useful for production?" (15:4 LXX).[99] More devastating is Jeremiah's sudden move from the metaphor of the people as a plant to their purification for slaughter: "You planted them, and they took root; they bred children and produced fruit; you are near to their mouths; and far from their kidneys. … Purify (ἁγνίζω) them for a day of their slaughter!" (12:2, 3b LXX).[100] This is an admittedly odd use of a term for purification, denoting something like preparing them or setting them apart for destruction. But Jeremiah also puts the figure of the vine in close proximity to the sin's defilement of the people. After Jeremiah says that God planted Israel as "a fruitful vine, entirely true," (ἄμπελον καρποφόρον πᾶσαν ἀληθινήν, 2:21 LXX; cf. ἡ ἄμπελος ἡ ἀληθινὴ, Jn 15:1) and indicts them for becoming a bitter, "foreign vine" (ἡ ἄμπελος ἡ ἀλλοτρία; 2:21 LXX), he immediately speaks of Israel's moral defilement by foreign idols:[101]

> Though you wash [ἀποπλύνω] yourself with nitre and multiply herbs for yourself, you have become stained by your injustices before me, says the Lord. How will you say, "I was not defiled [μιαίνω], and I did not go after the goddess Baal"? (Jer. 2:22–23a LXX)

Later, their defilement is blamed on Israel's leaders. "Many shepherds have destroyed my vineyard; they have defiled my portion" (ἐμόλυναν τὴν μερίδα μου, 12:10 LXX; cf. Jer. 23:11, 15). In other words, for Jeremiah moral defilement is the cause of the vine's failure to produce good fruit (8:10–13). The rhetoric of judgment on the vine throughout Israel's Scripture is that it would not be possible for a vine planted and cared for by God to bear anything but good fruit, but, somehow, it produced nothing but thorns or bitter fruit.

Even so, it is a vine that God will replant and restore (Isa. 27:6; Ps. 80), and this hope for its restoration informs the image of the vine and branches in the Farewell Discourse. In contrast to the prophetic judgment on the vine, the disciples' pruning by the Father increases their capacity to bear good fruit (Jn 15:2). Or, rather, makes it impossible for them not to bear good fruit, since the only branches left on the vine are those that bear fruit, the others having been removed (15:2a).[102] The defilement of sin that previously withered the vine and ruined its harvest would not be repeated in those branches remaining in *this* vine, which is God's provision for Israel's restoration to fruitfulness.[103] In this way, the image of the vine and branches connects the disciples'

---

[99] By contrast, in the Farewell Discourse, it is not the "purified" branches that are consumed by fire, but the branches that are removed from the vine (Jn 15:2, 6).

[100] Whereas the object of slaughter in the MT becomes sheep, in the LXX the implied object is still the plant and its fruit.

[101] On the language of moral impurity in Jer. 2, see the treatment in § 1.3.

[102] I no longer find any sense of warning in Jesus's words to his disciples in this passage, which, in any case, would betray his erstwhile confidence that he would lose none of those whom the Father gave him (Jn 6:39–40; 10:28–30). Instead, the removal of unfruitful or dead vines (15:2, 6) serves what is positively predicated of the disciples, namely, their capacity to bear much fruit as a result of their purification and companionship with Jesus. That is, they are in the vine, so they *will* bear fruit.

[103] So, Thompson, *John: A Commentary*, 322–7; Blumhofer, *The Gospel of John and the Future of Israel*, 188.

purification not only to the work of God in humanity's restoration, but also to their capacity to "work the works of God," that is, the restoration of their moral capacity (cf. 3:21; 6:28–29).[104] So, it is significant that immediately following Jesus's direct address to his disciples—"you are pure" (15:3)—are words about the impossibility of bearing fruit apart from vital union with him, which is constituted by abiding:

> Abide in me as I abide in you. Just as the branch cannot bear fruit [οὐ δύναται καρπὸν φέρειν] by itself unless it abides in the vine, neither can you unless you abide in me. I am the vine, you are the branches. Those who abide in me and I in them bear much fruit, because apart from me you can do nothing [οὐ δύνασθε ποιεῖν οὐδέν]. (15:4–5)

In these words of Jesus attention is given to the ability of the disciples to bear fruit. Their capacity to bear fruit depends on their abiding in Jesus as branches in a vine. The two-fold use of *cannot* (οὐ δύναμαι) in direct relation to bearing fruit (15:4) or doing anything (15:5) expresses moral inability without companionship with Jesus.[105] The moral purity of the disciples, then, serves the relational, responsive ethics of the Fourth Gospel insofar as their purity is what enables their response to God.[106] The vital relation of the disciples to Jesus, which is signified by the image of messianic vine and purified branches, is what makes it possible for them to bear much fruit. And because it is possible for them to bear fruit, fruit will be born in them.

4.4.2 The Word that Jesus Speaks Makes Pure

It is the word that Jesus has spoken that makes his disciples pure (15:3). Arguably, the Father's work of pruning and purifying the branches and the word that Jesus speaks in order to make them pure is a singular act.[107] Earlier in the Farewell Discourse, Jesus says that "the words that I say to you (τὰ ῥήματα ἃ ἐγὼ λέγω ὑμῖν) I do not speak on my own; but the Father who dwells in me does his works" (ποιεῖ τὰ ἔργα αὐτοῦ; 14:11). This suggests that the Father's works are enacted through Jesus's words.[108] In other

---

[104]   There is a vision in 1 En. 10.16–22 that is not dissimilar, in which the righteous who survive cataclysmic judgment plant righteousness and truth in the land, along with vineyards and vines, after which comes the purification of the earth from impurity and sin and the renewed worship of God.

[105]   Talbert interprets the language of abiding in God in Jn 15:1–17 in terms of divine enablement for the keeping of covenant ("The Fourth Gospel's Soteriology," 139–45).

[106]   Weyer-Menkhoff, for example, writes that "not even Jesus accomplishes the works of God autonomously but rather responsively," ("The Response of Jesus," 164). See also, Patrick J. Hartin, who is among the earliest to give a narratological approach to Fourth Gospel's ethics that focuses on responsiveness ("Remain in Me [John 15:5]: The Foundation of the Ethical and Its Consequences in the Farewell Discourses," *Neot* 25.2 [1991]: 341–56); see also Lindsey Trozzo, whose work on Johannine Christology leads her to conclude that what is to be imitated in the life of Jesus is his unity with and responsiveness to the Father (*Exploring Johannine Ethics: A Rhetorical Approach to Moral Efficacy in the Fourth Gospel Narrative*, WUNT 2/449 [Tübingen: Mohr Siebeck, 2017], 85–96).

[107]   *Contra* Thompson, who supposes that Jesus first purifies the disciples through the word, which the Father maintains through their pruning (*John: A Commentary*, 324).

[108]   So Michaels, who draws special attention to the word of Jesus in the work of "giving life and executing judgment" (*The Gospel of John*, 779), to which I would add the work of making morally pure.

words, the Father's work of pruning and purifying the disciples consists in the word that Jesus has spoken to them. The disciples' purity is neither the result of their good works nor their faith, but is wholly dependent on the action of God in Jesus.[109] As was seen in the preceding survey, purity was sometimes used in early Jewish discourse to speak of the divine restoration of human moral capacity. So the disciples' purity being the result of God's act in Jesus's word is not an implicit excoriation of early Jewish purity, but entails the deployment of a certain discourse of biblical and early Jewish purity to describe the work that God does in Jesus.

As for the λόγος that Jesus spoke being the medium of purification, I have found almost nothing like it in Israel's Scripture or in early Jewish writings. In the Psalms, the oracles of the Lord are once spoken of as pure (τὰ λόγια κυρίου λόγια ἀγνά, Ps. 11:7 LXX), but only in contrast to the deceitfulness of human beings (Ps. 11:2). There is no sense that the pure word of the Lord purifies human beings from such deceit. In the purification of Naaman from leprosy, the narrator focuses twice on the importance of Elisha's word (λόγος) to Naaman, but it was his washing in the Jordan that was ultimately purifying (2 Kgs 5:13–14). In Ps. Sol. 17, the messianic king is said to be pure from sin (17:36), and the word (λόγος) of this messianic king is supposed to destroy nations (17:24), strike the earth (17:35), and remove sinners (17:36). There may be a sense that these actions are involved in his work "to purify (καθαρίζω) Ierousalem from nations that trample her down in destruction" (17:22 LXX), but even if there was, it would be a completely different sort of purification than that envisioned in Jesus's vine discourse. That is, that purification results in the removal of sinners from Jerusalem, whereas the disciples' purification results in their good works.

The closest one comes to a word, that is, a λόγος, being conceptualized as purifying is found in several passages in Philo's *On Dreams* that focus on Jacob (1.148, 1.198).[110] Philo's Jacob arrives at virtue primarily through practice and struggle, in contrast to Abraham whose virtue comes by learning and Isaac whose virtue is innate (1.167–71). Integral to Jacob's moral purification for Philo is the imagery of angels on ladders and sheep and goats in Jacob's dreams, which he interprets allegorically as the words of God that make pure. Philo speaks first of those who are so morally pure that God promises to them that "I will walk in you, and will be your God" (1.148). Then he writes:

> But in the understandings of those who are still undergoing cleansing [τῶν ἔτι ἀπολουομένων] and have not yet fully washed their life defiled and stained [κατὰ τὸ παντελὲς ἐκνιψαμένων τὴν ῥυπῶσαν καὶ κεκηλιδωμένην] by the body's weight there walk angels, divine words [ἄγγελοι, λόγοι θεῖοι], making them bright and

---

[109] Stare focuses on how the Fourth Gospel represents purity as a divine gift, but her antithesis to purity as a ritual practice is unwarranted ("Die Reinheitsthematik," 91–3). Busse holds together divine action in purification by Jesus's word with practices of ritual purification in pursuit of God ("Reinigung und Heiligung," 154–8). These readings are to be preferred to those that assert the faith of Jesus's disciples replaces ritual purification, for which there is little basis in the Fourth Gospel. The primary example of such interpretations appears in comments on the wedding at Cana, on which, see § 1.1.

[110] Later in *Dreams*, when Philo says that "the holy word had cleansed us (ἐκάθηρεν ἡμᾶς ὁ ἱερὸς λόγος) with the water of sprinkling made ready for our sanctification" he is speaking allegorically about the high priest performing cultic duties (1.226 [Colson and Whitaker], cf. 1.215).

clean [φαιδρύνοντες] with the doctrines of all that is good and beautiful. (1.148, [Colson and Whitaker])

Philo's understanding of the word as purifying is made possible by an allegorical identification of angels as divine words (cf. 1.141–3). Such purification by these divine words involves being lifted out of the bodily, mortal realm toward heaven, from which these angels descended (1.146–8). Philo's language of ascent and descent and the connection he draws between divine words and mortality's removal have affinity with the Fourth Gospel, but are not identical. Philo appeals to a particular cosmology and anthropology involving soul-body dualism to warrant his judgments (1.144–7).

Later, Philo writes of Jacob's dream about the goats and rams (cf. Gen. 31:10–16) and interprets these creatures as symbols of "two perfect ways of thinking" (δυεῖν λόγων σύμβολα τελείων), explaining that

> the one cleanses and purges a soul from sin [καθαίρει καὶ κενοῖ ψυχὴν ἁμαρτημάτων], and the other nourishes it and renders it full of high achievements. Such are the leading thoughts [λόγοι] at the head of the herds within us; and the herds, possessed of dispositions answering to the names of sheep and goats which represent them, dart and go forward towards righteousness with earnestness [μετὰ σπουδῆς πρὸς δικαιοσύνην]. (*Dreams* 1.198 [Colson and Whitaker]).

Since Jacob's dream involved the generation of sheep and goats through mating, the λόγοι that they allegorically represent are also thought to be generative. Thus, the morally purifying λόγος is not simply a spoken word, but a particular rationality or way of thinking that purifies Jacob for the practice of virtue. In other words, the purification the λόγος effects is freedom from sin and for virtuous life. In this respect, this passage from Philo portrays moral purification by λόγος similarly to the disciples' purification by Jesus's λόγος, since their capacity for moral action is given by the word of Jesus (Jn 15:2). However, unlike Philo's exegetical and allegorical ruminations on the λόγος, the purifying λόγος in the Fourth Gospel is identified simply as that which Jesus spoke to the disciples (τὸν λόγον ὃν λελάληκα ὑμῖν, Jn 15:3). So Philo and the Fourth Gospel envision a similar moral result for the moral purification effected by a λόγος, but differ in how they conceive the content of that λόγος.

Given that the Fourth Gospel's portrayal of the word of Jesus as purifying is highly peculiar among extant early Jewish texts, one assumes that the Fourth Gospel gives its readers just enough to make some sense of it. In light of this, it seems that Busse rightly reads Jesus's statement about his word being the cause of his disciples' purity as a retrospective interpretation of Jesus's speeches and dialogues as having purifying power.[111] The Fourth Gospel briefly gives a window into the life of the disciples after Jesus's resurrection, which involved them remembering and trusting both Scripture and "the word that Jesus had spoken" (τῷ λόγῳ ὃν εἶπεν ὁ Ἰησοῦς, 2:22). These words of Jesus are described in the Fourth Gospel as "Spirit and life" (πνεῦμά ... καὶ ζωή,

---

[111]   Busse, "Reinigung und Heiligung," 154–5.

6:63) and "words of eternal life" (ῥήματα ζωῆς αἰωνίου, 6:68). This may suggest that the Fourth Gospel itself, as that which is supposed to mediate the word of Jesus, was received by its early readers as an instrument of God's work of moral purification.[112] Perhaps the desired rhetorical effect of nowhere directly narrating the disciples' purification by the word was to give the Fourth Gospel's readers the impression that they too had encountered the word of Jesus and so became pure.[113] That is, the word of Jesus that makes pure is the word heard by whosoever is addressed by the Fourth Gospel's account of Jesus's words, so that the purity predicated of Jesus's disciples becomes purity predicated of the Fourth Gospel's hearers. The purity of the disciples, then, is not a quality of character designed to be imitated, so much as a quality that becomes one's own having read the Fourth Gospel.[114] But this is all speculative, insofar as no concrete historical data is available for how the earliest readers of the Fourth Gospel received it.[115] Furthermore, the Fourth Gospel is a written book (βιβλίον, 21:24–25), which is not the same as a spoken word (λόγος). So, at the very least, it may be said that the Fourth Gospel's representation of the word of Jesus as morally purifying suggests that the discourses of Jesus in the Fourth Gospel are ethical in the sense that they are designed to make possible much good fruit in the lives of Jesus's companions.

The fruit that is to come out of pure branches that abide in the vine is the fruit of love, which is evident in the way that the discourse on the vine moves from the living union between branches and vine (15:1–8) to the loving union between Jesus and his disciples, among whom is to be repeated the love that Jesus has for them (15:9–17).[116] The loving union between Jesus and his disciples is dependent on their keeping of Jesus's commandments, which are summed up in the single commandment that they

---

[112] So Busse, "Reinigung und Heiligung," 154–5. Reinhartz argues with some reservation that the Fourth Gospel would have been received by its early readers as Scripture, because of (1) the equivocation between Jesus's word and Scripture in Jn 2:22, (2) the recorded fulfillment of Jesus's word (17:12; 18:8-9), and (3) the use of the phrase γέγραπται with reference to the Fourth Gospel (20:30; "The Jews of the Fourth Gospel," 131–3).

[113] Appealing to Aristotle's preference for the "probable impossibility" over the "improbable possibility," narratologist James Phelan argues that the rhetorical interest of a flesh-and-blood author often shapes how a story is told (*Somebody Telling Somebody Else: A Rhetorical Poetics of Narrative*, Theory and Interpretation of Narrative [Columbus, OH: Ohio State University Press, 2017], 33–60).

[114] James Phelan outlines three ways that a text's sympathetic readers respond to its rhetoric, which can be called "mimetic, thematic, and synthetic" (James Phelan, "Rhetoric/Ethics," in *The Cambridge Companion to Narrative*, ed. David Herman, Cambridge Companions to Literature [Cambridge: Cambridge University Press, 2007], 203–16). Whereas mimesis involves treating characters as possible models of desire and action and synthesis involves critical analysis of texts, thematic responses "involve an interest in characters as representative classes of people" (211). In this case, readers who also find themselves bound in faith to Jesus may come to understand the disciples' purity by Jesus's word as representing their own purity by Jesus's word. So, rhetorically speaking, Jesus's statement about his disciples' purity could be understood as representative of all true disciples of Jesus, both women and men.

[115] There is, however, enough material in the second and early third century on how the word or Scripture purifies its hearers that I suppose one could write a dissertation on it (cf., e.g., Barn. 8.1–4; Herm. Vis. 16.11; Clement of Alexandria, *Protr.* 10.79; *Paed.* 1.6; 3.9; Origen, *Comm. Jo.* 2.129; 6.220; 32.53).

[116] On the transition from focus on life to the focus on love, see Michaels, *The Gospel of John*, 809–10.

love one another as Jesus has loved them (15:12).[117] As with the love commandment given after the footwashing (13:34–35, cf. 13:15), the term καθώς in the phrase "love one another as [καθώς] I have loved you" carries ethical freight, as it makes the quality of Jesus's love for the disciples the paradigm for the disciples to imitate in their love for one another.[118] Jesus's love consists in the abandonment of mortal life (ψυχή) for his friends (15:13).[119] And so, the condition of life, love, and obedience that constitutes the disciples' union with Jesus leaves no remainder. The disciples will keep the commandment, having been made capable of producing such costly fruit in love not only by their vital relation to Jesus, but also by the moral purification effected by his word. Thus, the disciples' moral purification by the Father at work in Jesus's word makes possible the increase of love's work among them.

4.5 Conclusion

In the Farewell Discourse, Jesus twice tells his disciples, "you are pure" in the same passages in which he commands them to love one another (13:10–11; 15:2–3). Although the language of moral purity does have a soteriological dimension in the Fourth Gospel, it appears in these contexts with an ethical orientation. I argued that the disciples' moral purity is what enables them to keep Jesus's commandment to love one another. The Fourth Gospel employs biblical and early Jewish traditions of moral purity related to moral character and capacity in order to predicate of Jesus's disciples their restored capacity to live and love after the pattern of Jesus. Jesus evaluates his disciples with the language of moral purity. He discerns that Judas is impure because of his intention to shed blood. But he ascribes moral purity to the rest of his disciples, whom he is sure will do as he had done and enter blessedness. The disciples would be pure for the sake of love. Their love for one another would be responsive to the love that Jesus had for them, and that love would be pure from the defilement of sins such as bloodshed, sexual misdeeds, idolatry, or theft. The disciples' purity involves their capacity to do what Jesus asks of them, either to enact his pattern of life-giving love (13:15–17, 34–35) or to bear much fruit out of a vital union with Jesus constituted by abiding in his love and keeping his commandment to love (15:9–17). The disciples' purity is a result of the work of God in Jesus's word, and its placement in the discourse on the vine suggests that their purity is also a facet in the restoration of Israel. The disciples' purity is at once theological and ethical, as it signals the disciples' capacity for a mode of life in keeping with Jesus's love.

---

[117]   Jey J. Kanagaraj finds that there is a meaningful distinction between ἐντολή and ἐντολαί in Jn 15:10–12. He argues that the commandments are those of the decalogue, which are summed up in the singular commandment to love, which was sometimes "treated as the summary of the Law"; see "The Implied Ethics of the Fourth Gospel: A Reinterpretation of the Decalogue," *TynBul* 52.1 (2001): 36–7.

[118]   On imitation and the significance of the term καθώς in Jn 13:15, 34–35; 15:12, see Cornelis Bennema, "Mimetic Ethics in the Gospel of John," in *Metapher – Narratio – Mimesis – Doxologie: Begründungsformen frühchristlicher und antiker Ethik*, ed. Ulrich Volp, Friedrich Wilhelm Horn, and Ruben Zimmermann, WUNT 356 (Tübingen: Mohr Siebeck, 2016), 211–15.

[119]   Zimmermann, "Abundant and Abandoning Life," 44–8.

5

Conclusion: Purity Remains

The purpose of this book was to explore how the Fourth Gospel adopts and adapts biblical and early Jewish traditions of purity to make sense of the luminous figure at the center of its narrative, as well as those bound to him by faith. But this way of framing the matter is incommensurable with the twentieth-century interpretive consensus that the Fourth Gospel, in the words of Raymond Brown, includes "the theme of Jesus' replacement of Jewish institutions like ritual purification" and that "all previous religious institutions, customs and feasts lose meaning in his presence."[1] In this interpretive paradigm, the ablutions of John, the sign at Cana, the controversy over purification, and the purity of Jesus's disciples may all be understood in terms of the replacement of early Jewish forms of ritual purification with faith in Jesus. This way of interpreting purity explains why so few scholars have written anything constructive about it in the Fourth Gospel. If it is true that purity is replaced by Jesus, there is little else to say about it.

But purity in the Fourth Gospel is better approached as a symbolic system than as a fossil in a scheme of evolutionary development. In the influential work of William Robertson Smith, purity was treated like the fossilized remains of a primitive, irrational creature, and its only value was to demonstrate the advancement and vitality of that which superseded it.[2] Such a low estimation of purity is at best implausible in view of the pervasive, wide-ranging, reflective, and contested discourse on purity among ancient Jews, whose traditions of purity worked to construct holy space and sacred time, to organize social life, to contribute to ethical formation, and to inspire reflection on life before God. Purity's entanglement with early Jewish faith and practice is the reason that it is better to approach it as a symbolic system, in the same vein as Mary Douglas and Jonathan Klawans.[3] The disparate elements of purification are presumed to work together to create something dynamic and intelligible within early Jewish theology, cosmology, and practice. The conceptual density of early Jewish discourse on biblical traditions of purity is reflected in certain ways that the Fourth Gospel sets forth the work of God in Jesus. The argument of this book is that the Fourth Gospel employs biblical traditions of purity associated with the revelation of God and restoration of

---

[1] Brown, *The Gospel according to John*, 1:lxx and 1:104, respectively.
[2] Smith, *Lectures on the Religion of the Semites: First Series*, 132–49; 427–35.
[3] On which, see Douglas, *Purity and Danger*, 8–35; Klawans, *Impurity and Sin*, 21–42; Klawans, *Purity, Sacrifice, and the Temple*, 49–73.

Israel to narrate how God's people are prepared for the coming of Jesus and enabled by him to have life before God characterized by love.

In the Fourth Gospel, ritual purification is bound together with human perception and divine revelation.[4] The three elements form a kind of constellation, which is visible in John's ablutions with water for the revelation of Jesus to Israel (1:31), in the pure stone vessels at Cana that were instrumental in the revealing of Jesus's glory to his disciples (2:11), in the pool of Siloam where the man born blind was given sight by washing (9:1–7), and (just barely) in the ritual purity of the disciples for the Passover in which God's lowly love was revealed in the cross (11:55; 13:10a). The Fourth Gospel's treatment of ritual purity draws from a glimmering constellation of purity, perception, and revelation within early Jewish tradition. This constellation of elements may be traced back to Moses's washing of Israel to prepare them for the revelation of God in the giving of the Law at Sinai (Exod. 19:10–11). This constellation is visible in the reception of the Sinai account by a variety of early Jewish interpreters, and is applied in innovative ways in Philo, the deuterocanonical wisdom literature, and 1QS. Significantly, in this constellation of elements, ritual purification always prepares Israel to perceive what is revealed of God—whether the Law of God, the glory of God, the wisdom of God, or, in the case of the Fourth Gospel, the Word of God made flesh. The allusions to the giving of the law and limits of human perception at the end of the Prologue (Jn 1:16–18) interlock with the account of John's ablutionary witness (1:15, 19–34) and effectively align John's ablutions with Moses's washing of Israel at Sinai. By representing John's ablutions as a ritual purification that prepares for the perception of God's revelation, the Fourth Gospel employs Israel's embodied theology of purity in service of its Christology. What is revealed of God through John's ablutions is Jesus. In the Fourth Gospel, ritual purification is Israel's preparation to perceive what God reveals of God in Jesus (1:31).

Ritual purity is distinct from moral purity in the Fourth Gospel, but the way ritual purity prepares the body for the revelation of God corresponds to the way that moral purity enables Israel to live fully and obediently in the presence of God, with lives characterized by practice at the sort of love Jesus showed his disciples. Moral purity resonates with the prophetic expectation of a divine, eschatological purification of Israel from sin's impurity, caused by bloodshed, sexual misdeeds, and idolatry. In the Major Prophets, Israel's sin defiles the land, defiles the temple, and defiles the people, and this moral defilement is the cause for God's judgment on Israel and the land's desolation by the nations. These prophets expected that God would restore Israel, purify Israel's sin, enable Israel to keep God's commandment, and fill the land with life. Isaiah speaks of this restoration in terms of Israel's birth (Isa. 42:10–17; 46:1–7; 49:9–26; 54:1; 66:7–9), and Jeremiah speaks of it in terms of the consummate joy of the bridegroom and the bride (Jer. 33:7–11). The hope for God finally to purify Israel from sin was associated with Israel's restoration and carried forward in a number of early Jewish writings, including, as I have argued, the Gospel of John (especially Jn 3:1–4:2; cf., also, 2 Macc; 1 QS 3–4; *Jub.* 1:23–25; Pss. Sol. 17).

---

[4] On the terms *ritual purity* and *moral purity* used throughout this book, see §1.3 and Klawans, *Impurity and Sin*, 22–31.

The Fourth Gospel takes up the weight of this expectation for God to purify Israel from sin and focuses it onto Jesus when the Pharisees ask John (the Baptist), "Why then are you abluting if you are neither the Messiah, nor Elijah, nor the prophet?" (1:25 NRSV, trans. mod.). In this question, the Pharisees presuppose that the work of moral purification would be carried out by a figure associated with Israel's restoration, and that this figure would do so through some kind of ablution. The Pharisees' presupposition, which reflected biblical and early Jewish traditions about moral purification, was correct, but misplaced. John subsequently identifies Jesus as the Lamb of God who takes away the world's sin and as the one who ablutes with the Holy Spirit. In so doing, John indicates that Jesus is one who is pure and the one who purifies Israel from sin. When Jesus begins his ablutionary ministry, John responds to a controversy about purification by alluding to the only oracle in Jeremiah related to God's purification of Israel from sin (Jn 3:25; Jer. 33:7–11). John discovers in Jesus's ablutions God's moral purification of Israel and the restoration of life for God's people. Through the ablutions of Jesus, Israel was to be born from above and made able to see and enter the life of God (3:1–15). Thus, in his ministry Jesus does not replace purity with something else, but rather removes the impurity of sin so that his pure disciples might live fully before God. The work of God in Jesus to purify Israel from sin is instantiated in the giving of sight to the man born blind. The judgment that he is born in sin is removed along with his blindness when he washes with water, an act of ritual purification that corresponds to Jesus's work of moral purification through the word that he speaks to the man (9:35–38). The man comes to see that Jesus is from God and he enters through Jesus into life (9:1–10:21). Having been born blind, the work of God in restoring his sight is a birth from above, brought into effect through the water of Siloam and the word of Jesus.

The moral purification of Jesus's disciples is not narrated in the same way that the giving of sight to the man born blind is. The Fourth Gospel withholds the precise moment that these disciples came to be (morally) pure. But already at the Farewell Discourse, Jesus pronounces all his disciples to be (morally) pure, except for Judas (13:10–11; 15:2–3). In the image of the vine and branches, the disciples' companionship with Jesus locates them in Israel's restoration, and their purity is found to be the work of the Father through Jesus's word (15:2–3). But the disciples' purity does not indicate their possession of salvation, as though God's life were at their disposal to do with it whatever they willed. Each time Jesus calls the disciples pure, he also commands them to love one another just as he has loved them (13:1–38; 15:1–17). The disciples' purity is a matter of the moral quality of their lives and their moral capacity to keep Jesus's commandment. Jesus seems utterly confident that every disciple he calls pure will do as he had done, produce the fruit of love, and so enter blessedness (13:15–18; 15:4–5, 8–11). Moral purification in the Fourth Gospel is at once soteriological and ethical. It enables those who are purified to see and enter God's life, just as it enables God's life to be replicated in the pure disciples. The disciples' purity, given by God, consists in the repetition of the love and life of Jesus among them.

A striking feature of the Fourth Gospel's approach to purity is how both ritual and moral purity are conceptualized positively in relation to human ability, potential, and capacity, rather than negatively in relation to the absence of ritual impurities or defiling sins. Because purity is the result of the removal of impurities, scholars have sometimes used structural linguistics to define purity as "the absence of impurity."[5] This may indeed be fitting for a number of early Jewish writings. But the Fourth Gospel has almost nothing to say about ritual impurity. Instead, it is concerned with ritual *purity* as the bodily state needed to perceive what God revealed of God in Jesus. Likewise, moral purity is constituted by the moral qualities and capacity that made possible the kind of love that leads to abundant, abandoned life for others.[6] To be sure, it is not that the Fourth Gospel never speaks of sin in relation to moral purification. Jesus is called the lamb of God who takes away the sin of the world, and Judas was not regarded as pure on account of his complicity in bloodshed, a defiling sin. Even so, the Fourth Gospel's focus falls on the result of moral purification. Moral purity would make it possible for Israel to see and enter the life of God through Jesus, and the disciples' purity would enable them to bear love's fruit. The Fourth Gospel gives a bracing vision of purity in relation to human capacity, with almost no recourse to impurity of any kind. In the Fourth Gospel, purity is defined not by the absence of impurity, but by a fullness of perception, life, and love.

Surprisingly, the Fourth Gospel, for all its focus on faith, does not directly relate the purity of the disciples to their faith in Jesus. It is not clear whether faith precedes the word of Jesus that (morally) purifies, or whether the purifying word of Jesus makes the human response of faith possible. When it comes to the disciples of Jesus in the Fourth Gospel, faith is nearly always lexicalized as a verb (πιστεύω), but moral purity is adjectival (καθαρός).[7] As wind exists only by blowing, faith exists only in human responsiveness to Jesus. For this reason, faith can never be complete, and the Fourth Gospel itself is written for faith to come alive in those who read it (20:30–31). By contrast, Jesus calls his disciples pure, and their purity leaves nothing to be desired (13:10–11; 15:2–3). Those disciples who are pure are totally pure, and that purity is the result of God's work in Christ, not of human action. God has given to such disciples the moral capacity for life in its fullest sense. Of course, this is not the case for all disciples. Jesus judged Judas not to be pure, and this judgment inclines one to think that concepts of purity continued to be used within the circle of Jesus's disciples for moral and theological deliberation (cf. 1 Jn 1:5–10). To put it another way, judgment about purity is reserved for insiders, not outsiders. Jesus calls none of the *Ioudaioi* impure, only his chosen disciple Judas. While purity and faith, then, cannot be brought into a clear logical relationship based on the Fourth Gospel, they can be brought into clear sociological relation: purity pertains to those who are among Jesus's disciples.

---

[5] Feder refers to James Barr's interpretation of purity as the "absence of impurity" through the application of structural linguistics, then offers an interesting rebuttal in his etymological study of purity's positive relation to radiance in ancient Semitic languages ("The Semantics of Purity," 88–90). On the claim that ritual purity is the absence of ritual impurity, see, for example, Harrington, *The Purity Texts*, 9; Leonhardt, *Jewish Worship in Philo*, 257; Bockmuehl, "Keeping It Holy," 104; Thiessen, *Jesus and the Forces of Death*, 6, fn. 18.

[6] Again, I am borrowing this lovely turn of phrase from Zimmermann, "Abundant and Abandoning Life."

[7] The one time faith is lexicalized as an adjective is when Jesus tells Thomas "become faithful" (γίνου … πιστός; 20:27), but Christopher Seglenieks argues that the adjective stresses faithfulness enacted in witness, rather than the responsive, relational character John's Gospel ascribes to having faith; see "Thomas the (Un)Faithful: Πιστός in John 20.27," *JSNT* 45.2 (2022): 135–56.

The argument of *Purity Remains* can be taken as a case study in the complex relationship between the Fourth Gospel and its early Jewish context. The Fourth Gospel's treatment of purity is often interpreted in terms of its departure from early Judaism.[8] However, the Fourth Gospel is quite at home in the controverted discourse of early Jewish (im)purity. An intelligence about purity is at work in the Fourth Gospel, and it demonstrates far more continuity with early Jewish concepts of purity than previously supposed. At the same time, these early Jewish conceptions of purity are employed in service of the Fourth Gospel's Christology, soteriology, and ethics, which involves discontinuity and conflict with other early Jewish traditions. It is astonishing, for example, that ritual purification would prepare Israel for the revelation of a human being named Jesus. The scandal of such an act forces the question of Jesus's relation to God, which was the source of conflict between Jesus and the *Ioudaioi* (see, e.g., 5:17–18; 10:31–33). That is, the Fourth Gospel inscribes Jesus's identity with God into early Jewish practices of worship, and, in so doing, transforms ritual purification into a site of Christological controversy.

The Fourth Gospel also relates Jesus's work of moral purification to the restoration of Israel in a way that complicates how scholars conceptualize the relationship between John's Gospel and early Judaism. The relation of purity to Israel's restoration complements recent scholarly contentions that the Fourth Gospel does envision a future for Israel "in continuity with its basic beliefs, traditions, and practices."[9] At the same time, God's eschatological, moral purification is enacted through Jesus, and the Fourth Gospel develops its claims about moral purification through conflict—the conflict between Jesus and Nicodemus over birth from above (3:1–15), the conflict between John's disciples' and an *Ioudaios* over purification (3:22–30), and the conflict between the Pharisees about the giving of sight to the man born blind (9:16; 10:21).[10] Those who do not receive God's purifying work in Jesus will be unable to perceive and enter the life of God that Jesus mediates.

For many ancient Jews, the worst thing that could have happened happened when the Jerusalem Temple was destroyed in 70 CE.[11] The Fourth Gospel, likely not published until after that destruction, proclaims that the restoration of Israel had taken place with the arrival of Jesus.[12] Appearances were to the contrary. What one could see

---

[8] See, for example, Brown, *The Gospel according to John*, 1:lxxv, 1:103–4; Hakola, *Identity Matters*, 87–8. See also § 1.2.

[9] Blumhofer, *The Gospel of John and the Future of Israel*, 46.

[10] On the way that the Fourth Gospel develops its soteriological claims by means of conflict, see Blumhofer, *The Gospel of John and the Future of Israel*, 1–47; Van der Watt, "Salvation," 102–3.

[11] On ancient Jewish perception of the temple's destruction as a crisis see Motyer, *Your Father the Devil?*, 77–87. The connection to the temple even among ancient Jews dispersed throughout the Mediterranean is evident in their payment of a temple tax, sometimes despite the resistance of local authorities (as, e.g., in the Lycus Valley; see Ulrich Huttner, *Early Christianity in the Lycus Valley*, Ancient Judaism and Early Christianity 85 [Leiden: Brill, 2013], 70–2). That said, the significance of the destruction of the temple to ancient Jews is a complex historical phenomenon, some of the dimensions of which are addressed in Daniel R. Schwartz and Zeev Weiss, *Was 70 CE a Watershed in Jewish History? On Jews and Judaism before and after the Destruction of the Second Temple*, Ancient Judaism and Early Christianity 78 (Leiden: Brill, 2012).

[12] Motyer helpfully argues that there are certain points of sensitivity in the Fourth Gospel that reflect its response to the catastrophe of the temple's destruction (*Your Father the Devil?*, 35–73).

from Judea at the end of the first century was the desolate remains of the temple, the stubborn presence of foreign powers, and the dispersion of Jews throughout the known world—in other words, the very situation from which certain ancient Jews expected restoration. To see anything else would require an entirely different way of seeing, as well as a rationale for why the restoration of Israel by Jesus was not inclusive of all ancient Jews. The Fourth Gospel's concept of moral purity and the conflict it entails constructs an imaginative grid that can hold together the catastrophe of the temple's destruction with the conviction of Israel's restoration through Jesus Christ. Only those born of God through moral purification can see and enter the kingdom of God. That is, God's salvation is here and now, but one must have it to see it, and because not all have it, not all can see it. In the Fourth Gospel, God's work of moral purification through Jesus opens up a future the Prophets expected for Israel at the same time as it envisions a division within Israel.

Purity can no longer be understood simply as a sign of the Fourth Gospel's departure from early Judaism. Instead, the Fourth Gospel simultaneously adopts early Jewish conceptions of purity as its very own, and adapts them to serve its Christology, soteriology, and ethics. In the Fourth Gospel, purity remains, even if "it doth suffer a sea-change, into something rich and strange."

Bibliography

Adler, Yonatan. "Between Priestly Cult and Common Culture: The Material Evidence of Ritual Purity Observance in Early Roman Jerusalem Reassessed." *JAJ* 7.2 (2016): 228–48.

Adler, Yonatan. "Ritual Purity in Daily Life after 70 CE: The Chalk Vessel Assemblage from Shuʿafat as a Test Case." *JSJ* 52.1 (2020): 39–62.

Adler, Yonatan. "Watertight and Rock Solid: Stepped Pools and Chalk Vessels as Expressions of Jewish Ritual Purity." *BAR* 47.1 (2021): 44–51.

Agamben, Giorgio. "Potentialities: Collected Essays in Philosophy." Pages 177–84 in *Meridian: Crossing Aesthetics*. Edited and translated by Daniel Heller-Roazen Stanford: Stanford University Press, 2007.

Allison Jr., Dale C. "Kingdom of God." *EDEJ*, 860–1.

Alon, Gedalyahu. *Jews, Judaism, and the Classical World: Studies in Jewish History in the Times of the Second Temple and Talmud*. Jerusalem: Magnes, 1977.

Aquinas, Thomas. *Commentary on the Gospel of John: Chapters 1–5*. Translated by Fabian R. Larcher and James A. Weisheipl. Thomas Aquinas in Translation Series. Washington, DC: Catholic University of America Press, 2010.

Argall, Randal A. *1 Enoch and Sirach: A Comparative Literary and Conceptual Analysis of the Themes of Revelation, Creation, and Judgment*. EJL 8. Atlanta, GA: Scholars Press, 1995.

Assis, Elie. "A Disputed Temple (Haggai 2,1–9)." *ZAW* 120 (2008): 582–96.

Assis, Elie. "Haggai: Structure and Meaning." *Bib* 87 (2006): 531–41.

Assis, Elie. "To Build or Not to Build: A Dispute between Haggai and His People (Hag 1)." *ZAW* 119 (2007): 514–27.

Atkinson, Kenneth. "Herod the Great, Sosius, and the Siege of Jerusalem (37 B.C.E.) in Psalm of Solomon 17." *NovT* 38.4 (1996): 313–22.

Attridge, Harold W. "Genre Bending in the Fourth Gospel." *JBL* 121.1 (2002): 3–21.

Bal, Mieke. *Narratology: Introduction to the Theory of Narrative*. 3rd ed. Toronto: University of Toronto Press, 2009.

Bal, Mieke. "The Point of Narratology." *Poetics Today* 11.4 (1990): 727–53.

Balberg, Mira. *Purity, Body, and Self in Early Rabbinic Literature*. S. Mark Taper Foundation Imprint in Jewish Studies. Berkeley: University of California Press, 2014.

Barclay, John M. G. *Flavius Josephus: Translation and Commentary. Against Apion*. Edited by Steve Mason. BJP 10. Leiden: Brill, 2007.

Barrett, C. K. *The Gospel according to St. John: An Introduction with Commentary and Notes on the Greek Text*. 2nd ed. Philadelphia, PA: Westminster, 1978.

Bauckham, Richard. *Gospel of Glory: Major Themes in Johannine Theology*. Grand Rapids, MI: Baker Academic, 2015.

Bauckham, Richard. *Jesus and the God of Israel: God Crucified and Other Studies on the New Testament's Christology of Divine Identity*. Grand Rapids, MI: Eerdmans, 2009.

Bauckham, Richard. *The Testimony of the Beloved Disciple: Narrative, History, and Theology in the Gospel of John*. Grand Rapids, MI: Baker Academic, 2007.

Bauckham, Richard. "Messianism according to the Gospel of John." Pages 34–68 in *Challenging Perspectives on the Gospel of John*. Edited by John Lierman. WUNT 2/219. Tübingen: Mohr Siebeck, 2006.

Bauckham, Richard. "Sacraments and the Gospel of John." Pages 83–96 in *The Oxford Handbook of Sacramental Theology*. Edited by Hans Boersma and Matthew Levering. Oxford: Oxford University Press, 2015.

Bauckham, Richard. "The Holiness of Jesus and His Disciples in the Gospel of John." Pages 95–113 in *Holiness and Ecclesiology in the New Testament*. Edited by Kent E. Brower and Andy Johnson. Grand Rapids, MI: Eerdmans, 2007.

Bauckham, Richard, James R. Davila, and Alexander Panayotov, eds. *Old Testament Pseudepigrapha: More Noncanonical Scriptures*. Vol. 1. Grand Rapids, MI: Eerdmans, 2013.

Baur, F. C. *The Church History of the First Three Centuries*. Translated by Allan Menzies. 3rd ed. Vol. 1. London: Williams and Norgate, 1878.

Beasley-Murray, George R. *Baptism in the New Testament*. Grand Rapids, MI: Eerdmans, 1973.

Beasley-Murray, George R. *John*. 2nd ed. WBC. Nashville: Thomas Nelson, 1999.

Bell, Catherine. *Ritual Theory, Ritual Practice*. New York: Oxford University Press, 1992.

Bennema, Cornelis. "Mimetic Ethics in the Gospel of John." Pages 205–17 in *Metaphor – Narratio – Mimesis – Doxologie: Begründungsformen frühchristlicher und antiker Ethik*. Edited by Ulrich Volp, Friedrich Wilhelm Horn, and Ruben Zimmermann. WUNT 356. Tübingen: Mohr Siebeck, 2016.

Bennema, Cornelis. "Spirit-Baptism in the Fourth Gospel: A Messianic Reading of John 1:33." *Bib* 84.1 (2003): 35–60.

Blidstein, Moshe. *Purity, Community, and Ritual in Early Christian Literature*. Oxford Studies in the Abrahamic Religions. New York: Oxford University Press, 2017.

Blumhofer, Christopher. *The Gospel of John and the Future of Israel*. SNTSMS 177. Cambridge, MA: Cambridge University Press, 2020.

Bockmuehl, Markus. "'Keeping It Holy': Old Testament Commandment and New Testament Faith." Pages 95–124 in *I Am the Lord Your God: Christian Reflections on the Ten Commandments*. Edited by Christopher R. Seitz and Carl E. Braaten. Grand Rapids, MI: Eerdmans, 2005.

de Boer, Martinus C. "Jesus the Baptizer: 1 John 5:5–8 and the Gospel of John." *JBL* 107.1 (1988): 87–106.

Boismard, M. E. "Le lavement des pieds (Jn 13:1–17)." *RB* 71.1 (1964): 5–24.

Bolen, Edward Roland. "Purity and Pollution in the Fourth Gospel." PhD diss., Southern Baptist Theological Seminary, 1993.

Boucher, Pierre-Marin. "Jn 3,3.7: γεννηθῆναι ἄνωθεν* (IV)." *ETL* 88.1 (2012): 71–93.

Boyarin, Daniel. "What Kind of Jew Is an Evangelist?" Pages 109–53 in *Those Outside: Noncanonical Readings of Canonical Gospels*. Edited by George Aichele and Richard G. Walsh. London: T&T Clark, 2006.

Brant, Jo-Ann A. *Dialogue and Drama: Elements of Greek Tragedy in the Fourth Gospel*. Peabody, MA: Hendrickson, 2004.

Brant, Jo-Ann A. *John*. Paideia Commentaries on the New Testament. Grand Rapids, MI: Baker Academic, 2011.

Brawley, Robert L. *Text to Text Pours Forth Speech: Voices of Scripture in Luke-Acts*. Bloomington: Indiana University Press, 1995.

Brower, Kent. "Purity in the Gospel of John." Pages 114–33 in *Purity: Essays in Bible and Theology*. Edited by Andrew Brower Latz and Arseny Ermakov. Eugene, OR: Wipf & Stock, 2014.

Brown, Raymond E. *The Gospel According to John*. 2 vols. AB 29–29A. Garden City, NY: Doubleday, 1966.

Bultmann, Rudolf. *The Gospel of John: A Commentary*. Translated by George R. Beasley-Murray. Philadelphia, PA: Westminster, 1971.

Bultmann, Rudolf. *Theology of the New Testament*. Translated by Kendrick Grobel. Vol. 2. New York: Charles Scribner's Sons, 1955.

Burge, Gary M. "Siloam, Bethesda, and the Johannine Water Motif." Pages 259–70 in *John, Jesus, and History*, Vol. 3: *Glimpses of Jesus through the Johannine Lens*. Edited by Paul N. Anderson, Felix Just, and Tom Thatcher. ECL 18. Atlanta, GA: SBL Press, 2016.

Burge, Gary M. *The Anointed Community: The Holy Spirit in the Johannine Tradition*. Grand Rapids, MI: Eerdmans, 1987.

Busse, Ulrich. "Reinigung und Heiligung im Johannesevangelium." Pages 141–58 in *The Scriptures of Israel in Jewish and Christian Tradition: Essays in Honour of Maarten J. J. Menken*. Edited by B. J. Koet, S. Moyise, and J. Verheyden. NovTSup 148. Leiden: Brill, 2013.

Charles, R. H. *The Greek Versions of the Testaments of the Twelve Patriarchs: Edited from Nine MSS Together with the Variants of the Armenian and Slavonic Versions and Some Hebrew Fragments*. Oxford: Clarendon Press, 1908.

Childs, Brevard S. *Isaiah*. OTL. Louisville, KY: Westminster John Knox, 2001.

Cicero. *On Duties*. Translated by Walter Miller. LCL 30. Cambridge, MA: Harvard University Press, 1913.

Cirafesi, Wally V. *John within Judaism: Religion, Ethnicity, and the Shaping of Jesus-Oriented Jewishness in the Fourth Gospel*. Ancient Judaism and Early Christianity 112. Leiden: Brill, 2021.

Colautti, F. M. *Passover in the Works of Josephus*. JSJSup 75. Leiden: Brill, 2002.

Collins, John J. "Early Judaism in Modern Scholarship." Pages 1–23 in *The Eerdmans Dictionary of Early Judaism*. Edited by John J. Collins and Daniel C. Harlow. Grand Rapids, MI: Eerdmans, 2010.

Collins, John J. "Testaments." Pages 325–56 in *Jewish Writings of the Second Temple Period: Apocrypha, Pseudepigrapha, Qumran, Sectarian Writings, Philo, Josephus*. Edited by Michael E. Stone. Assen; Philadelphia, PA: Van Gorcum; Fortress Press, 1984.

Coloe, Mary L. "Welcome into the Household of God: The Foot Washing in John 13." *CBQ* 66.3 (2004): 400–15.

Conway, Colleen M. "Gender and the Fourth Gospel." Pages 220–36 in *The Oxford Handbook of Johannine Studies*. Edited by Judith Lieu and Martinus C. de Boer. Oxford Handbooks. Oxford: Oxford University Press, 2018.

Culpepper, R. Alan. *Anatomy of the Fourth Gospel: A Study in Literary Design*. Philadelphia, PA: Fortress, 1983.

Culpepper, R. Alan. "The Johannine Hypodeigma: A Reading of John 13." *Semeia* 53 (1991): 133–52.

Davila, James. *The Provenance of the Pseudepigrapha: Jewish, Christian, or Other?* JSJSup 105. Boston, MA: Brill, 2005.

Deines, Roland. *Jüdische Steingefässe und pharisäische Frömmigkeit: Ein archäologisch-historischer Beitrag zum Verständnis von Joh 2,6 und der jüdischen Reinheitshalacha zur Zeit Jesu* WUNT 2/52. Tübingen: Mohr Siebeck, 1993.

Dennis, John A. *Jesus' Death and the Gathering of True Israel: The Johannine Appropriation of Restoration Theology in the Light of John 11.47–52* WUNT 2/217. Tübingen: Mohr Siebeck, 2006.

Dennis, John A. "Jesus' Death in John's Gospel: A Survey of Research from Bultmann to the Present with Special Reference to the Johannine Hyper-Texts." *CBR* 4.3 (2006): 331–63.

DeSilva, David A. *Introducing the Apocrypha: Message, Context, and Significance.* Grand Rapids, MI: Baker Academic, 2004.

DiFransico, Lesley. "Identifying Inner-Biblical Allusion through Metaphor: Washing Away Sin in Psalm 51." *VT* 65 (2015): 542–57.

Dimant, Devorah, and Donald W. Parry, eds. *Dead Sea Scrolls Handbook.* Leiden: Brill, 2014.

Dodd, C. H. *Historical Tradition in the Fourth Gospel.* Cambridge, MA: Cambridge University Press, 1963.

Dodd, C. H. *The Interpretation of the Fourth Gospel.* Cambridge, MA: Cambridge University Press, 1953.

Doran, Robert. *2 Maccabees.* Edited by Harold W. Attridge. Hermeneia. Minneapolis, MN: Fortress, 2012.

Douglas, Mary. *Purity and Danger: An Analysis of the Concepts of Pollution and Taboo.* London: Routledge & Kegan Paul, 1966.

Du Rand, Jan A. "A Syntactical and Narratological Reading of John 10 in Coherence with Chapter 9." Pages 94–115 in *The Shepherd Discourse of John 10 and Its Context: Studies.* Edited by Johannes Beutler and Robert Tomson Fortna. SNTSMS 67. Cambridge, MA: Cambridge University Press, 1991.

Duschinsky, Robbie, Simone Schnall, and Daniel H. Weiss, eds. *Purity and Danger Now: New Perspectives.* Abingdon: Routledge, 2017.

Ego, Beate. "Purity Concepts in Jewish Traditions of the Hellenistic Period." Pages 477–92 in *Purity and the Forming of Religious Traditions in the Ancient Mediterranean World and Ancient Judaism.* Edited by Christian Frevel and Christophe Nihan. Dynamics in the History of Religions 3. Leiden: Brill, 2013.

Elowsky, Joel C., ed. *John 1–10.* Ancient Christian Commentary on Scripture, New Testament 4a. Downers Grove, IL: IVP Academic, 2006.

Embry, Bradley. "The Psalms of Solomon and the New Testament: Intertextuality and the Need for a Re-Evaluation." *JSP* 13.2 (2002): 99–136.

Engberg-Pedersen, Troels. *John and Philosophy: A New Reading of the Fourth Gospel.* Oxford: Oxford University Press, 2017.

Engberg-Pedersen, Troels. "Philosophy and Ideology in John 9–10." Pages 295–306 in *"The One Who Sows Bountifully": Essays in Honor of Stanley K. Stowers.* Edited by Caroline E. Johnson Hodge, Saul M. Olyan, Daniel C. Ullucci, and Emma Wasserman. BJS 356. Providence, RI: Brown Judaic Studies, 2013.

Erbele-Küster, Dorothea. *Body, Gender and Purity in Leviticus 12 and 15.* LHBOTS 539. London: T&T Clark, 2017.

Evans, Craig A. *Word and Glory: On the Exegetical and Theological Background of John's Prologue.* JSNTSup 89. Sheffield: JSOT, 1993.

Fatkin, Danielle Steen. "Invention of a Bathing Tradition in Hasmonean Palestine." *JSJ* 50 (2019): 155–77.

Feder, Yitzhaq. "Contagion and Cognition: Bodily Experience and the Conceptualization of Pollution (Ṭum'ah) in the Hebrew Bible." *JNES* 72.2 (2013): 151–67.

Feder, Yitzhaq. "The Semantics of Purity in the Ancient Near East: Lexical Meaning as a Projection of Embodied Experience." *JANER* 14 (2014): 87–113.

Ferguson, Everett. *Baptism in the Early Church: History, Theology, and Liturgy in the First Five Centuries.* Grand Rapids, MI: Eerdmans, 2009.

Filtvedt, Ole Jakob. "Revisiting Nicodemus's Question in John 3:9." *JTS* 70.1 (2019): 110–40.

Fonrobert, Charlotte Elisheva. *Menstrual Purity: Rabbinic and Christian Reconstructions of Biblical Gender.* Contraversions: Jews and Other Differences. Stanford: Stanford University Press, 2002.

Foster, Timothy D. "John 3:5: Redefining the People of God." *BBR* 27.3 (2017): 351–60.

Fraade, Steven D. "Hearing and Seeing at Sinai: Interpretive Trajectories." Pages 247–68 in *The Significance of Sinai: Traditions about Sinai and Divine Revelation in Judaism and Christianity.* Edited by George J. Brooke, Hindy Najman, and Loren T. Stuckenbruck. TBN 12. Leiden: Brill, 2008.

Freedman, David Noel, ed. *Anchor Bible Dictionary.* 6 vols. New York: Doubleday, 1992.

Frevel, Christian, and Christophe Nihan, eds. *Purity and the Forming of Religious Traditions in the Ancient Mediterranean World and Ancient Judaism.* Dynamics in the History of Religions 3. Leiden: Brill, 2013.

Frey, Jörg. *Theology and History in the Fourth Gospel: Tradition and Narration.* Waco, TX: Baylor University Press, 2018.

Frey, Jörg. "Between Jewish Monotheism and Proto-Trinitarian Relations: The Making and Character of Johannine Christology." Pages 189–221 in *Monotheism and Christology in Greco-Roman Antiquity.* Edited by Matthew V. Novenson. NovTSup 180. Leiden: Brill, 2020.

Furstenberg, Yair. "Defilement Penetrating the Body: A New Understanding of Contamination in Mark 7.15." *NTS* 54.2 (2008): 176–200.

Gadot, Yuval, and Yonatan Adler "A Quantitative Analysis of Jewish Chalk Vessel Frequencies in Early Roman Jerusalem: A View from the City's Garbage Dump." *IEJ* 66.2 2016: 202–19.

Ganzel, Tova. "The Defilement and Desecration of the Temple in Ezekiel." *Bib* 89 (2008): 369–79.

Ganzel, Tova. "The Descriptions of the Restoration of Israel in Ezekiel." *VT* 60 (2010): 197–211.

García Martínez, Florentino. *The Dead Sea Scrolls Translated: The Qumran Texts in English.* Translated by Wilfred G. E. Watson. 2nd ed. Leiden: Brill, 1996.

Gorman, Frank H. "Pagans and Priests: Critical Reflections on Method." Pages 96–110 in *Perspectives on Purity and Purification in the Bible.* Edited by Baruch J. Schwartz, David P. Wright, Jeffrey Stackert, and Naphtali S. Meshel. LHBOTS 474. New York: T&T Clark, 2008.

Gorman, Frank H. "Ritual Studies and Biblical Studies: Assessment of the Past, Prospects for the Future." *Semeia* 67 (1994): 13–36.

Grabbe, Lester L. "Eschatology in Philo and Josephus." Pages 163–85 in *Judaism in Late Antiquity 4. Death, Life-After-Death, Resurrection and The World-to-Come in the Judaisms of Antiquity.* Edited by Alan Avery-Peck and Jacob Neusner. Handbook of Oriental Studies. Section 1 The Near and Middle East 49. Leiden: Brill, 2000.

Green, Joel B. "Kingdom of God/Heaven." *Dictionary of Jesus and the Gospels*, 468–81.

Green, Joel B. "Rethinking 'History' for Theological Interpretation." *JTI* 5.2 (2011): 159–73.

Greenblatt, Stephen. "Culture." Pages 225–32 in *Critical Terms for Literary Study*. Edited by Frank Lentricchia and Thomas McLaughlin. Chicago: University of Chicago Press, 1990.

Grigsby, Bruce H. "The Cross as an Expiatory Sacrifice in the Fourth Gospel." *JSNT* 15 (1982): 51–80.

Grimes, Ronald L. *The Craft of Ritual Studies*. Oxford Ritual Studies. New York: Oxford University Press, 2013.

Haber, Susan. *"They Shall Purify Themselves": Essays on Purity in Early Judaism*. Edited by Adele Reinhartz. EJL 24. Atlanta, GA: Society of Biblical Literature, 2008.

Haenchen, Ernst. *John: A Commentary on the Gospel of John*. Translated by Robert W. Funk. Philadelphia, PA: Fortress, 1984.

Hakola, Raimo. *Identity Matters: John, the Jews, and Jewishness*. NovTSup 118. Leiden: Brill, 2005.

Harrington, Hannah K. "Purification in the Fourth Gospel in Light of Qumran." Pages 117–38 in *John, Qumran, and the Dead Sea Scrolls Sixty Years of Discovery and Debate*. Edited by Mary L. Coloe and Tom Thatcher. EJL 32. Atlanta, GA: Society of Biblical Literature, 2011.

Harrington, Hannah K. *The Impurity Systems of Qumran and the Rabbis: Biblical Foundations*. SBLDS 143. Atlanta, GA: Scholars Press, 1993.

Harrington, Hannah K. *The Purity Texts*. Companion to the Qumran Scrolls. London: T&T Clark International, 2004.

Hartin, Patrick J. "Remain in Me (John 15:5): The Foundation of the Ethical and Its Consequences in the Farewell Discourses." *Neot* 25.2 (1991): 341–56.

Hayes, Christine E. *Gentile Impurities and Jewish Identities: Intermarriage and Conversion from the Bible to the Talmud*. Oxford: Oxford University Press, 2002.

Hayes, Christine E. *What's Divine about Divine Law?: Early Perspectives*. Princeton, NJ: Princeton University Press, 2015.

Hays, Richard B. *Echoes of Scripture in the Gospels*. Waco, TX: Baylor University Press, 2016.

Hays, Richard B. *Echoes of Scripture in the Letters of Paul*. New Haven, CT: Yale University Press, 1989.

Hayward, Charles Thomas Robert. "The Giving of the Torah: Targumic Perspectives." Pages 269–85 in *The Significance of Sinai: Traditions about Sinai and Divine Revelation in Judaism and Christianity*. Edited by George J. Brooke, Hindy Najman, and Loren T. Stuckenbruck. TBN 12. Leiden: Brill, 2008.

Hengel, Martin, and Roland Deines. "E.P. Sanders' 'Common Judaism,' Jesus, and the Pharisees." *JTS* 46.1 (1995): 1–70.

Hogan, Karina Martin. *Theologies in Conflict in 4 Ezra: Wisdom, Debate, and Apocalyptic Solution*. JSJSup 130. Leiden: Brill, 2008.

Hollander, H. W. *Joseph as an Ethical Model in the Testaments of the Twelve Patriarchs*. SVTP 6. Leiden: Brill, 1981.

Holleran, J. W. "Seeing the Light: A Narrative Reading of John 9." *ETL* 69.4 (1993): 354–82.

Holleran, J. W. "Seeing the Light: A Narrative Reading of John 9." *ETL* 69.1 (1993): 5–26.

Holtz, Gudrun. "Purity Conceptions in the Dead Sea Scrolls: 'Ritual-Physical' and 'Moral' Purity in a Diachronic Perspective." Pages 519–36 in *Purity and the Forming of Religious Traditions in the Ancient Mediterranean World and Ancient Judaism*. Edited by Christian Frevel and Christophe Nihan. Dynamics in the History of Religions 3. Leiden: Brill, 2013.

Hoskyns, Edwyn C. *The Fourth Gospel*. Edited by Francis Noel Davey. London: Faber and Faber, 1947.

Hrobon, Bohdan. *Ethical Dimension of Cult in the Book of Isaiah*. BZAW. Berlin: de Gruyter, 2010.

Hull, John. "Open Letter from a Blind Disciple to a Sighted Saviour." Pages 154–77 in *Borders, Boundaries and the Bible*. Edited by Martin O'Kane. JSOTSup 313. London: Sheffield Academic, 2002.

Hultgren, Arland J. "The Johannine Footwashing (Jn 13:1–11) as Symbol of Eschatological Hospitality." *NTS* 28.4 (1982): 539–46.

Hurtado, Larry W. *How on Earth Did Jesus Become a God? Historical Questions about Earliest Devotion to Jesus*. Grand Rapids, MI: Eerdmans, 2005.

Hurtado, Larry W. *Lord Jesus Christ: Devotion to Jesus in Earliest Christianity*. Grand Rapids, MI: Eerdmans, 2005.

Huttner, Ulrich. *Early Christianity in the Lycus Valley*. Ancient Judaism and Early Christianity 85. Leiden: Brill, 2013.

Jensen, Robin M. *Living Water: Images, Symbols, and Settings of Early Christian Baptism*. Supplements to Vigiliae Christianae 105. Leiden: Brill, 2011.

Jervis, L. Anne. "Worlds of Judgment: John 9." Pages 48–57 in *Conception, Reception and the Spirit: Essays in Honour of Andrew T. Lincoln*. Edited by J. Gordon McConville and Lloyd K. Pietersen. Cambridge, MA: James Clarke, 2015.

Jones, Larry P. *The Symbol of Water in the Gospel of John*. JSNTSup 145. Sheffield: Sheffield Academic, 1997.

de Jonge, Marinus. *Jewish Eschatology, Early Christian Christology and the Testaments of the Twelve Patriarchs: Collected Essays*. NovTSup 63. Leiden: Brill, 1991.

Josephus. *Jewish Antiquities*, Vol. 3: *Books 7–8*. Translated by Ralph Marcus. LCL 281. Cambridge, MA: Harvard University Press, 1934.

Josephus. *Jewish Antiquities*, Vol. 4: *Books 9–11*. Translated by Ralph Marcus. LCL 326. Cambridge, MA: Harvard University Press, 1937.

Josephus. *The Jewish War*, Vol. 1: *Books 1–2*. Translated by H. St. J. Thackeray. LCL 203. Cambridge, MA: Harvard University Press, 1927.

Josephus. *The Jewish War*, Vol. 2: *Books 3–4*. Translated by H. St. J. Thackeray. LCL 487. Cambridge, MA: Harvard University Press, 1927.

Josephus. *The Jewish War*, Vol. 3: *Books 5–7*. Translated by H. St. J. Thackeray. LCL 210. Cambridge, MA: Harvard University Press, 1928.

Kanagaraj, Jey J. "The Implied Ethics of the Fourth Gospel: A Reinterpretation of the Decalogue." *TynBul* 52.1 (2001): 33–60.

Käsemann, Ernst. *The Testament of Jesus: A Study of the Gospel of John in the Light of Chapter 17*. Translated by Gerhard Krodel. The Johannine Monograph Series 6. Eugene, OR: Wipf & Stock, 2017.

Kazen, Thomas. "Dirt and Disgust: Body and Morality in Biblical Purity Laws." Pages 43–64 in *Perspectives on Purity and Purification in the Bible*. Edited by Baruch J. Schwartz, David P. Wright, Jeffrey Stackert, and Naphtali S. Meshel. LHBOTS 474. New York: T&T Clark, 2008.

Kazen, Thomas. *Jesus and Purity Halakhah: Was Jesus Indifferent to Impurity?* Rev. ed. ConBNT 38. Winona Lake, IN: Eisenbrauns, 2010.

Kazen, Thomas. "Levels of Explanation for Ideas of Impurity: Why Structuralist and Symbolic Models Often Fail While Evolutionary and Cognitive Models Succeed." *JAJ* 9.1 (2018): 75–100.

Kee, Howard C. "Ethical Dimensions of the Testaments of the XII as a Clue to Provenance." *NTS* 24.2 (1978): 259–70.

Kee, Howard C. "Testaments of the Twelve Patriarchs." *Old Testament Pseudepigrapha.* Edited by James H. Charlesworth. Vol. 1 of 2. New York: Hendrickson, 1983.

Keener, Craig S. *The Gospel of John: A Commentary.* Peabody, MA: Hendrickson, 2003.

Keener, Craig S. *The Spirit in the Gospels and Acts: Divine Purity and Power.* Peabody, MA: Hendrickson, 1997.

Kerr, Alan R. *The Temple of Jesus' Body: The Temple Theme in the Gospel of John.* JSNTSup 220. London: Sheffield Academic, 2002.

Klawans, Jonathan. *Impurity and Sin in Ancient Judaism.* Oxford: Oxford University Press, 2000.

Klawans, Jonathan. *Josephus and the Theologies of Ancient Judaism.* Oxford: Oxford University Press, 2012.

Klawans, Jonathan. "Methodology and Ideology in the Study of Priestly Ritual." Pages 84–95 in *Perspectives on Purity and Purification in the Bible.* Edited by Baruch J. Schwartz, David P. Wright, Jeffrey Stackert, and Naphtali S. Meshel. LHBOTS 474. New York: T&T Clark, 2008.

Klawans, Jonathan. "Purity in the Dead Sea Scrolls." Pages 377–402 in *The Oxford Handbook of the Dead Sea Scrolls.* Edited by Timothy H. Lim and John J. Collins. Oxford Handbooks in Religion and Theology. Oxford: Oxford University Press, 2010.

Klawans, Jonathan. *Purity, Sacrifice, and the Temple: Symbolism and Supersessionism in the Study of Ancient Judaism.* New York: Oxford University Press, 2005.

Klein, Anja. "From the 'Right Spirit' to the 'Spirit of Truth': Observations on Psalm 51 and 1QS." Pages 171–91 in *The Dynamics of Language and Exegesis at Qumran.* Edited by Devorah Dimant and Reinhard Gregor Kratz. FAT 2.35. Tübingen: Mohr Siebeck, 2009.

Klink, Edward W. *The Sheep of the Fold: The Audience and Origin of the Gospel of John.* SNTSMS 141. Cambridge, MA: Cambridge University Press, 2007.

Köstenberger, Andreas J. *A Theology of John's Gospel and Letters.* Biblical Theology of the New Testament. Grand Rapids, MI: Zondervan, 2009.

Köstenberger, Andreas J. "The Destruction of the Second Temple and the Composition of the Fourth Gospel." Pages 69–108 in *Challenging Perspectives on the Gospel of John.* Edited by John Lierman. WUNT 2/219. Tübingen: Mohr Siebeck, 2006.

Kraft, Robert A. *Exploring the Scripturesque: Jewish Texts and Their Christian Contexts.* JSJSup 137. Leiden: Brill, 2009.

Kraft, Robert A. "Setting the Stage and Framing Some Central Questions." *JSJ* 32.4 (2001): 371–95.

Kugel, James L. *A Walk through Jubilees: Studies in the Book of Jubilees and the World of Its Creation.* JSJSup 156. Leiden: Brill, 2012.

Kugler, Robert A. *Testaments of the Twelve Patriarchs.* Guides to Apocrypha and Pseudepigrapha. Sheffield: Sheffield Academic, 2001.

Labahn, Michael. "'It's Only Love'—Is That All? Limits and Potentials of Johannine 'Ethic'—A Critical Evaluation of Research." Pages 3–44 in *Rethinking the Ethics of John: "Implicit Ethics" in the Johannine Writings.* Edited by Jan G. van der Watt and Ruben Zimmermann. WUNT 291. Tübingen: Mohr Siebeck, 2012.

Lakoff, George, and Mark Johnson. *Metaphors We Live By.* Chicago, IL: University of Chicago Press, 1980.

Lam, Joseph. *Patterns of Sin in the Hebrew Bible: Metaphor, Culture, and the Making of a Religious Concept.* New York: Oxford University Press, 2016.

Laporte, Jean. *Eucharistia in Philo*. Studies in the Bible and Early Christianity 3. New York: Edwin Mellen, 1983.

Lawrence, Jonathan David. *Washing in Water: Trajectories of Ritual Bathing in the Hebrew Bible and Second Temple Literature*. AcBib 23. Atlanta, GA: Society of Biblical Literature, 2006.

Lee, Dorothy. *The Symbolic Narratives of the Fourth Gospel: The Interplay of Form and Meaning*. JSNTSup 95. Sheffield: JSOT Press, 1994.

Lemos, T.M. "Where There Is Dirt, Is There System?: Revisiting Biblical Purity Constructions." *JSOT* 37.3 (2013): 265–94.

Leonhardt, Jutta. *Jewish Worship in Philo of Alexandria*. TSAJ 84. Tübingen: Mohr Siebeck, 2001.

Lightfoot, R. H. *St. John's Gospel: A Commentary*. Edited by C. F. Evans. Oxford Paperbacks 5. London: Oxford University Press, 1960.

Lincoln, Andrew T. *The Gospel According to Saint John*. BNTC. Grand Rapids, MI: Baker Academic, 2013.

Loader, William R. G. "The Law and Ethics in John's Gospel." Pages 143–58 in *Rethinking the Ethics of John: "Implicit Ethics" in the Johannine Writings*. Edited by Jan G. van der Watt and Ruben Zimmermann. WUNT 291. Tübingen: Mohr Siebeck, 2012.

Longenecker, Bruce W. *Rhetoric at the Boundaries: The Art and Theology of New Testament Chain-Link Transitions*. Waco, TX: Baylor University Press, 2005.

Low, Maggie. *Mother Zion in Deutero-Isaiah. A Metaphor for Zion Theology*. StBibLit 155. New York: Peter Lang, 2013.

Lucian. *How to Write History. The Dipsads. Saturnalia. Herodotus or Aetion. Zeuxis or Antiochus. A Slip of the Tongue in Greeting. Apology for the "Salaried Posts in Great Houses." Harmonides. A Conversation with Hesiod. The Scythian or The Consul. Hermotimus or Concerning the Sects. To One Who Said "You're a Prometheus in Words." The Ship or The Wishes*. Translated by K. Kilburn. LCL 430. Cambridge, MA: Harvard University Press, 1959.

Mackie, Scott D. "Seeing God in Philo of Alexandria: Means, Methods, and Mysticism." *JSJ* 43.2 (2012): 147–79.

Manning, Gary T. *Echoes of a Prophet: The Use of Ezekiel in the Gospel of John and in Literature of the Second Temple Period*. JSNTSup 270. London: T&T Clark, 2004.

Marcus, Joel. *John the Baptist in History and Theology*. Studies on Personalities of the New Testament. Columbia: The University of South Carolina Press, 2018.

Marcus, Joel. "The Testaments of the Twelve Patriarchs and the Didascalia Apostolorum: A Common Jewish Christian Milieu?" *JTS* 61.2 (2010): 596–626.

Martyn, J. Louis. *History and Theology in the Fourth Gospel*. 3rd ed. NTL. Louisville, KY: Westminster John Knox, 2003.

Martyn, J. Louis. "The Johannine Community among Jewish and Other Early Christian Communities." Pages 183–90 in *What We Have Heard from the Beginning: The Past, Present, and Future of Johannine Studies*. Edited by Tom Thatcher. Waco, TX: Baylor University Press, 2007.

Mason, Steve. "Pollution and Purification in Josephus's Judean War." Pages 181–207 in *Purity, Holiness, and Identity in Judaism and Christianity: Essays in Memory of Susan Haber*. Edited by Carl S. Ehrlich, Anders Runesson, and Eileen M. Schuller. WUNT 305. Tübingen: Mohr Siebeck, 2013.

Matera, Frank J. "'On Behalf of Others,' 'Cleansing,' and 'Return': Johannine Images for Jesus' Death." *LS* 13.2 (1988): 161–78.

Mathew, Bincy. *The Johannine Footwashing as the Sign of Perfect Love: An Exegetical Study of John 13:1–20.* WUNT 2/464. Tübingen: Mohr Siebeck, 2018.

McNamara, Martin, Kevin Cathcart, and Michael Maher, eds. *Targum Neofiti 1, Exodus.* Translated by Martin McNamara. Collegeville, MN: Liturgical Press, 1994.

McWhirter, Jocelyn. *The Bridegroom Messiah and the People of God: Marriage in the Fourth Gospel.* SNTSMS 138. Cambridge, MA: Cambridge University Press, 2006.

Meeks, Wayne A. "The Ethics of the Fourth Evangelist." Pages 317–26 in *Exploring the Gospel of John: In Honor of D. Moody Smith.* Edited by R. Alan Culpepper and C. Clifton Black. Louisville, KY: Westminster John Knox, 1996.

Meeks, Wayne A. "The Man from Heaven in Johannine Sectarianism." *The Interpretation of John.* Edited by John Ashton. Issues in Religion and Theology 9. Philadelphia, PA: Fortress, 1986.

Meier, John P. *A Marginal Jew: Rethinking the Historical Jesus,* Vol. IV: *Law and Love.* ABRL. New York: Yale University Press, 2009.

Mermelstein, Ari. *Creation, Covenant, and the Beginnings of Judaism: Reconceiving Historical Time in the Second Temple Period.* JSJSup 168. Leiden: Brill, 2014.

Michaels, J. Ramsey. "By Water and Blood: Sin and Purification in John and First John." Pages 149–62 in *Dimensions of Baptism: Biblical and Theological Studies.* Edited by Stanley E. Porter and Anthony R. Cross. JSNTSup 234. London: Sheffield Academic, 2002.

Michaels, J. Ramsey. *The Gospel of John.* NICNT. Grand Rapids, MI: Eerdmans, 2010.

Milgrom, Jacob. *Leviticus 1–16: A New Translation with Introduction and Commentary.* Vol. 1. AB 3. New York: Doubleday, 1991.

Miller, Stuart S. "Stepped Pools, Stone Vessels, and Other Identity Markers of 'Complex Common Judaism.'" *JSJ* 41 (2010): 214–43.

Motyer, Stephen. *Your Father the Devil?: A New Approach to John and "the Jews."* Paternoster Biblical and Theological Studies. Carlisle: Paternoster, 1997.

Najman, Hindy. "The Idea of Biblical Genre: From Discourse to Constellation." Pages 307–21 in *Prayer and Poetry in the Dead Sea Scrolls and Related Literature: Essays in Honor of Eileen Schuller on the Occasion of Her 65th Birthday.* STDJ 98. Leiden: Brill, 2011.

Najman, Hindy. "Towards a Study of the Uses of the Concept of Wilderness in Ancient Judaism." *DSD* 13.1 (2006): 99–113.

Nässelqvist, Dan. *Public Reading in Early Christianity: Lectors, Manuscripts, and Sound in the Oral Delivery of John 1–4.* NovTSup 163. Leiden: Brill, 2016.

Nestle, Eberhard, Erwin Nestle, Barbara Aland, Kurt Aland, Iōan D. Karavidopoulos, Carlo Maria Martini, Bruce M. Metzger, and Holger Strutwolf, eds. *Novum Testamentum Graece.* 28th ed. Stuttgart: Deutsche Bibelgesellschaft, 2012.

Neusner, Jacob. *Judaism in the Beginning of Christianity.* Philadelphia, PA: Fortress, 1984.

Neusner, Jacob. *The Idea of Purity in Ancient Judaism.* Leiden: Brill, 1973.

Nielsen, Jesper Tang. "The Lamb of God: The Cognitive Structure of a Johannine Metaphor." Pages 217–58 in *Imagery in the Gospel of John: Terms, Forms, Themes, and Theology of Johannine Figurative Language.* Edited by Jörg Frey, Ruben Zimmermann, Jan G. Van der Watt, and Gabriele Kern. WUNT 1/200. Tübingen: Mohr Siebeck, 2006.

Nisbet, Robert A. *Metaphor and History: The Western Idea of Social Development.* New Brunswick, NJ: Transaction Publishers, 2009.

Orian, Matan. "Josephus's Seven Purities and the Mishnah's Ten Holinesses." *JSJ* 47.2 (2016): 183–211.

Owanga-Welo, Jean. "The Function and Meaning of the Footwashing in the Johannine Passion Narrative: A Structural Approach." PhD diss., Emory University, 1980.

Parker, Robert. *Miasma: Pollution and Purification in Early Greek Religion.* Oxford: Clarendon, 1983.

Parsenios, George L. *Departure and Consolation: The Johannine Farewell Discourses in Light of Greco-Roman Literature.* NovTSup 117. Leiden: Brill, 2005.

Phelan, James. "Rhetoric/Ethics." Pages 203–16 in *The Cambridge Companion to Narrative.* Edited by David Herman. Cambridge Companions to Literature. Cambridge, MA: Cambridge University Press, 2007.

Phelan, James. *Somebody Telling Somebody Else: A Rhetorical Poetics of Narrative.* Theory and Interpretation of Narrative. Columbus, OH: Ohio State University Press, 2017.

Philo. *On Flight and Finding. On the Change of Names. On Dreams.* Translated by F. H. Colson and G. H. Whitaker. LCL 275. Cambridge, MA: Harvard University Press, 1934.

Philo. *On the Decalogue. On the Special Laws, Books 1–3.* Translated by F. H. Colson. LCL 320. Cambridge, MA: Harvard University Press, 1937.

Philo. *On the Unchangeableness of God. On Husbandry. Concerning Noah's Work as a Planter. On Drunkenness. On Sobriety.* Translated by F. H. Colson and G. H. Whitaker. LCL 247. Cambridge, MA: Harvard University Press, 1930.

Pietersma, Albert, and Benjamin G. Wright, eds. *A New English Translation of the Septuagint.* New York: Oxford University Press, 2007.

Poirier, John C. "'Day and Night' and the Sabbath Controversy of John 9." *Filología Neotestamentaria* 19.37 (2006): 113–19.

Poirier, John C. "Purity beyond the Temple in the Second Temple Era." *JBL* 122.2 (2003): 247–65.

Poulsen, Frederik. *Representing Zion: Judgement and Salvation in the Old Testament.* Copenhagen International Seminar. London: Routledge, 2015.

Rabens, Volker. "Johannine Perspectives on Ethical Enabling in the Context of Stoic and Philonic Ethics." Pages 114–39 in *Rethinking the Ethics of John: "Implicit Ethics" in the Johannine Writings.* Edited by Jan G. van der Watt and Ruben Zimmermann. WUNT 291. Tübingen: Mohr Siebeck, 2012.

Rahlfs, Alfred and Robert Hanhart, eds., *Septuaginta: id est Vetus Testamentum Graece iuxta LXX interpretes,* 2nd ed. Stuttgart: Deutsche Bibelgesellschaft, 2006.

Rahmsdorf, Olivia. "'You Shall Not Wash My Feet εἰς τὸν αἰῶνα' (John 13.8): Time and Ethics in Peter's Interactions with Jesus in the Johannine Narrative." *JSNT* 41.4 (2019): 458–77.

Reed, Annette Yoshiko. *Jewish-Christianity and the History of Judaism: Collected Essays.* TSAJ 171. Tübingen: Mohr Siebeck, 2018.

Regev, Eyal. "Abominated Temple and a Holy Community: The Formation of the Notions of Purity and Impurity in Qumran." *DSD* 10.2 (2003): 243–78.

Regev, Eyal. "Pure Individualism: The Idea of Non-Priestly Purity in Ancient Judaism." *JSJ* 31.2 (2000): 176–202.

Reinhartz, Adele. "'And the Word Was Begotten': Divine Epigenesis in the Gospel of John." *Semeia* 85 (1999): 83–103.

Reinhartz, Adele. *Cast out of the Covenant: Jews and Anti-Judaism in the Gospel of John.* Lanham, MD: Lexington Books – Fortress Academic, 2018.

Reinhartz, Adele. "The Jews of the Fourth Gospel." Pages 121–37 in *The Oxford Handbook of Johannine Studies.* Edited by Judith Lieu and Martinus C. de Boer. Oxford Handbooks. Oxford: Oxford University Press, 2018.

Resseguie, James L. "Point of View." Pages 79–96 in *How John Works: Storytelling in the Fourth Gospel.* Edited by Douglas Estes and Ruth Sheridan. RBS 86. Atlanta, GA: SBL Press, 2016.

Reynolds, Benjamin E. "The Testimony of Jesus and the Spirit: The 'We' of John 3:11 in Its Literary Context." *Neot* 41.1 (2007): 157–72.

Reynolds, Benjamin E. "The Use of the Son of Man Idiom in the Gospel of John." Pages 101–29 in *"Who Is This Son of Man?": The Latest Scholarship on a Puzzling Expression of the Historical Jesus.* Edited by Larry W. Hurtado and Paul Owen. LNTS 390. London: T&T Clark, 2011.

Reynolds, Benjamin E., and Gabriele Boccaccini, eds. *Reading the Gospel of John's Christology as Jewish Messianism: Royal, Prophetic, and Divine Messiahs.* Ancient Judaism and Christianity 106. Leiden: Brill, 2018.

Richter, Georg. "Die Fußwaschung Joh 13, 1–20." *MTZ* 16.1–2 (1965): 13–26.

Rogan, Wil. "Purity in Early Judaism: Current Issues and Questions." *CBR* 16.3 (2018): 309–39.

Rogerson, J. W. *The Bible and Criticism in Victorian Britain: Profiles of F. D. Maurice and William Robertson Smith.* JSOTSup 201. Sheffield: Sheffield Academic, 1995.

Rosenblum, Jordan D. *The Jewish Dietary Laws in the Ancient World.* New York: Cambridge University Press, 2016.

Royse, James R. *Scribal Habits in Early Greek New Testament Papyri. Scribal Habits in Early Greek New Testament Papyri.* NTTSD 36. Leiden: Brill, 2007.

Royse, James R., and Adam Kamesar. "The Works of Philo." Pages 32–64 in *The Cambridge Companion to Philo.* Edited by Adam Kamesar. Cambridge Companions to Philosophy. Cambridge, MA: Cambridge University Press, 2009.

Runesson, Anders. "Purity, Holiness, and the Kingdom of Heaven in Matthew's Narrative World." Pages 144–80 in *Purity, Holiness, and Identity in Judaism and Christianity: Essays in Memory of Susan Haber.* Edited by Carl S. Ehrlich, Anders Runesson, and Eileen M. Schuller. WUNT 305. Tübingen: Mohr Siebeck, 2013.

Runge, Steven E. *Discourse Grammar of the Greek New Testament: A Practical Introduction for Teaching and Exegesis.* Lexham Bible Reference. Peabody, MA: Hendrickson, 2010.

Sanders, E. P. *Jewish Law from Jesus to the Mishnah: Five Studies.* London: SCM, 1990.

Schmid, Konrad, and Odil Hannes Steck. "Restoration Expectations in the Prophetic Tradition of the Old Testament." Pages 41–81 in *Restoration: Old Testament, Jewish, and Christian Perspectives.* Edited by James M. Scott. JSJSup 72. Leiden: Brill, 2001.

Schuchard, Bruce G. "Form versus Function: Citation Technique and Authorial Intention in the Gospel of John." Pages 23–45 in *Abiding Words: The Use of Scripture in the Gospel of John.* Edited by Alicia D. Myers and Bruce G. Schuchard. RBS 81. Atlanta, GA: SBL Press, 2015.

Schwartz, Daniel R., and Zeev Weiss. *Was 70 CE a Watershed in Jewish History? On Jews and Judaism before and after the Destruction of the Second Temple.* Ancient Judaism and Early Christianity 78. Leiden: Brill, 2012.

Seglenieks, Christopher. "Thomas the (Un)Faithful: Πιστός in John 20.27." *JSNT* 45.2 (2022): 135–56.

Segovia, Fernando F. "John 13:1–20: The Footwashing in the Johannine Tradition." *ZNW* 73.1–2 (1982): 31–51.

Seim, Turid Karlsen. "Descent and Divine Paternity in the Gospel of John: Does the Mother Matter?" *NTS* 51.3 (2005): 361–75.

Shakespeare, William. *The Tempest: The Cambridge Dover Wilson Shakespeare*. Edited by Sir Arthur Quiller-Couch and John Dover Wilson. Cambridge Library Collection—Literary Studies. Cambridge, MA: Cambridge University Press, 2009.

Shin, Sookgoo. *Ethics in the Gospel of John: Discipleship as Moral Progress*. Biblical Interpretation Series 168. Leiden: Brill, 2019.

Skinner, Christopher W. "Misunderstanding, Christology, and Johannine Characterization: Reading John's Characters through the Lens of the Prologue." Pages 111–27 in *Characters and Characterization in the Gospel of John*. Edited by Christopher W. Skinner. LNTS 461. London: T&T Clark, 2013.

Slingerland, Dixon. "The Nature of Nomos (Law) within the Testaments of the Twelve Patriarchs." *JBL* 105.1 (1986): 39–48.

Smith, D. Moody. *John*. ANTC. Nashville: Abingdon, 1999.

Smith, William Robertson. *Lectures on the Religion of the Semites: First Series, The Fundamental Institutions*. New York: D. Appleton, 1889.

Smith, William Robertson. *Lectures on the Religion of the Semites: Second and Third Series*. Edited by John Day. JSOTSup 183. Sheffield: Sheffield Academic, 1995.

Stare, Mira. "Die Reinheitsthematik im Johannesevangelium." *SNTSU* 40 (2015): 79–95.

Stare, Mira. "Ethics of Life in the Gospel of John." Pages 213–28 in *Rethinking the Ethics of John: "Implicit Ethics" in the Johannine Writings*. Edited by Jan G. van der Watt and Ruben Zimmermann. WUNT 291. Tübingen: Mohr Siebeck, 2012.

Streett, Andrew. *The Vine and the Son of Man: Eschatological Interpretation of Psalm 80 in Early Judaism*. Emerging Scholars. Minneapolis, MN: Fortress, 2014.

Talbert, Charles H. "The Fourth Gospel's Soteriology between New Birth and Resurrection." *PRSt* 37.2 (2010): 133–45.

Talmon, Shemaryahu. "The Emergence of Jewish Sectarianism in the Early Second Temple Period." *Ancient Israelite Religion: Essays in Honor of Frank Moore Cross*. Edited by Patrick D. Miller, Paul D. Hanson, and S. Dean McBride. Philadelphia, PA: Fortress, 1987.

Taylor, Joan E. *The Immerser: John the Baptist within Second Temple Judaism*. Grand Rapids, MI: Eerdmans, 1997.

Thatcher, Tom. "John and the Jews: Recent Research and Future Questions." Pages 3–38 in *John and Judaism: A Contested Relationship in Context*. Edited by R. Alan Culpepper and Paul N. Anderson. RBS 87. Atlanta, GA: SBL Press, 2017.

Theobald, Michael. *Das Evangelium nach Johannes*. RNT. Regensburg: Friedrich Pustet, 2009.

Thiessen, Matthew. *Jesus and the Forces of Death: The Gospels' Portrayal of Ritual Impurity within First-Century Judaism*. Grand Rapids, MI: Baker Academic, 2020.

Tholuck, Augustus. *Commentary on the Gospel of John*. Translated by Charles P. Krauth. 7th ed. Philadelphia, PA: Smith, English & Co., 1859.

Thomas, John Christopher. *Footwashing in John 13 and the Johannine Community*. 2nd ed. Cleveland, TN: CPT Press, 2014.

Thomas, John Christopher. "The Fourth Gospel and Rabbinic Judaism." *ZNW* 82.3–4 (1991): 159–82.

Thompson, Marianne Meye. "Baptism with Water and with Holy Spirit: Purification in the Gospel of John." Pages 59–78 in *The Opening of John's Narrative (John 1:19–2:22): Historical, Literary, and Theological Readings from the Colloquium Ioanneum 2015 in Ephesus*. Edited by R. Alan Culpepper and Jörg Frey. WUNT 385. Tübingen: Mohr Siebeck, 2017.

Thompson, Marianne Meye. "Eternal Life in the Gospel of John." *ExAud* 5 (1989): 35–55.

Thompson, Marianne Meye. "Hearing Voices: Reading the Gospels in the Echo Chamber of Scripture." *JTI* 11.1 (2017): 37–48.

Thompson, Marianne Meye. "'His Own Received Him Not': Jesus Washes the Feet of His Disciples." Pages 258–73 in *The Art of Reading Scripture*. Edited by Ellen F. Davis and Richard B. Hays. Grand Rapids, MI: Eerdmans, 2003.

Thompson, Marianne Meye. "Jesus and the Victory of God Meets the Gospel of John." Pages 21–38 in *Jesus, Paul, and the People of God: A Theological Dialogue with N.T. Wright*. Edited by Nicholas Perrin, Richard B. Hays, and N. T. Wright. Downers Grove, IL: IVP Academic, 2011.

Thompson, Marianne Meye. *John: A Commentary*. NTL. Louisville, KY: Westminster John Knox, 2015.

Thompson, Marianne Meye. *The God of the Gospel of John*. Grand Rapids, MI: Eerdmans, 2001.

Thompson, Marianne Meye. *The Promise of the Father: Jesus and God in the New Testament*. Louisville, KY: Westminster John Knox, 2000.

Tigchelaar, Eibert. "A Cave 4 Fragment of Divre Mosheh (4QDM) and the Text of 1Q22 1:7–10 and Jubilees 1:9, 14." *DSD* 12.3 (2005): 303–12.

Trozzo, Lindsey. *Exploring Johannine Ethics: A Rhetorical Approach to Moral Efficacy in the Fourth Gospel Narrative*. WUNT 2/449. Tübingen: Mohr Siebeck, 2017.

Uro, Risto. *Ritual and Christian Beginnings: A Socio-Cognitive Analysis*. Oxford: Oxford University Press, 2016.

Vahrenhorst, Martin. "Johannes und die Tora: Überlegungen zur Bedeutung der Tora im Johannesevangelium." *KD* 54.1 (2008): 14–36.

Vermès, Géza. "A Summary of the Law by Flavius Josephus." *NovT* 24.4 (1982): 289–303.

Vermès, Géza. "Jewish Literature and New Testament Exegesis: Reflections on Methodology." *JJS* 33 (1982): 361–76.

von Wahlde, Urban C. "The Gospel of John and Archeology." Pages 101–20 in *The Oxford Handbook of Johannine Studies*. Edited by Judith Lieu and Martinus C. de Boer. Oxford Handbooks. Oxford: Oxford University Press, 2018.

von Wahlde, Urban C. "The Pool(s) of Bethesda and the Healing in John 5: A Reappraisal of Research and of the Johannine Text." *RB* 116.1 (2009): 111–36.

van der Watt, Jan G. "Ethics and Ethos in the Gospel According to John." *ZNW* 97 (2006): 147–76.

van der Watt, Jan G. "Ethics in Community in the Gospel and Letters of John." Pages 363–80 in *The Oxford Handbook of Johannine Studies*. Edited by Judith Lieu and Martinus C. de Boer. Oxford Handbooks. Oxford: Oxford University Press, 2018.

van der Watt, Jan G. "Salvation in the Gospel According to John." Pages 101–31 in *Salvation in the New Testament: Perspectives on Soteriology*. Edited by Jan G. van der Watt. Leiden: Brill, 2005.

van der Watt, Jan G. "The Meaning of Jesus Washing the Feet of His Disciples (John 13)." *Neot* 51.1 (2017): 25–39.

Weiss, Daniel H., and Holger Zellentin. "Purity and the West: Christianity, Secularism, and the Impurity of Ritual." Pages 181–200 in *Purity and Danger Now: New Perspectives*. Edited by Robbie Duschinsky, Simone Schnall, and Daniel H. Weiss. Abingdon: Routledge, 2017.

Wenham, Gordon J. *The Book of Leviticus*. NICOT. Grand Rapids, MI: Eerdmans, 1979.

Werrett, Ian C. *Ritual Purity and the Dead Sea Scrolls*. STDJ 72. Leiden: Brill, 2007.

Weyer-Menkhoff, Karl. *Die Ethik des Johannesevangeliums im sprachlichen Feld des Handelns*. WUNT 2/359. Tübingen: Mohr Siebeck, 2014.

Weyer-Menkhoff, Karl. "The Response of Jesus: Ethics in John by Considering Scripture as Work of God." Pages 159–74 in *Rethinking the Ethics of John: "Implicit Ethics" in the Johannine Writings*. Edited by Jan G. van der Watt and Ruben Zimmermann. WUNT 291. Tübingen: Mohr Siebeck, 2012.

Whitenton, Michael R. *Configuring Nicodemus: An Interdisciplinary Approach to Complex Characterization*. LNTS 549. London: T&T Clark, 2019.

Whitenton, Michael R. "The Dissembler of John 3: A Cognitive and Rhetorical Approach to the Characterization of Nicodemus." *JBL* 135.1 (2016): 141–58.

Williams, Megan Hale. "No More Clever Titles: Observations on Some Recent Studies of Jewish-Christian Relations in the Roman World." *JQR* 99.1 (2009): 37–55.

Wright, David P. "Clean and Unclean (OT)." *ABD* 6:729–41.

Zangenberg, Jürgen K. "Pure Stone: Archeological Evidence for Jewish Purity Practices in Late Second Temple Judaism (Miqwaʾot and Stone Vessels)." Pages 537–72 in *Purity and the Forming of Religious Traditions in the Ancient Mediterranean World and Ancient Judaism*. Edited by Christian Frevel and Christophe Nihan. Dynamics in the History of Religions 3. Leiden: Brill, 2013.

Zimmerli, Walther. *Ezekiel 1: Commentary on the Book of the Prophet Ezekiel, Chapters 1–24*. Edited by Leonard J. Greenspoon. Translated by Ronald E. Clements. Hermeneia. Philadelphia, PA: Fortress, 1979.

Zimmerli, Walther. *Ezekiel 2: A Commentary on the Book of the Prophet Ezekiel, Chapters 25–48*. Edited by Paul D. Hanson and Leonard J. Greenspoon. Translated by James D. Martin. Hermeneia. Philadelphia, PA: Fortress, 1983.

Zimmermann, Ruben. "Abundant and Abandoning Life: Towards an 'Ethic of Life' in the Gospel of John." *ABR* 64 (2016): 31–53.

Zimmermann, Ruben. "Is There Ethics in the Gospel of John?" Pages 44–80 in *Rethinking the Ethics of John: "Implicit Ethics" in the Johannine Writings*. Edited by Jan G. van der Watt and Ruben Zimmermann. WUNT 291. Tübingen: Mohr Siebeck, 2012.

Zimmermann, Ruben. "The 'Implicit Ethics' of New Testament Writings: A Draft on a New Methodology for Analyzing New Testament Ethics." *Neot* 43.2 (2009): 399–423.

Index of References

Subject Index